FAITH AND PRACTICE

FAITH AND PRACTICE

ADOPTED 1955

REVISED 1972
15,000 COPIES

REPRINTED WITH
LIMITED EDITORIAL CHANGES 1978
8,000 COPIES

REPRINTED 1984
6,000 COPIES

REVISED 1997
10,000 COPIES

REPRINTED JANUARY 1998
5,000 COPIES

REPRINTED MAY 1998
5,000 COPIES

REVISED JUNE 2002
8,000 COPIES

REPRINTED DECEMBER 2007
7,000 COPIES

PHILADELPHIA YEARLY MEETING
FIFTEENTH AND CHERRY STREETS
PHILADELPHIA, PENNSYLVANIA
19102-1479

Faith &

Practice

PHILADELPHIA YEARLY MEETING
OF THE
RELIGIOUS SOCIETY OF FRIENDS

A Book of Christian Discipline

CONTENTS

As Friends use this Faith and Practice, we should heed the admonition stemming from the Meeting of Elders held at Balby, England in 1656:

> *Dearly beloved Friends, these things we do not lay upon you as a rule or form to walk by, but that all with the measure of the light which is pure and holy may be guided, and so in the light walking and abiding, these may be fulfilled in the Spirit, —not from the letter, for the letter killeth, but the Spirit giveth life.*

This edition of Faith and Practice of Philadelphia Yearly Meeting of the Religious Society of Friends is intended to be a guide for our members and all those who seek to understand in greater detail the ways we endeavor to apply our fundamental affirmations.

Early Friends proclaimed that from the beginning every person has been endowed with the capacity to enter directly, without mediator or mediation, into an empowering holy communion with God. They rejected, therefore, the assumption that this communion, which is essential to spiritual health, occurs primarily in the presence of designated persons in an established religious institution using sacred language and rituals. Friends, both in individual worship and in meetings for worship and for business, continue to experience the presence of the living God not only as awe and healing but also as guidance for conduct. Like the prophets of Israel they proclaim the unity of religious faith and social justice.

The Religious Society of Friends continues to affirm that refreshment of spirit and the ability both to know and do right come when families and individuals, in daily life and in meeting, trust in the Light that enlightens and empowers everyone who comes into the world.

What is presented herein represents the labor of nearly a decade by almost a score of committee members and by many, many members of Philadelphia Yearly Meeting in their home Meetings and in sessions of yearly meeting.

Of importance has been the recognition that formerly latent differences among yearly meeting members have become explicit and vigorous. During the decades in which the two Philadelphia Yearly Meetings were preparing for and consummating reunion, Friends remembered that the separation of 1828 seemed to have arisen over theological words and phrases and were wary of using such terms for fear of renewing the schism. In recent years that worry has faded and there is more outspoken diversity of expression among us. It has also become clear that Friends sometimes find clarity of communication difficult because of the lack of a commonly understood religious vocabulary, as members from many different religious backgrounds and experience have joined the Society of Friends.

From the beginning it was determined by those entrusted with the task of revising the 1972 Faith and Practice that more was expected than to update that version. As a matter of policy, sexist language has been removed except in direct quotations. We have returned to the understanding of early Friends that Faith and Practice, as a whole and as a book of discipline, comprises advices regarding the 'good order used among us' which have been confirmed by experience. Still, we have included – at the beginning of the section of quotations—the extracts from Epistles of the Yearly Meeting of Pennsylvania and the Jerseys, 1694 and 1695, which many Friends find especially helpful, and which appeared in the 1972 edition under the heading Advices.

In conclusion, we have tried to respect the deeply felt leadings of sometimes diverse groups and of individual Friends without attempting to represent them in detail. The quotations section, extracts from the works of Friends past and present, is intended to reflect more directly the richness of our diversity.

Commitment to a life of obedience to the Spirit has been of essential importance to Friends both as individuals and as Meetings. This commitment has led us to support much that is creative in public life, education, business, and concern for the oppressed. It also has led us to oppose practices and institutions that result in violence and exploitation in the world around us. Our history, however, demonstrates that our discernment has not always been complete: we have not always been united in our perceptions of what obedience to the Spirit requires, and we have fallen into conflict and misunderstanding even among ourselves. Yet out of such conflicts, painful as they have been, have come greater clarity of commitment and unity in witness.

The following account divides our history into five periods, from the origins of Quakerism in England to recent developments within Philadelphia Yearly Meeting.

I   BEGINNINGS   1652-1689

The Religious Society of Friends arose in England in the middle of the seventeenth century. This was a time of turbulence and change in both religion and politics. In the established Church of England, great emphasis was placed upon outward ceremony; there, and in such dissenting churches as the Baptists and Presbyterians, religious faith was also generally identified with the authority of the Bible or the acceptance of a formal creed. Many individuals, however, became increasingly dissatisfied with ceremonies and creeds, and broke away from these churches. Singly or in small groups, they turned inward in search of a religion of personal experience and direct communion with God.

George Fox (1624 – 1691) was one of these seekers. Even as a child, he was serious and thoughtful, often pondering the Scriptures and engaging in solitary reflection. At age nineteen, after being urged to engage in conduct that violated his religious scruples, he decided to leave home in order to seek spiritual direction. For four years he wandered through the English midlands and as far south as London. Though he consulted various ministers and professors (that is, professing Christians), none could give rest to his troubled soul. Finally, as he recorded in his Journal,

> *...when all my hopes in [Christian ministers and professors] and in all men was gone, so that I had nothing outwardly to help me, nor could tell what to do, then, Oh! then, I heard a voice which said, "There is one, even Christ Jesus, that can speak to thy condition," and when I heard it, my heart did leap for joy. ...My desires after the Lord grew stronger, and zeal in the pure knowledge of God and of Christ alone, without the help of any man, book, or writing.*

And so, in 1647, at the age of twenty-three, George Fox began to preach.

His basic message was simple enough: first, that his own dramatic and life-changing experience of a direct, unmediated revelation from God confirmed the possibility of a religion of personal experience and direct communion with God, a religion of continuing revelation instead of a closed, written canon; and second, that this same possibility was available to every person. Fox's message, combined with his charismatic personality, soon attracted a small group of women and men who joined him in spreading the "good news" that "Christ has come to teach His people himself." These first "publishers of Truth" believed the good news to be a revival of primitive Christianity rather than a new gospel. Gradually, Fox and his associates began to enlist others in this revival; and in 1652, Fox persuaded many of the Westmorland Seekers, a numerous and already well-established religious movement, to become Friends (or Friends of Truth), as his followers called themselves, or Quakers, as they came to be called by others. Also in 1652, with the permission of Judge Fell, Fox and Margaret Fell turned Swarthmoor Hall, the Fells' home, into the headquarters for the infant Religious Society of Friends. These two events – the absorption of the Westmorland Seekers into the Quaker movement, and the establishment of a home base—warrant the choice of 1652 as the birthtime of the Religious Society of Friends.

While many religious dissenters who welcomed Fox's message of direct communion and continuing revelation became Friends, those persons who were committed to the Church of England or to other churches regarded his message as unwelcome, heretical, and treasonable. It was unwelcome, since Fox and some of his followers often invaded and disrupted the church services of others. It was heretical, since the idea of continuing revelation displaced the church and even the Scriptures as finally authoritative. It was treasonable, since those who embraced this idea also refused to acknowledge the authority of the state (with its established church) as taking precedence over the authority of individual conscience, and consequently refused to take any oath of allegiance to the state and to pay tithes towards the maintenance of the Anglican Church. Accordingly, the meetings of early Quakers were frequently disrupted by angry mobs, their meetinghouses were vandalized and burned, and they were themselves subjected to imprisonment and cruel treatment by officials of the state. Such persecution continued until 1689 and the so-called Glorious Revolution, when a Toleration Act was adopted that gave legal sanction to the principle of religious liberty. (Some restrictions on rights continued, however, into the 19th century.) Yet, like the early Christian church, the Quaker movement gained more adherents despite—or because of—the persecution. Some historians claim that the Quakers constituted ten percent of the British population by the end of the seventeenth century.

This combination of persecution and expansion yielded several important consequences. First, the Quakers' sense of themselves as a distinct people with a divine mission became stronger. Their refusal to take oaths under any circumstances, to serve in the army, to take off their hats to persons in authority, to use formal speech (the plural "you" when speaking to one's so-called betters), and to dress like the "world's people" all date from this period. Unlike other dissenters, they insisted on holding their meetings publicly in spite of persecution, and thus began earning their reputation for scrupulous honesty. (The fact that Quaker merchants adopted a fixed price system significantly enhanced this reputation.)

Second, though unwilling to formulate any explicit creed or profession of faith, the early Friends were more than willing to engage in religious controversy and to defend their basic beliefs. Thus began the publication of numerous books and tracts intended to explain and justify Quaker principles. Undoubtedly, Robert Barclay's *Apology* (first published in Latin in 1676 and then in English in 1678) was the most theologically sophisticated of these books. Both Margaret Fell and George Fox wrote pamphlets defending a woman's right to preach and prophesy, one of the more controversial of basic Quaker beliefs.

Third, the early Friends realized that their movement required at least some kind of institutional structure: to provide material assistance and emotional support for those being persecuted, and also to nurture and discipline the individual and group life of its adherents. Thus was initiated, at Fox's urging, the bottom-up system of monthly, quarterly, and yearly meetings. Though this system has often seemed undisciplined to non-Friends, it has given stability and continuity to our Religious Society. Separate men's and women's meetings for business were established as another institutional innovation. The latter afforded opportunities for women to exercise administrative and decision-making skills that were not generally available to them in the larger society.

During this initial period of Quakerism, Friends were not only engaged in sharing their "good news" with others in England. They also went to countries on the continent of Europe and in the Near East. Mary Fisher, for instance, was one of six Friends who undertook a mission to Turkey, but was the only one to be received by the Sultan in 1658. Of particular importance were the missions to the British colonies in North America and the West Indies. And under the leadership of William Penn (1644 – 1718), Quaker colonies were established in West Jersey and Pennsylvania.

Friends first came to New England as early as 1656, just four years after the birth of their religious society. In Massachusetts, the Quaker missionaries were imprisoned, tortured and expelled; four of them were put to death between 1659 and 1661, including Mary Dyer, whose statue is near the entrance of Friends Center at 1515 Cherry St. in Philadelphia. In the more tolerant Rhode Island, however, they were not only permitted to proselytize but also to settle. Meetings for worship were soon formed, and the first yearly meeting to be established was held in 1661, though meetings for business were apparently not held until some ten years later.

Quakers began to settle in the Delaware Valley in 1675, following the purchase of land near the present city of Burlington, New (then West) Jersey by two Friends. In 1681, Charles II repaid a sizable debt to the estate of William Penn's father by granting to Penn the land to the west of the Delaware River. The King named this land Pennsylvania in honor of Admiral Penn. William Penn intended to establish there a veritable "holy experiment"—an enlightened proprietorship based on New Testament principles and with liberty of conscience guaranteed.

Unfortunately, Penn's tenure as proprietor of his colony was frequently marked by conflict, and things only worsened when his sons came to power. Perhaps the most lasting vestige of Penn's "holy experiment" is a form of creative tension. Penn's political practice was by no means consistent with his theory, nor was his theory of governance adequately developed. Then as now, the tension between practice and theory, social engagement and mystical illumination, yielded as much heat as light. And yet the underlying principles of Penn's vision are as pertinent as ever: participatory decision making, religious liberty, justice as fair dealing with one's neighbors (the Native Americans, for instance), non-violent resistance rather than military defense, and the abolition of oaths.

II. CONSOLIDATION & WITHDRAWAL   1689-CIRCA 1800

Quakers continued to be maligned and occasionally persecuted, even after the adoption of the Toleration Act by the English Parliament in 1689. But for the most part, Quakers were left alone. Perhaps ironically, their enthusiasm—or in other words, missionary zeal—diminished almost as soon as they won toleration; and the maintaining of discipline among a "peculiar people" tended to replace the expansive evangelism of the early years. What had once been a glorious and creative movement now took on the characteristics of a closed sect.

By 1720, the Quakers had become a minority of the population of Pennsylvania, but they retained political control of the colony until 1755 when, at the onset of the French and Indian Wars, most Friends gave up their seats in the Assembly rather than vote war measures. There was, during this period, a kind of "interlocking directorate" of the political leaders of Pennsylvania and the leading figures within Philadelphia Yearly Meeting. Nevertheless, Quakers throughout the eighteenth century tended more and more to withdraw from active public life; increasingly, they sought to deepen their own spiritual lives and to hedge their Society about with distinctive rules and customs. But there were some, Betsy Ross for instance, who chose actively to support the American cause during the revolution and who formed a movement called the Free Quakers; others sought to avoid the conflict by moving to Canada; and a few Quaker leaders were exiled to Virginia.

During this period yearly meetings established requirements for membership and adopted, then frequently revised, Books of Discipline, which were intended to define more precisely the code of Quaker conduct and to prescribe the means of enforcing this code on members. For instance, Philadelphia Yearly Meeting's 1704 Book of Discipline included a provision discouraging the marriage of Friends to non-Friends; its 1712 Discipline recommended disownment (that is, expulsion) of members who married "out of meeting"; and its 1722 Discipline required immediate disownment for this conduct. Such policies obviously enhanced the exclusivity of the Religious Society of Friends, as did the Queries and Advices formulated in order to increase Friends' mindfulness of their distinctive code of conduct.

But this period of consolidation was also a period of creativity. Even as Friends turned their energies from worldly matters, and particularly as they withdrew from governing Pennsylvania in 1755, they clarified and refined the testimonies for which Friends are known today. For instance, they became more deeply involved as leaders in the movement to abolish slavery and to achieve racial justice; they expressed concern for the treatment of prisoners; they established a number of philanthropies benefitting Native Americans; and they opposed the payment of taxes for war purposes and adhered generally to the principle of nonviolence.

An unprecedented number of reforming ministers arose at this time and traveled widely in the ministry, combining an effort to improve the discipline and to perfect the setting up of meetings, to preach against slavery and other social evils, and to hold public meetings in which they preached to the general public, just as their spiritual ancestors had done a century earlier. One such minister was John Woolman (1720 – 1772), who exemplified what a Quaker life could be when governed by the testimonies of Friends. His untiring efforts to eliminate the holding of slaves, to improve the treatment of Native Americans, and to end economic exploitation gave substance to the Quaker testimony on equality; and his choice of a way of life "free from much Entanglement and the Desire of outward Greatness," as he records in his Journal, likewise demonstrated the practical import of the Quaker testimony on simplicity. Though he directed his energies primarily to reform within the Religious Society of Friends, his work and his public writings were also clearly intended to influence the practice of the larger society.

III. SCHISM AND REFORM   CIRCA 1800-1900

Even before the opening of the nineteenth century, American Friends exhibited two divergent tendencies: on the one hand, an emphasis on continuing revelation; on the other, an emphasis on the Christian origins of Quakerism and the authority of the Bible. For instance, in the 1690s George Keith formed a separatist movement called the Christian Quakers which strongly emphasized the life and teachings of the historical Jesus. Keith—one of the earliest and most effective "publishers of Truth"—had emigrated to East Jersey in 1685, and then to Philadelphia in 1689, where he became the first headmaster of the Quaker school from which both Friends Select and William Penn Charter claim descent. Though previously he had written some thirty books and tracts defending basic Quaker beliefs, he had increasing doubts about those beliefs and also about the structure of governance within monthly meetings. Accordingly, he began a campaign to establish deacons and elders as the guardians of the theological views of those who spoke in meetings for worship. He also proposed that all members be required to affirm a confession of faith or creed. After being rebuffed by Philadelphia Yearly Meeting (and then by London Yearly Meeting as well), he established the Christian Quakers, with some fifteen monthly meetings. This movement did not last very long; by 1700 it had all but disappeared, and Keith himself had returned to England and joined the Anglican Church. But it clearly anticipates one of the tendencies of American Friends in the nineteenth century, which has been labeled (or perhaps, mislabeled) the evangelical.

The other nineteenth-century tendency continued to emphasize the Inward Light, or immediate and continuing revelation, as the primary basis for religious faith and practice. The most eloquent and charismatic leader of this movement was Elias Hicks (1748 – 1830), a Quaker farmer from Long Island. Hicks personally believed in the divinity of Jesus Christ, but emphasized the primacy of the Inner Light, and deplored creedal statements. He urged Friends to live apart from the world, he opposed public education, he opposed the construction of the Erie Canal and a system of railroads. But he was a strong abolitionist, and criticized those Friends who used any products of slave labor. His opposition to the wealth and power of city Friends in such centers as Philadelphia drew support from many, though some leading Philadelphia Quakers believed that his remarks were intended to undermine their authority. Hicks became a catalyst for existing differences among members of Philadelphia Yearly Meeting.

Finally, in 1827 there was a formal schism within Philadelphia Yearly Meeting into "Orthodox" and "Hicksite" branches. Economic, geographic, kinship, and governance considerations were involved, in addition to theological differences. Many Orthodox Friends emphasized the importance of establishing a personal relationship with the bibilical Christ; some evidenced the influence of John and Charles Wesley, founders of the Methodist movement. Those who generally sympathized with the religious teachings of Elias Hicks became the Hicksite Yearly Meeting.

Many Hicksite Friends believed that experience of the Inward Christ was more important than understanding the biblical Christ. Orthodox Friends in Philadelphia met at the 4th and Arch Streets meetinghouse, while Philadelphia Hicksite Friends built a meetinghouse at 15th and Race Streets. To confuse matters further, each group continued to refer to itself as Philadelphia Yearly Meeting: that is, each assumed that it alone represented the authentic Quaker perspective and practice. Orthodox Friends were dominant in the city of Philadelphia; and Hicksite Friends, elsewhere in the region previously under the jurisdiction of a single Philadelphia Yearly Meeting. This split was soon followed by similar schisms in Baltimore, New York, New England, Ohio, and Indiana Yearly Meetings.

Further schisms occurred subsequently, occasioned by disagreements among Friends regarding faith and practice, but clearly exacerbated by the strong personalities of the principal controversialists. An English Friend, Joseph John Gurney (1788 – 1847), brother of Elizabeth Fry, who was a well-known advocate of prison reform, also took an evangelical position, emphasizing the Bible and playing down the Inward Light. His teachings influenced the Orthodox Friends in America, and some of his followers in England separated from London Yearly Meeting in 1835. John Wilbur (1774 – 1856) attempted to establish a position that would reconcile differences—that is, he stressed Orthodox Quaker views but also acknowledged the importance of the Inward Light; some of his followers formed another separatist movement among Friends in 1845. Still, it was the basic schism between Orthodox and Hicksite Friends that largely defined Quaker experience in Philadelphia Yearly Meeting for the remainder of the nineteenth century and well into the twentieth century. (Precisely because this schism defined the Quaker experience in America for such a long time, no definitive account nor interpretation has gained universal assent among Friends even today.)

Despite these divergent trends and conflicts, American Quakers made notable advances and contributions during the nineteenth century. Friends participated in the westward expansion, forming monthly and yearly meetings wherever they settled—but especially in Ohio, Indiana, Iowa, and on the Pacific coast. Many of these meetings adopted a pastoral system. Education, always a major Quaker concern, was promoted by the establishment of a number of Quaker schools and colleges. Friends also worked for the abolition of slavery and war, for the welfare of African-Americans and Native Americans, for prison reform, for temperance, and for the rights of women. Some Quakers played a prominent role in the formation of the underground railroad, giving aid and shelter to escaping slaves on their way to the Northern states or to Canada. And it is note-worthy that of the five women who organized the first women's rights convention at Seneca Falls in 1848, four were Quakers: Lucretia Mott; her sister, Martha Coffin Wright; Mary Ann McClintock; and Jane Hunt. Such activities obviously placed members of the Religious Society of Friends in conflict with many in the larger society.

IV. RECONCILIATION CIRCA 1900-1955

Appropriately enough, it was the continuing commitment of both Orthodox and Hicksite Friends to the peace testimony that paved the way for their gradual reconciliation and, in 1955, for the reunification of Philadelphia Yearly Meeting. Orthodox and Hicksite members attended the Lake Mohonk Conferences on International Arbitration held near the end of the nineteenth century. In 1897, they worked together to support American participation in an arbitration treaty. And in 1901 the two separate (and occasionally contentious) Philadelphia Yearly Meetings jointly organized a conference for world peace to which all American Quakers were invited.

There were other developments in the early 1900s which contributed to the eventual reconciliation of Orthodox and Hicksite Friends. The formation of Friends General Conference in 1900 laid the foundation for cooperation in nurturing Quakers and Quakerism, though it was in itself a Hicksite enterprise.

After the Manchester Conference of 1895, London Yearly Meeting began shifting to a more liberal stance and to develop contacts with Hicksite Friends, inviting some to their summer schools. When Woodbrooke was set up as a Quaker study center in 1903, a number of Hicksite young people were recruited to attend, and thus met Orthodox young people for the first time on British soil. Both British and American Young Friends began to work actively to heal the breach. In January of 1913 Henry Cadbury organized a group of Philadelphia Young Friends from each branch to meet regularly to study the separation. Their report, issued in 1914, stated that it was not a matter of doctrine but of authority which had caused the separation. The group continued to meet, and to develop social occasions in which young people of both branches could get together. In time a few marriages resulted.

In 1916 Joseph Elkinton—a prominent Orthodox Friend—personally conveyed a letter of friendship from his own yearly meeting to the Hicksite Yearly Meeting. In 1917, both branches united with Friends Five Years Meeting to organize the American Friends Service Committee to provide service opportunities for conscientious objectors of all American yearly meetings, and implement Quaker testimonies in response to the First World War. Formation of the Friends Committee on National Legislation in 1943 played a similar bridging role, as did Pendle Hill and, at least in the immediate Philadelphia area, the Friends Neighborhood Guild. Working together proved efficient, and by 1930 a number of committees with similar objectives merged as a means of gaining greater effectiveness: of particular significance was the formation of a unified Peace Committee. At the same time, the Disciplines of the two yearly meetings were revised in the direction of commonalities rather than differences: for instance, at least some of the queries included in the two Disciplines were, after a time, identical. The process of healing was further helped by two social groups organized for the purpose—the Friends Social Union and the Divotee Golf Club of Atlantic City. Women of the two yearly meetings worked together on issues of suffrage and of peace.

The two yearly meetings both took action in the 1920s to lay down their separate women's and men's meetings for business. This was done at the request of the women. Thus ended an institution that in the seventeenth century had been radical—acknowledging women's spiritual gifts; that in the nineteenth century had been an important training ground for Quaker women entering public life; but that came to be seen in the age of female suffrage as second class status in religious life. That this step was taken by both yearly meetings at about the same time was further evidence of their readiness to come together.

These developments, which resulted from the individual and shared efforts of a number of Orthodox and Hicksite Friends, established a growing desire for reunification. In 1933, changes were made in the Disciplines of the two Philadelphia Yearly Meetings to provide for the formation of united monthly meetings, that is, monthly meetings with membership in both Orthodox and Hicksite yearly meetings. An even more decisive step towards unity was taken in 1946, when the two Philadelphia Yearly Meetings agreed to establish the Philadelphia General Meeting which would be held in the autumn and attended by both Orthodox and Hicksite Friends, though separate sessions would continue to be held in the spring. Also in the mid-1940s, the two yearly meetings formed a Religious Life Committee which met for its own spiritual nourishment and also to prepare for visiting monthly meetings in both yearly meetings; clearly, the need had been felt to affirm religious unity. Finally, in 1950, a committee was formed with representatives from both yearly meetings to prepare a common book of discipline. This committee submitted its work, entitled Faith and Practice, to both yearly meetings and to the General Meeting in 1954. The following year, a schism that had lasted for 128 years was amicably brought to an end, and a single, reunified Philadelphia Yearly Meeting convened—with standing room only—at Arch Street Meetinghouse.

V. UNITY AMIDST DIVERSITY 1955-

Friends in Canada and in New York were reconciled and reunited at about the same time as those in Philadelphia Yearly Meeting. New England Yearly Meeting had already experienced this process some ten years earlier. And indeed, there was among Friends throughout North America a growing interest in dialogue and cooperation. The Friends World Committee for Consultation, which had been founded in 1937 following the Friends World Conference at Swarthmore College, encouraged this development. Even more, the Fourth World Conference of Friends held at Guilford College yielded what became known as the Faith and Life Movement, with regional and then national meetings during the 1970s and early 1980s in which all North American yearly meetings participated; all shared the objective of finding common ground. On the other hand, there were important differences that continued to divide Friends, both within and between the various yearly meetings, and not the least concerned how to respond to two major social and political issues of the 1960s—the Vietnam war and the civil rights movement.

SOCIAL CONCERNS

Members of Philadelphia Yearly Meeting (PYM) were encouraged to participate in efforts to end the war in Vietnam. For instance, the PYM News for May 1965 included a call to attend a vigil at the Pentagon sponsored by the Interreligious Committee on Vietnam, of which Philadelphia Yearly Meeting was itself a member. Then, at the 1967 yearly meeting sessions, the decision was reached to support the Phoenix project sponsored by an Action Group of Concerned Friends. This project involved sending medical supplies to North Vietnam despite the illegality of such action. The clerk of Philadelphia Yearly Meeting resigned his clerkship soon thereafter, because as a sitting federal judge he was personally and officially committed to uphold the law; other Friends likewise wrestled with the question of whether civil disobedience was an appropriate method of registering opposition to the Vietnam war.

Following its 1964 sessions Philadelphia Yearly Meeting issued A Quaker Call to Action in Race Relations. In that call, Friends acknowledged failure in carrying out the implications of the Quaker testimony regarding human equality and advocated various steps to promote fair housing and fair employment. During the summer of 1964, Philadelphia Yearly Meeting sponsored a project in Mississippi to rebuild churches and construct a local community center. Many Friends, however, felt that their efforts should be focused on the needs of disadvantaged minorities in their own geographic area. Accordingly, in 1966, Friends in Philadelphia Yearly Meeting initiated a community action project in Chester, Pennsylvania. Philadelphia Friends were thus already attempting to respond to the urban crisis when they were presented with the Black Manifesto.

In the summer of 1969, the Black Economic Development Conference confronted various religious groups, including Philadelphia Yearly Meeting, with the demand that they pay reparations, given the alleged participation or complicity of such groups in the institutional arrangements that had disadvantaged African-Americans over the years. Shortly thereafter Philadelphia Yearly Meeting scheduled three called sessions in order to consider how it should respond to the Black Manifesto. Some 27 members of the local Black Economic Development Conference attended the third session, on 31 January 1970, and stood at the front of the meetinghouse for 45 minutes, with brief speeches by three of its leaders. Though the yearly meeting decided to reject the demand for payment of reparations, it did establish a Minorities Economic Development Fund which allocated funds (established in part through individual contributions and in part from the yearly meeting endowment) to support various community action projects in the Philadelphia area, including some sponsored by the Black Economic Development Conference.

Subsequently, Philadelphia Yearly Meeting wrestled with other manifestations of the ongoing problems of race relations and war. In the spring of 1978, it attempted to establish a "Friendly Presence" in West Philadelphia to encourage nonviolent resolution of the growing conflict between MOVE, a local commune, and the city of Philadelphia. In 1984 and again in 1988, the yearly meeting became the object of an IRS suit resulting from its refusal to levy the salary of one of its employees who did not pay the military portion of federal taxes.

The members of Philadelphia Yearly Meeting have confronted other social concerns since 1955. Among these have been gender roles within monthly meetings and the general society, the rights of homosexuals, the investment of yearly meeting funds in companies with business interests in South Africa under apartheid, the Sanctuary movement for refugees in the US without credentials, the AIDS crisis, and the need for conflict resolution skills in families and schools.

REORGANIZATION OF PHILADELPHIA YEARLY MEETING

When *The Messenger* (the newsletter of Philadelphia Yearly Meeting [Hicksite]) began publication in late 1928, there were some 10 yearly meeting committees with 3 devoted to social concerns. The latter were the Committee on Peace and Service, the Committee on the Interests of the Colored Race, and the Committee on Philanthropic Labor (which was charged to support prohibition, prison reform and child welfare agencies, among other things). A similar distribution of committees existed in the Philadelphia Yearly Meeting [Orthodox]. By the mid 1960s, following reunification and even with the merger of committees from the two yearly meetings that had not merged previously, there were still 40 distinct yearly meeting committees and some 15 of these were independently operated and funded. Clearly, some kind of restructuring was needed.

And so, in 1966, Representative Meeting solicited responses from monthly meetings and from individual Friends to two basic questions: How should our religious society be organized so that it allows its members the most effective opportunities for service to the world and its own members? How should the finances of the yearly meeting be handled in order to use our moneys and funds most effectively in the service of God? The first question has been answered with decisions to restructure Philadelphia Yearly Meeting in the mid-1970s and then in the mid-1990s. And likewise, the second question has been answered with the adoption of different approaches to fund raising and budgeting in the late 1960s and then in the late 1990s.

The first restructuring of Philadelphia Yearly Meeting occurred in 1974, which coincided with ground breaking for the new Friends Center at 15th and Cherry Streets in Philadelphia. The new organization included three general committees—Worship and Ministry (which replaced the previously separate Yearly Meeting on Worship and Ministry), Nominating, and Personnel: and also three coordinating committees. The latter were to provide oversight and support for various committees and working groups dealing with specific programs and functions in relation, respectively, to the education and care of members, testimonies and concerns, and general services. Also, Representative Meeting was reorganized so that, in addition to members appointed by yearly meeting committees and a small number of at-large members, each monthly meeting appointed its own members. And finally, a committee formed in 1964 to undertake the revision of **Faith and Practice** completed its work, which was approved at the 1972 sessions of Philadelphia Yearly Meeting.

Beginning in 1994, a Structures and Workings Committee formed primarily of the clerks of monthly and quarterly meetings, began to consider once again how our yearly meeting might best be organized. It recommended a general plan to replace the three coordinating committees with five standing committees: Worship and Care, Education, Peace and Concerns, Support and Outreach, and General Services. Philadelphia Yearly Meeting in its 1996 sessions approved this plan, and also the formation of an Implementation Committee, charged with working out the details—in particular the roles and responsibilities of the standing committees. This was completed by the 1998 annual sessions. Apart from the standing committees, there were to be two independent committees— Nominating Committee and a Financial Stewardship Committee; and Representative Meeting was renamed Interim Meeting. Otherwise, all yearly meeting services, programs and working groups were to come under the general oversight of an appropriate standing committee. In particular, the Worship and Ministry Committee, which had been independent of the previous coordinating committee structure, was brought under the aegis of the Worship and Care Standing Committee, though it has been renamed the Meeting on Worship and Ministry; similarly, the Personnel Committee became the Personnel Services Group under the aegis of the General Services Standing Committee. To complement this reorganization, the yearly meeting staff changed its basic role from committee support to general provision of services, so that assistance in coordinating volunteers or planning conferences, for instance, might be available to any of the project, service, or working groups that operate under the aegis of the five standing committees.

There have also been two approaches to financing yearly meeting activities. In early 1969, Philadelphia Yearly Meeting adopted centralized budgeting and a new pattern of fund raising. Each monthly meeting was expected to pay an assessment or quota based on its adult membership;

and a Combined Appeal (subsequently named the Annual Appeal, and then the Annual Fund) replaced separate appeals issued on behalf of some 13 different yearly meeting committees. In addition to the funds from meetings and individuals, a significant portion of the yearly meeting budget comes from bequests and income from bequests. Then in 1997, concurrently with its restructuring, the yearly meeting replaced the quota system with a covenant mechanism, such that each monthly meeting voluntarily pledges the level of its support for quarterly and yearly meeting activities and services based on the resources that it can make available for these purposes (rather than the number of its adult members). The yearly meeting also adopted a procedure for increasing the involvement of monthly and quarterly meetings in the setting of priorities for the activities and services of Philadelphia Yearly Meeting, and hence for its budget.

RECENT GROWTH AND CHANGE

Since reunification in 1955, Philadelphia Yearly Meeting experienced significant growth in its associated institutions. The number of Friends schools proliferated. Several life care retirement communities were formed, beginning with Foulkeways in 1964. And the Burlington Meetinghouse was renovated and expanded as a conference center for the increasing number of younger Friends and families.

Philadelphia Yearly Meeting had some 30,000 members in 1775, and about half that number by 1925, which were unevenly divided between two yearly meetings. Since then, the yearly meeting has continued to experience a gradual reduction in recorded membership. In 1994, Philadelphia Yearly Meeting recorded 12,100 members. Of these, about half had newly joined the Religious Society of Friends during the past 15 years. Many of our monthly meetings experienced an influx of active attenders. A large number of young families participated in the revitalization of the First Day Schools. At this time, attenders were not included in the membership statistics of the yearly meeting.

Our monthly meetings, our yearly meeting, and Friends institutions have continued to offer a vital and active service to members, attenders, and the community at large. We remain committed to a life of obedience to the Spirit, and seek to be faithful witnesses to the Truth.

The Light Within

The Light Within is the fundamental and immediate experience for Friends. It is that which guides each of us in our everyday lives and brings us together as a community of faith. It is, most importantly, our direct and unmediated experience of the Divine.

Friends have used many different terms or phrases to designate the source and inner certainty of our faith—a faith which we have gained by direct experience. The Inward Light, the Way, the Truth and the Life, the Spirit of Truth, the Divine Principle, the Christ Within, the Seed, and the Inner Light are examples of such phrases. George Fox refers in his Journal to "that Inward Light, Spirit, and Grace by which all might know their salvation" and to "that Divine Spirit which would lead them into all truth." He wrote: "There is one, even Christ Jesus, that can speak to thy condition" and encouraged Friends "to walk cheerfully over the world, answering that of God in every one." Many Friends interpret "that of God" as another designation for the Light Within.

For Friends, the Light Within is not the same as the conscience or moral faculty. The conscience is a human faculty, which is conditioned by education and the cultural environment; it is not, therefore, an infallible guide to moral practice. It should nevertheless be attended to, for it is one of the faculties through which the Light shines. Friends are encouraged to test the leadings of conscience by seeking clearness, through direct communion in the meeting for worship, and through the clearness process (see p. 29). Such testing enhances and clarifies insight so that the conscience may be purged of misconceptions and become more truly obedient to the Light Within. When conscience has been transformed by experiencing the Light, it gives more reliable direction even though it may seem to point in a direction that is contrary to generally accepted authorities.

Friends' experience has been that following an enlightened conscience brings a release of the spirit and also a state of peace that are independent of the tangible results of the action taken. Spiritual power arises from living in harmony with the divine will. George Fox often spoke of the power he experienced in times of need, and of that relationship between power and the Light. For instance, he writes that "the power of God sprang through me," and, he admonishes us, "hearken to the Light, that ye may feel the power of God in every one of you."

Continuing obedience to the Light increases our gratitude for God's gifts. Among these are an awareness of enduring values, the joy of life, and the ability to resolve problems in accord with divine leading, as individuals or as a Meeting. Under the guidance of the Light, the monthly meeting is enabled to use and transform the aspirations and judgments of its members. This practice helps the Meeting make decisions and face undertakings in a spirit detached from self-interest or prejudice. Basic Quaker testimonies such as equality, simplicity, nonviolence, integrity, and community have arisen from a deep sense of individual and corporate responsibility guided by the Light Within.

Recognizing that God's Light is in every person overcomes our separation and our differences from others and leads to a sympathetic awareness of their need and a sense of responsibility toward them. Friends believe that the more widely and clearly the Light is recognized and followed, the more will humanity come into accord. "Therefore," writes George Fox, "in the Light wait, where unity is."

Worship and the Meeting for Worship

The meeting for worship is the heart of the Religious Society of Friends. It draws us together in the enlightening and empowering presence of God, sending us forth with renewed vision and commitment.

WORSHIP

Our word "worship" has its roots in the concept of "worth-ship." Worship is our response to what we feel to be of ultimate importance. Our expression of that feeling of ultimate worthship may take many forms. Worship is always possible, alone or in company, in silence, in music or speech, in stillness or in dance. It is never confined to place or time or form.

When Friends worship, we reach out from the depths of our being to God, the giver of life and of the world around us. Our worship is the search for communion with God and the offering of ourselves—body and soul— for the doing of God's will. The sense of worship can be experienced in the awe we feel in the silence of a meeting for worship or in the awareness of our profound connectedness to nature and its power. In worship we know repentance and forgiveness in the acknowledgment of God as the ultimate source of our being, and the serenity of accepting God's will.

In worship we discover direction for our lives and the uses of our resources. Leadings are often made clearer by reference to the life and teachings of Jesus and by the transforming power of the Inner Light. From worship there comes a fresh understanding of the two great commandments: to love "your God with all your heart, and with all your soul, and with all your strength, and with all your mind; and your neighbor as yourself." (Luke 10:27).

Careful listening to the Inward Teacher can lead to fresh openings: an inpouring of love, insight, and interdependence. True listening can also bring the worshiper to new and sometimes troubling perceptions, including clear leadings that may be a source of pain and anxiety; yet it can also bring such wholeness of heart that hard tasks can become a source of joy. Even when we worship torn with our own pain or that of another, it is in worship that we discover new strength for what faces us in our everyday lives.

Each experience of worship is different. There is no right way to prepare for spiritual communion, no set practice to follow when worship grows from expectant waiting in the Spirit. Vital worship depends far more on a deeply felt longing for God than upon any particular practice. "Ask, and it will be given you; seek, and you will find; knock, and it will be opened to you." (Matthew 7:7)

THE MEETING FOR WORSHIP

Friends find it useful to come to meeting with hearts and minds prepared for worship by daily prayer, meditation, and study, especially of the Bible and of the experience of others. We deepen thereby our awareness of the wonder of God and of God's love, and acquire the words with which to understand and to express that awareness. Many also find help through thoughtful reflection and listening to the Inward Teacher in the course of daily life and service.

As Friends arrive for meeting, such preparation helps us set aside our preoccupation with ourselves and our affairs and so settle into worship in a manner described by Alexander Parker in 1660:

The first that enters into the place of your meeting ... turn in thy mind to the light, and wait upon God singly, as if none were present but the Lord; and here thou art strong. Then the next that comes in, let them in simplicity of heart sit down and turn in to the same light , and wait in the spirit; and so all the rest coming in, in the fear of the Lord, sit down in pure stillness and silence of all flesh, and wait in the light. Those who are brought to a pure still waiting upon God in the Spirit are come nearer to the Lord than words are; for God is spirit and in the spirit he is worshiped.

Worship in meeting may thus begin with stilling the mind and body, letting go of tensions and everyday worries, feeling the encompassing presence of others, and opening oneself to the Spirit. It may include meditation, reflection on a remembered passage from the Bible or other devotional literature, silent prayer, thanksgiving, praise of God, consideration of one's actions, remorse, request for forgiveness, or search for direction. Even in times of spiritual emptiness, Friends find it useful to be present in worship.

Worshiping together strengthens the members of the worshiping community and deepens the act of worship itself. Such communal worship is like a living organism whose individual but interdependent members are essential to one another and to the life of the greater whole. It is like the luminous unity and individual fulfillment that arise when musicians, responding to the music before them, offer up their separate gifts in concert. Friends sometimes use Paul's image and speak of the meeting for worship as a body whose head is Christ (I Cor. 12:27). The gifts and participation of each member are important in maintaining and enriching the spiritual life of the meeting for worship.

There is a renewal of spirit when we turn away from worldly matters to rediscover inward serenity. Friends know from experience the validity of Jesus' promise that "Where two or three are gathered together in my name, there am I in the midst of them" (Matthew 18:20). Often we realize our hopes for a heightened sense of the presence of God through the cumulative power of group worship, communicated in silent as well as vocal ministry. When we experience such a profound and evident sense of oneness with God and with one another, we speak of a "gathered" or "covered" meeting for worship.

Communion and Communication

Direct communion with God constitutes the essential life of the meeting for worship. Into its living stillness may come leadings and fresh insights that are purely personal, not meant to be shared. At other times they are meant for the Meeting at large to hear.

When a leading is to be shared, the worshiper feels a compelling inward call to vocal ministry. The very name "Quaker" is by tradition derived from the evident quaking of early Friends witnessing under the power of the Spirit. Though ministry is seldom accompanied by such out-ward signs, some still feel the inward quaking. Vocal ministry may take many forms, as prayer, praise of God, song, teaching, witnessing, or shar-ing. These messages may center upon a single, vital theme; often appar-ently unrelated leadings are later discovered to have an underlying unity. Such ministry and prayer may answer the unrecognized or unvoiced needs of other seekers.

When someone accepts the call of the Spirit to speak, fellow wor-shipers are likewise called to listen with openness of minds and hearts. Diffident and tender spirits should feel the Meeting community's loving encouragement to give voice, even if haltingly, to the message that may be struggling to be born within them. Friends whose thought has been long developing and whose learning and experience are profound serve the meeting best when they, like all others, wait patiently for the prompting of the Inward Teacher. Anyone moved to speak following another should first allow others to absorb and respond inwardly to what has already been said.

Friends should not put obstacles in the way of the call, whether by deciding in advance to speak or not to speak, or by feeling a duty to speak to provide some balance between silence and the spoken word. Even if not a word is spoken, meetings for worship can be profoundly nurturing.

Hindrances to Worship
All present should remember that spiritual opportunities entail responsi-bilities as well, including attention to the time of assembling and consid-eration for those already settled. Speaking carried on in a spirit of debate or lecturing or discussion is destructive to the life of the meeting for wor-ship and of the meeting community. It is rarely helpful to answer or rebut what has been said previously. Friends moved to vigorous support of caus-es need to find brief and sensitive ways to voice their insights. Similar sen-sitivity should be practiced by those who bring material to be posted or shared during worship. Any who habitually settle into silent reading or sit in inattentive idleness cut themselves off from their fellow worshipers and from the pervasive reach of the Spirit. If hindrances to worship occur within a meeting for worship, members of Worship and Ministry or oth-ers as appropriate should move quickly and in love to provide counsel.

In Closing

Friends gather for worship in quiet waiting upon God. We come together out of our care for one another and out of our shared hunger to know God, to follow the leading of the Spirit, to feel with clarity our shortcomings and the reality of forgiveness, to give voice to our anguish, faith, praise, joy, and thanksgiving. At the close of the meeting for worship, we shake hands in acknowledgment of our commitment to one another and to God, and go forth with renewed trust in the power and reality of God's grace and love.

Decision-Making

The presuppositions of the corporate meeting for worship have, from the very beginning, profoundly affected the method of decision-making in the meeting for business. In both, there is faith in the Guide. There is faith in a continuous revelation that is always open to produce fresh disclosures. And there is respect and affection for each other that cuts through all diversity and that helps to kindle a faith that, with patience and openness, the group can expect to come to clearness and to resolve the problems that come before it.

– Source unknown

From Faith Into Business

Friends' decision-making is rooted in the spiritual oneness of a religious community. We reject majority rule for the higher goal of reaching decisions in unity, through distinctive attitudes developed by Friends over the centuries. Our process is democratic in the sense that everyone is encouraged to participate. However, it also goes beyond democracy in that it does not rely solely on human will or ability. Participants are expected to put aside personal desires and allow themselves to be led by a Guide beyond the self.

When this decision-making process is used carelessly, its lack of formal rules of order can lead to abuse by neglect or by design. When used with care, it is deeply satisfying and produces practical decisions that are in harmony with the Spirit.

The act of choosing is inescapably religious, in that it reveals our fundamental values and deepest loyalties. Friends must therefore be rigorous in discerning the ultimate source of their leadings, always looking beyond the self, and never letting their own wills become a substitute for God.

The Religious Basis of Our Decision-Making
Despite the difference in format, meetings for business are meetings for worship in which our business is held and are conducted in the same openness to the leading of the Spirit. For our religious community to thrive, it is essential that we nurture our love for one another, maintain our spiritual unity, and live in harmony with the Spirit. These beliefs underlie every attitude and practice in our meetings for business.

As we wrestle with outward issues, the Inward Light gives us new perspectives and creative responses. On all matters, even the mundane, its presence promises a fresh revelation of truth and a clearer understanding of God's will.

It is also our experience that new openings to truth may come at any time and from any source. Each Friend should therefore listen to all efforts to express that truth, testing them against accumulated experience, the life and teachings of Jesus, and moral and spiritual guides in Scripture and elsewhere. Yet we are careful to rely not on the letter of the text, but to read as George Fox enjoined us to read the Scriptures: "in the Spirit in which they were given forth."

The Goal of Friends' Decision-making
The goal of Friends' decision-making is a Spirit-led sense of the meeting – a crystallization of the search for clarity on the topic under consideration. Even in the face of strong difference of opinion, that goal is achievable when there is spiritual unity.

Our search is for unity, not unanimity. We consider ourselves to be in unity when our search for Truth is shared; when our listening for God is faithful; when our wills are caught up in the presence of Christ; and when our love for one another is constant. A united meeting is not necessarily all of one mind, but it is all of one heart.

We believe that this unity, transcending apparent differences, springs from God's empowering love, and that a Meeting, trusting in the leadership of that love and gathered in its spirit, will enjoy unity in its search for truth.

A Meeting is a living spiritual entity which may encompass strong differences of opinion. It is like an individual who may have many conflicting inclinations but who still has a final sense of how to act. The sense of the meeting is not designed and fitted together, but is conceived, born, and nurtured; the Meeting's care for the quality of its decision-making process is essential to the rightness of its decisions in the same way that an expectant mother's care for her own health is essential to the strength of her child.

Sense of the meeting is not synonymous with consensus. Consensus is a widely used and valuable secular process characterized by a search for general agreement largely through rational discussion and compromise. Sense of the meeting is a religious process characterized by listening for and trusting in God. Both result in a course of action agreed to by all of the participants, but the sense of the meeting relies consciously on the Spirit. Although reasoned argument and lively debate may often play a role in Friends' decision-making, they are useful only to the extent that they are the expressions of spiritual leadings.

When the sense of the meeting has been rightly discerned, those present will know that they have faithfully followed their Guide, and will feel a continued affection for each other.

Expectations of Participants

Among Friends, the decisions made by a group are enriched when all members commit themselves to regular attendance at meetings for worship as well as at decision-making sessions.

By maintaining a spirit of worship throughout the meeting, participants nurture their openness to the leadings of the Spirit and its gifts of trust, humility, compassion, and courage.

Although an individual Friend has the designated role of clerk, all share the responsibility for the maintenance of a Spirit-led gathering, for the wise use of time, and for a steadfast search for truth. All are expected to be attentive and to offer concisely such insight as each may have. None should remain silent in the belief that the conclusion is foregone, or that an insight apparently counter to that of the body of the Meeting will be divisive.

Friends who feel they cannot agree with what they perceive to be the weight of the Meeting must not yield to the temptation to absent themselves from the meeting for business in order to spare both themselves and the Meeting. Such an absence implies a lack of faith in the Meeting's access to divine guidance and its ability to find unity.

Both speaking and listening should be marked by respect for others, with speakers saying only what they know to be worth others' hearing, and with listeners seeking the Light as it is revealed through others. An openness of spirit is crucial, especially when differing views are being expressed.

Friends have learned the value of contributions from serious and consistent attenders who are not members. Many Meetings welcome all who care to attend at decision-making sessions. Non-members should show sensitive restraint when addressing Meeting affairs. Each Meeting is at liberty to limit the participation of attenders; such limits should be clearly defined and communicated in advance to avoid embarrassment and hurt feelings. Prior definition is particularly important with respect to any sessions which involve confidential information or evaluations of individuals.

No one should take action on the Meeting's behalf in anticipation of a minute's approval, but should wait for actual approval.

The Role of the Clerk

Ideally, the clerk is both servant and leader who thoughtfully prepares for the meeting; maintains a worshipful spirit in the meeting; sets a helpful pace; discerns the sense of the meeting when it is present; and expresses it clearly or identifies those who can do so. Such a clerk sensitively searches for the right course of action and helps maintain the meeting's spiritual unity. All these tasks are accomplished in an active, informed, helping spirit, facilitating but never dominating, carefully free from partisanship.

When nominated and appointed by members of the Meeting, the clerk accepts the obligation to focus time, energies, and gifts in the fulfillment of that trust.

The clerk helps the Meeting move through the agenda with efficient but unhurried dispatch, keeping the members' attention on the matters to be considered. The clerk listens, learns, and sifts, searching for the sense of the meeting, possibly suggesting tentative minutes or periods of silent worship to help clarify or focus Friends' leadings. The clerk encourages those who are reluctant to speak, and in like manner restrains those who tend to speak at undue length or to speak too often.

When the sense of the meeting seems to be clear, the clerk lays it before the Meeting. If there are objections or reservations, the clerk opens the way for further seeking and refinement. When there are no further objections or refinements, the clerk directs that the sense of the meeting be so recorded.

It is especially important that the clerk make clear what previous decisions or customs have been established on a given issue since lack of unity on a proposed change normally means that the status quo will be preserved.

When the sense of the meeting seems elusive, the clerk should be sensitive to the potential benefit of deferring the matter to a later time, to a different body, or to a different forum.

The clerk should be careful to refrain from opinionated participation in the discussion. Further, the clerk should be alert to those occasions when his or her ability to read the sense of the meeting may be blurred by deep personal convictions. In that event, the clerk stands aside and asks the Meeting to recognize someone else as clerk for the moment.

After the meeting is concluded it is the clerk's duty to ensure that those charged by the Meeting with new tasks or specific actions are informed of their responsibilities. The clerk also takes care that matters held over appear in later agenda. Finally, letters or documents whose drafting has been entrusted to the clerk are promptly dispatched.

The Role of the Recording Clerk

The proceedings of a meeting should be carefully and appropriately minuted by someone designated to serve as recording clerk.

Since meetings are held for different purposes, the recording clerk's minutes reflect the essential purpose of each meeting, be it for decision, for discussion, or for inspiration. The recording clerk should state precisely the nature, extent, and timing of actions directed to be taken and the persons responsible. Ambiguity and inaccuracy must be avoided.

Minutes should be written in the knowledge that at a later date the Meeting may well need a full and circumstantial account of its decision and how it was reached.

In the writing of minutes, the recording clerk is more effective when there has been detailed prior consultation with the presiding clerk so that names, dates, and proposals are already familiar. It is then also possible for the recording clerk to prepare tentative introductory sentences for each item of business, especially those that are routine.

A recording clerk does not hesitate to ask for help in formulating minutes. Where the action to be taken is clear but the wording of the proposed minute is not, it is sometimes useful to ask a few Friends to withdraw to prepare a final draft for the Meeting's later consideration. In some cases, the presiding clerk rather than the recording clerk will be in a better position to write the minute.

The recording clerk may at times be asked to prepare a minute on a matter of substance while the Meeting waits. All others present should settle into silent and supportive prayer until this task is complete.

In some instances a meeting may approve a minute in principle, being satisfied that its later refinement need not come before the Meeting again.

Once adopted, minutes retain their authority until amended by a subsequent minute.

To prevent confusion and misunderstanding, some Meetings find it useful for the recording clerk to read the minutes and have them approved from time to time during the course of the meeting or at the end; others read only those minutes referring to weighty and difficult matters and approve the complete minutes at the following session. Meetings follow a variety of practices in this regard, each of which has merit. If minutes are considered at a later session, those not present when business was discussed and actions taken should refrain from sharing in the approval of the minutes.

Recording clerks and clerks are granted the freedom to make only editorial changes or correct inaccuracies in the minutes, taking care that their meaning is in no way changed thereby. If other correction is needed, it should be brought before the Meeting at a later session.

All minutes are preserved in ways that will ensure their availability and permanence.

The Good Order Used Among Us

Thoughtful preparation frees the Meeting to follow the leadings of the Spirit, preventing frustration arising from poor arrangements, incomplete information, or unclear procedure.

The clerks or other designated persons prepare the agenda and, if appropriate, distribute the agenda and other essential information in advance. They may need to remind persons who are to bring matters before the meeting to come prepared. They must be careful to call members' attention to issues of special moment.

Arrangements are made for the time and place of gathering, child care, meals, hospitality, and other organizational matters as needed, to permit as many as possible to attend and to provide ample opportunity for the unhurried disposition of business.

Members who are prompt in arrival and disciplined in settling into worship contribute much to the depth and power of the meeting. It is also important that this time of settling and focusing not become a brief formality.

Where a presiding or recording clerk has not already been appointed or is unable to serve, the Meeting may ask any member to serve until a regular appointment is made.

Decision-making by sense of the meeting applies to easy issues as well as to difficult ones. Matters felt to be routine but necessary are dealt with quickly in a spirit of trust. The Meeting may accept without extended discussion a suggestion volunteered by the clerk or other member, or may empower an individual or a committee to act on the matter.

Matters of importance are best presented by someone who is familiar with the issues. However, the Meeting must also be open to hear the concerns of others who may not be as widely experienced or well informed, but who nevertheless feel strongly led.

The promptings of the Inward Teacher may come with power to any present, without respect to age or experience. Friends know that sensitive and powerful insights come to newer and younger members They also know the importance of those whose experience and advice in similar matters have been helpful in the past.

THE MEETING IN CONFLICT

Friends often find themselves most challenged when matters before them call forth strongly held but incompatible responses. A Meeting which goes forward for whatever reason without real unity in the Spirit does so at its peril. When any member present feels so strongly led as to wish to prevent the Meeting from acting, it is important that the Meeting take the time to test this leading in a loving spirit, and examine responsibly the consequences if the action is not taken.

The search for the course of action that will keep the meeting in unity —or the resolution of the problems caused by disunity itself—rests as much with the individual or group in opposition as it does with the other members.

Questions for a Meeting in Conflict

When disagreement on an issue threatens to divide a Meeting, it may be helpful for the Meeting and each Friend to consider the following questions:

• Have all Friends taken care to fully examine, in a loving and prayerful spirit, the perspective of those with whom they disagree?

• Have all Friends truly tried to leave behind their personal desires, the better to be led by the Spirit?

- Do all Friends seek to discern God's will in all viewpoints?
- Have Friends considered whether God's will for them as individuals may differ from God's will for the Meeting?
- Do those in conflict regularly reaffirm, in voice and attitude, the love they feel for one another?

Moving Forward in Unity

In situations of conflicting insights, Friends have found helpful several ways of moving forward in unity:

- The Meeting may move to a deeper spiritual searching and sharing, often entering periods of silent worship. Every conviction is examined in the Light as Friends wait together to discern whether their convictions stem from a genuine motion of the Spirit. Friends may thus be empowered to lay aside those convictions which are not so based. While seeking new light, Friends should also remain faithful to the leadings they sense as authentic, even when these seem contrary to the weight of the Meeting.
- The Meeting may wait or proceed with other business while a small representative ad hoc committee withdraws, in the hope that they can bring forward a minute or course of action that will lead to unity.
- The Meeting may reschedule the matter for another time, encouraging members in the interim to continue their search for the right action, whether in solitary prayer and meditation, or in small informal groups.
- After patient searching over a considerable period, the Meeting may conclude that the sense of the meeting is clear and unity in the Spirit can be maintained if that sense is translated into action, but acknowledge that a few Friends continue to have reservations about the substance of the proposed action. In that event, those Friends may feel led to withdraw their objections, being unwilling to stand in the way of the Meeting. Or those Friends may say that they feel released from the burden of their concern, having laid it on the conscience of the Meeting. Or they may stand aside while maintaining their objections, asking that their names and the grounds of their objections be minuted.

Friends who stand aside are affirming their continuing spiritual unity with the Meeting. That unity will require of those Friends acceptance with good grace of the decision's consequences for the Meeting and for themselves. It will require the rest of the Meeting to keep the objections firmly in mind as they proceed.

Each of these avenues expresses trust in divine guidance and a commitment to remaining in unity in the Spirit.

Committees for Clearness

Friends may be most familiar with clearness as the process a Meeting uses to decide whether to take a marriage under its care, or to accept someone into membership. More and more, however, Friends are rediscovering the power of committees for clearness to guide and support members facing a crisis in their lives, sensing a leading towards a personal witness or considering a change in life's direction.

Those who wish the help of a clearness committee may ask the clerk of the Meeting that such a committee be formed. Meetings are encouraged to establish a procedure for the forming of clearness committees so that the Meeting may be prepared and supportive when a Friend so requests.

Members of a clearness committee are chosen based on their willingness to devote prayerful time and energy, their knowledge and experience, and their ability to ask searching questions and provide support and guidance in a spirit of loving worship. Those seeking clearness may suggest Friends who would bring significant gifts to the committee.

When Friends gather in a committee for clearness, we find ourselves under the same loving discipline as when we gather for meetings for worship and business: an openness to the Holy Spirit and a commitment to one another and to discerning God's will. We listen deeply to those who have asked for guidance. We do not come intent on giving advice or taking a position. The gathering includes an explanation of the issue or problem for which clearness has been sought, periods of worship, time for questions, and an opportunity for the sharing of insight and inspiration. The clerk of the committee guides this process, mindful of the needs of the Friend seeking clearness and of the promptings of the Spirit.

Whether or not clearness is reached, it is helpful to report to the monthly meeting, being careful to respect confidentiality. This enables the Meeting to continue to respond to the Friend who requested clearness, and to support any changes or witness this Friend undertakes.

Committees for clearness can help Friends be obedient to the Spirit and enable Meetings to better support and nurture their members, build trust, and deepen spiritual community.

Friends and the Bible

Friends' appreciation of the Bible and other scriptures springs from our faith that there is in everyone the capacity to be open and responsive to the experience of the Divine. The possibility of that experience has been present in every place and time, even before the Bible was written, whenever and wherever people have earnestly sought communion with God and an understanding of God's will.

The influence of the Bible upon the Society of Friends has been both unique and profound. George Fox knew the Bible intimately prior to his great "openings"—openings that dealt radically with both religious and social issues and that continue to influence our Society. He insisted that his openings came first by God's "immediate spirit and power" but were later found to be "agreeable to Holy Scriptures." Like Fox, Friends since have found the Bible to be the record of direct experiences of the Holy Spirit, serving as an important touchstone against which to test our leadings.

Friends at all times have brought to their reading of these scriptures light from other sources. Through historical, literary, and cultural studies as well as sifted experience we have enriched the insights provided by our reading of the Bible. As a Society we have been generally freed from the so-called conflict between science and faith, finding instead therein a mutual illumination.

Friends know from experience that knowledge of the Bible widely shared in a Meeting deepens the spiritual power of both spoken ministry and inward listening. The Bible, moreover, even in those parts that seem alien and uncongenial, challenges us to examine more closely our current assumptions and leadings. Maturing insight and experience often discover that passages once apparently irrelevant and lifeless speak truth with power.

Given the Bible's importance in shaping the ways Friends have expressed their experience of the presence and leading of God and its power to illumine our worship and our vocal ministry, we are encouraged to know it well.

We do not, however, consider scriptures, whether Hebrew or Christian or those of other religious faiths, to be the final revelation of God's nature and will. Rather, we believe in continuing revelation. This term emphasizes our ongoing communion with the Living God, our expanding sensitivity in our relationships with one another, and our growing knowledge of the universe.

Since it also has great nurturing power for individuals, knowledge of the Bible opens our spirits to the religious power of art, music, and literature. The Bible warns us as well of the violence that can spring from our individual self-righteousness and of the hard-heartedness rooted in our alienation from God. It offers the words to express the guidance that can flow from our responsiveness to the Light Within, as in Amos' call that we "let justice roll down like waters, and righteousness like an everflowing stream" (Amos 5:24); as in Jesus' citing the two great commandments (Matt. 22: 37-39); and as in Paul's injunction that we speak the truth in love (Eph. 4:15). Yet most importantly, the Bible offers us hope, as in Jesus' assurance: "Ask, and it shall be given you; seek, and you shall find; knock, and it shall be opened to you" (Matt. 7:7).

Prayer

The continuing experience of Friends has been that opening ourselves in prayer to the Divine is essential for deepening worship and rightly ordered lives. Since Friends have no prescribed form of prayer, we are free to choose those practices and those words to designate the Divine that meet our individual needs.

There are many ways to pray. Prayer can be sung, thought, spoken, or expressed through the work of our hands or the movements of our bodies. We may use formal prayers, such as the one that Jesus taught us, or pour forth our own heartfelt words. Prayer can be as simple as delighted gratitude for the day. It can be the quiet outpouring of the desire of the heart or even wordless, simply being in the Presence. It can be as complex as digging into ourselves in order to remove blocks to openness to the Spirit's action in our lives.

For many, prayer also grows out of a desire for a closer relationship with God as we discover that God reaches for us even as we reach for God. God loves us first. To center and be close to God can be a difficult exercise; yet, sometimes, with no apparent effort, one feels prayed through as an instrument of the Holy Spirit. Our prayers and lives of service are a response to this Infinite Love as we experience who we are and from whom we come.

Prayer with others or in solitude or in the attentive listening in the quiet of the meeting for worship often becomes the seedbed for leadings to service. When action proceeds out of lives of prayer, it serves neither the ego nor the need to succeed but instead fulfills our desire to be faithful to the leadings of the Light.

For many, asking God for healing for ourselves and for others is an integral part of prayer. It is their experience that mind and spirit, though wounded even at the deepest levels, can be healed through prayer and so become whole. Listening to our inmost being where the Inward Christ dwells enables us to go out and touch others in love and acceptance. Through prayer, Friends can enter with those of other faiths into a unity deeper than words or forms.

Many Friends have found that regular times for prayer are an important discipline, for it is through regular practice that prayer becomes central to our lives. Indeed, through the regular practice of prayer, our spirits grow and flourish in unanticipated ways. In the assurance that our Creator hears and cares, prayer can be a time of humble confession and yearning for forgiveness, a time when we do not ask for answers but seek to return to the order of God's world. In prayer we can pour forth our sorrow, our anger, our love, our joy, our thanksgiving for inward peace.

While prayer is most often intensely private, vocal prayer can be a helpful ministry in meetings for worship and for business. It may also spring up or be requested in the company of another or in small groups. Whether as individuals or families or Meetings, in spoken or silent grace before meals, we gratefully acknowledge our dependence upon God.

In prayer we may open ourselves to God's loving, teaching, healing, and recreating us so that we become people who worship in spirit and in truth and do God's work with joy on earth.

Friends and the Sacraments

The absence from Friends' worship of the outward observance of the Lord's Supper, water baptism, and other sacraments emphasizes the reality of inward experience. Friends are aware of the power of a true, inward baptism of the Holy Spirit; in meeting for worship at its best they know direct communion with God and fellowship with one another. These experiences make the outward rites seem unnecessary and, to some Friends, a hindrance to full attainment of the spiritual experiences which are symbolized.

While fully appreciative of the help that has come through the outward forms to many generations of Christians, Friends symbolize by their very lack of symbols the essentially inward nature of the sacraments. However, just as rituals and forms may become ends in themselves and thus diminished in spiritual power, so doctrinaire repudiation of form and ritual may become an end in itself, devoid of life.

Friends affirm the sacramental nature of the whole of life when it is under the leading of the Spirit. Any moment, any relationship, any object when so touched can serve as a sacrament. Insofar as we are faithful in our testimonies, our very lives may thus serve for others as the outward and visible evidence of inward and invisible communion.

Membership

THE MEANING OF MEMBERSHIP

The Religious Society of Friends is a community of faith based on experience of a transforming power named many ways: the Inner Light, the Spirit of Christ, the Guide, the Living God, the Divine Presence. Membership includes openness to an ongoing relationship with God and willingness to live one's life according to the leadings of the Spirit as affirmed by the community of faith. For generations of Friends, membership has been an outward sign of an inward experience of Christ, the "true light which gives light to everyone" (John 1:9).

In Philadelphia Yearly Meeting, Friends gather to worship in stillness, waiting upon the Divine Presence. From this have come revelations of the love and guiding will of God, revelations inwardly experienced that may be shared in words with others present and expressed in attitude and action. Participation in this form of worship is intrinsic to membership, since ours is above all an experiential religion. Friends do not require acceptance of a creed as a test of membership, believing that no creedal statement can adequately describe spiritual reality.

Membership establishes a commitment. It means that for each member the Religious Society of Friends provides the most promising home for spiritual enlightenment and growth. It commits a person to the daily pursuit of truth after the manner of Friends and commits the Meeting to support the member in that pursuit. Membership includes a willingness to live in spiritual unity with other members of the Religious Society of Friends.

Members are expected to participate in communal worship, to share in the work and service of the Society, and to live in harmony with its basic beliefs and practices. Membership entails readiness to live as part of the monthly, quarterly, and yearly meeting. Specifically, this means participation in meeting for worship, meeting for business, committee work, and giving time, skills, and financial support to Meeting activities such as religious education, pastoral care, and witness to the broader community. Since Friends reject the distinction between clergy and laity, responsibility for the full range of Meeting activities rests with the membership.

Friends Meetings are often visited by people from other religious backgrounds or with no religious ties. All visitors should be made welcome, with continuing attention given to those who return frequently and become regular attenders. Meeting members should endeavor to get acquainted with attenders and be available for spiritual support and guidance. Some Meetings have committees concerned specifically for the care of visitors and attenders.

The Meeting should invite regular attenders to participate in its life, recognizing that they may become members. They should be made familiar with Friends' way of worship, manner of conducting business, organizational structure, finances, and major spiritual and historical writings, as well as Friends' periodicals. They should be encouraged to attend business meetings and, at the discretion of the monthly meeting, to serve on committees. Attenders should also be urged to attend sessions of quarterly and yearly meeting and gatherings of Friends General Conference. Information about groups such as the American Friends Service Committee, Friends Committee on National Legislation, and Friends World Committee for Consultation should be made available. All regular attenders should be provided a copy of Faith and Practice.

Attenders who seem nourished through their involvement with the Meeting, are comfortable with Friends' basic beliefs and practices, and understand the responsibilities of membership, should apply for membership. The Meeting, for its part, should encourage such attenders to apply.

Before attenders apply, they may find it valuable to discuss their spiritual goals and concerns with Friends in whose wisdom, experience, and personal sympathy they have confidence. These Friends will guide the attender in deciding whether he or she is ready to apply or should first become more familiar with the Religious Society of Friends.

Application for Membership
The monthly meeting is the final authority in all matters concerning an individual's membership. A person joining a monthly meeting becomes thereby a member of a quarterly meeting, the yearly meeting, and the Religious Society of Friends. There is no membership in Philadelphia Yearly Meeting other than membership in a particular monthly meeting.

Attenders who apply for membership should do so in a formal request to the clerk of the monthly meeting, stating why they are moved to join the Religious Society of Friends and relating briefly their response to Friends' beliefs and practices. The clerk may share such requests with the Meeting and then refer them to the overseers, or may refer them directly to the overseers, who in either case promptly appoint a clearness committee to visit the applicant.

The clearness committee should undertake this visit as a serious responsibility both to the Meeting and to the applicant. The visit should take place in an atmosphere of openness and caring so that both the committee members and the applicant feel comfortable in exploring fundamental questions of religious belief and practice and the responsibilities involved in membership in the Society. Some questions the committee might ask are:

• What are some milestones in your spiritual journey? How do you expect membership in the Meeting to help you in this journey?

• What gifts do you believe you might bring to the Meeting community? In what ways would you like to share your time and talents with the Meeting?

• How familiar are you with Friends' beliefs and practices? Are there some in particular which attracted you to Friends? Are there some you find puzzling or disturbing?

• Are you comfortable with a Society whose unity of spirit coexists with a diversity of beliefs? Are you prepared to join a Meeting family which includes people whose perspectives may differ considerably from yours?

• Have you weighed the Queries and Advices? Does their guidance speak to you?

• How closely are you in harmony with Friends' testimonies? With Friends' work for social justice?

• Are you prepared to suffer (as Friends have done) if God calls you to take actions which are difficult, unpopular, or even contrary to the civil laws?

• Do you understand the relationship between the monthly, quarterly, and yearly meeting? Are you aware of and willing to meet our expectation of financial support for programs, services, and facilities at these three levels of our organizational structure?

The clearness committee needs to be prepared to respond faithfully to a wide range of questions that the applicant may ask. The applicant should be encouraged to share expectations concerning the Meeting and the significance of membership.

Applicants who are members of another religious body are expected to give up that membership as they join the Meeting, formally advising the other organization of their intent to join the Religious Society of Friends, and endeavoring to obtain a letter of release from their previous religious affiliation.

If the overseers approve the application, they recommend acceptance to the monthly meeting. Action may be postponed until a later session to give time where needed for members to become well acquainted with the prospective member.

If the monthly meeting approves the application, it records the acceptance into membership and appoints two or more Friends to welcome the new member.

While the desire of an attender to become a member is generally a cause for rejoicing, the overseers should not hesitate to advise the Meeting to postpone acceptance or even to reject an application if there is good reason to do so, such as an applicant's inflexible disagreement with some significant aspect of Friends' religious practice or belief. In cases where the overseers recommend postponement of a decision and the Meeting agrees, the overseers should keep in sympathetic touch with the applicant, explaining the reason for the hesitancy and seeking to help remove it. If and when the overseers judge the applicant to be ready for membership, they should encourage the Meeting to reconsider and accept the application.

If a person whose residence is remote from Meetings of Friends wishes to become a member, the monthly meeting should consider carefully whether the applicant's needs, as well as those of the Meeting, will be served by membership in absentia. Quakerism grows as we give and receive within a living community. It may help to recommend participation in the Wider Quaker Fellowship rather than membership in a particular monthly meeting.

CHILDREN

All children from birth to maturity need to feel themselves full participants in the fellowship of the Meeting, to be nurtured in their spiritual development and their understanding of the faith and practice of Friends, and to be guided and encouraged in preparation for Quaker adulthood. The Meeting should sympathetically help children prepare for the decisions they must face, such as those regarding cultural conformity and military service. As they mature, if they have received this care from their Meeting, they will become increasingly conscious of the full meaning of the responsibilities of membership in the Religious Society of Friends and be ready to make their own decision regarding membership. Growing up in a Meeting offers children an extended religious family. It is the Meeting's joyful responsibility to provide an atmosphere of care, love, and recognition—in short, a spiritual home—for all young people in the Meeting, regardless of their membership status or that of their parents.

A monthly meeting's approach to membership for children should promote the goal of a Religious Society of Friends made up of members by mature convincement. Some Friends believe the process of nurture of the young toward mature convincement is aided by a child's sense of belonging fully to a Meeting, a sense that comes only with membership. Other Friends believe the process is aided by a status of associate member that calls for a child to make an assertion of mature convincement when ready to do so. Still others believe that any form of involuntary membership limits a child's freedom to choose. Monthly meetings are encouraged to respect parents' sense as to what is best for their children.

Thus, either on their own initiative or in response to an inquiry from the Meeting, parents who are members may, at the time of their child's birth or adoption or later: [1] request membership for their child; [2] request associate membership for their child; [3] not request any enrollment for the child. If the parents are members of different Meetings, the parents decide which Meeting records the child. When only one parent is a member, children may be recorded upon the request of one parent and with the permission of the other or, under unusual circumstances, upon the request of one parent. Where there is only one legal parent, that member may request membership or associate membership for the child. Meetings are urged to recognize the diversity of family patterns and be sensitive to the concerns of all involved.

Parents requesting membership for their child should intend to raise the child as a Friend in a Meeting community. The parents and the Meeting should help the child to grow gradually into the responsibilities of membership, and should encourage the child to take on specific responsibilities when ready. The meeting has an obligation to those recorded as members at a young age to ensure that as they reach adulthood they are aware that they should thoughtfully consider their own commitment to membership.

Associate membership is available only to children. It carries with it the full responsibilities and privileges of membership up to age 21. (For yearly meeting statistical purposes associate members will not be recorded after their 21st birthday.) Associate members, when they are led, may request full membership. The monthly meeting should encourage associate members nearing the age of 21 to apply. If an associate member does not take this step by the age of 21, that person's name will be dropped from membership. If an associate member is not clear by that age about applying and is dropped from membership, it is the Meeting's responsibility to continue a caring relationship. Such a person may be encouraged to apply for membership when ready.

A person may apply for membership in a Meeting at any age, following the procedure set forth above. Meetings are urged to show a loving flexibility which recognizes the uniqueness of each person's spiritual growth. Some people are spiritually ready for membership early in their lives; others are ready only as adults. In the case of younger applicants, it may be desirable to ascertain the support of the parents or guardian.

TRANSFER OF MEMBERSHIP TO ANOTHER MEETING

Friends who live at a distance from their own monthly meeting but near another will do well to transfer their membership to the nearer one unless there is some very special reason not to do so. Residence in the vicinity makes it possible to enjoy the benefits, and to carry out the responsibilities, of membership in a particular Meeting. Inability to participate in the life of one's own Meeting means a loss to both the individual and the Meeting. A member of one monthly meeting who moves to the area of another is normally accepted as a member of the Religious Society of Friends and welcomed into membership.

Pending transfer of membership, both Meetings should cooperate in discharging their responsibility toward the member.

Duties of the monthly meeting from which the member is moving

To initiate the transfer of membership, Friends who have moved away from their Meeting should apply to that Meeting for a letter of transfer to a Meeting near their new place of residence.

When a monthly meeting receives such an application for transfer, the overseers should, unless there is a strong reason to doubt their member's willingness to contribute to the life of another Meeting, prepare in duplicate a letter of transfer, recommending the Friend to the care of the Meeting to which transfer is requested.

If the monthly meeting approves the application for transfer, the clerk should sign the letter, the principal copy being forwarded to the receiving monthly meeting, the duplicate being retained for the records.

When the Meeting issuing the transfer receives acknowledgment that the new Meeting has accepted the Friend into membership, the original Meeting terminates the Friend's membership, noting its action in the minutes.

Duties of the monthly meeting to which the Friend is moving
The clerk of the monthly meeting to which a member is being transferred should acknowledge receipt of the letter. Then the clerk should refer it to the overseers who should recommend action to the monthly meeting. If there is ground for serious objection to the transfer, the letter should be returned to the Meeting which issued it. If there is no objection, the monthly meeting should accept the transfer and record the Friend as a member, sending information to that effect to the issuing Meeting, to which the Friend in the interim has continued to belong.

Following a transfer, the monthly meeting should appoint one or more Friends to welcome the new member, including an invitation to attend meetings for worship and business, serve on committees, and share in the financial support of the Meeting.

Duties of the recorder concerning letters of transfer
The recorder should keep a list of all letters of transfer issued and accepted by the Meeting. The accepting Meeting's recorder should notify the yearly meeting of the new member.

On occasion, Friends request a transfer of membership for reasons other than a change of residence. The procedure noted above applies in any case.

Sojourning members
Friends may attend a monthly meeting because they have moved temporarily into its vicinity, but may not wish to give up membership in their home Meeting, to which they expect to return eventually. Their desires in this regard should be set forth in a minute from their home Meeting. Such Friends are listed as sojourning members of the Meeting they attend. Sojourning Friends may fulfill all functions that they are willing to undertake and that the host Meeting sees fit to assign to them. However, they should not be counted in the statistical reports of the host Meeting. Their sojourning membership ends when they leave the area of the Meeting where they have sojourned. Its clerk should then notify their home Meeting. Those who continue as sojourning Friends for an extended

period should be asked to examine their reasons for remaining in that status, and to consider a transfer of membership.

Joining other religious bodies

If members wish to leave the Religious Society of Friends and join some other religious body, they should notify their monthly meeting. The monthly meeting may give them a letter stating their good standing in the Religious Society of Friends. When they have been received in membership by another religious group, their membership with Friends shall cease.

Requests for dual membership

Membership is a major commitment to participate in a particular community of Friends, and full participation in two religious bodies at once is usually impractical. Except in unusual circumstances, a member of Philadelphia Yearly Meeting belongs to a particular monthly meeting and should not hold membership in any other religious body, including another monthly meeting.

Termination of membership

Resignation by the individual

Members may find that they are not in accord with the faith and practice of Friends or do not feel led to be involved actively in a monthly meeting over a significant period of time. They should seek the advice of the overseers or of others in the Meeting in whom they have confidence and try with their help to examine their own beliefs and practices and the reasons for disagreement or uninvolvement with Friends. If no resolution results, they may resign from the Religious Society of Friends in a letter to the clerk of their Meeting.

When a member resigns, the Meeting is not absolved from further care. A committee appointed either from overseers or from the Meeting at large should visit the Friend, inquire in love and forbearance into the cause of the resignation and, if appropriate, endeavor to bring the member back into the fellowship of Friends. A resignation may be accepted without appointing a committee when the Meeting is already well acquainted with the case and is satisfied that the member's decision will not be altered by friendly efforts.

When the Meeting accedes to a member's decision to resign, a minute should be made stating that this Friend is released at his/her own request.

The individual should be informed of this action and is no longer a member of the Religious Society of Friends.

Letters written in acceptance of a resignation should always manifest a considerate regard for the person leaving membership.

Release by the monthly meeting

When a member disregards the obligations of membership and exhibits lack of interest or responsibility, fails to reply to communications from the overseers or others, or passes out of the knowledge of the Meeting, then being part of the Meeting is obviously of little value to that member. In such cases it is normally the task of overseers to attempt to restore interest and involvement. Under exceptional circumstances the monthly meeting may appoint a special committee for this purpose.

If continued efforts prove unavailing, the monthly meeting should make a minute noting the circumstances and recording removal of the individual from membership. The clerk of the Meeting should promptly send written notice of this action to the individual. Such notice should also remind the released individual that an appeal to quarterly meeting is possible; in such a case the quarterly meeting may be able to play a mediating role. It is, however, the monthly meeting's responsibility to make the final decision.

In the case of a Friend whose actions seem out of harmony with the standard of conduct appropriate to the Religious Society of Friends, the Meeting, primarily through the overseers, may seek to renew the commitment of the member to Friends' practice. If these efforts fail, and if the overseers believe that they can accomplish nothing further, they should report this to the monthly meeting, which may appoint a special committee to make further attempts to reach a satisfactory solution.

If all these efforts are to no avail, the monthly meeting should take steps toward removal of the Friend from membership. The overseers or a special committee should present in writing a proposed minute recommending such action. When the minute is received by the monthly meeting, a copy should be given promptly to the person involved, and action should be deferred to a future meeting. Friends toward whom the monthly meeting has acted in this way should be advised that they may explain their position to the monthly meeting in person or in writing.

If the monthly meeting subsequently believes that the membership of the Friend in question should be discontinued, the minute of removal should be adopted and the Friend notified of the action and of the potential mediating role of quarterly meeting. All dealings involving removal from membership should be handled with the utmost patience, forbearance, and consideration, for the sake of both the individual and the Meeting.

A person whose membership has been ended either by resignation or by action of the monthly meeting, and who desires to rejoin either the same or a different monthly meeting, may do so by following the procedure outlined earlier for application for membership.

Some persons may wish to retain membership in the Religious Society of Friends when, over a period of many years, they are not active in any monthly meeting. At its discretion, a monthly meeting may carry inactive persons on its membership rolls, while recognizing its obligation to report them as part of the basis for financial assessment by the quarterly and yearly meeting. Long-term nominal membership is generally discouraged, however, except when active Meeting participation is not possible because of poor health, residence far away from any Meeting (so that transfer of membership or sojourning membership is not feasible), or some other compelling factor.

Membership records

Accurate information on the membership status of each member is kept by the recorder of each monthly meeting and shared with the quarterly meeting and yearly meeting as requested.

Friends and Education

Since its beginnings in the mid-seventeenth century, the Religious Society of Friends has emphasized the importance of education both for its members and for society generally. Friends have held that all persons are potential channels for the Inner Light and that all can benefit from education. Such benefit is more likely if education is spiritual in its nature and objectives, if it draws people ever nearer to a concern for others and strengthens their commitment to live in accordance with spiritual principles.

For guidance in word and deed, we look first to the Spirit as revealed in ourselves and in others. We recognize as did George Fox that education in itself does not necessarily lead to a deeper spiritual sensitivity and that there are many who lack extensive formal education yet who bring pure water from the spiritual springs of life. But we also know from experience that the perspective provided by sound education, which includes the development of skills in listening and communicating, helps us to identify what is faithful to the Light in our own leadings, to interpret and communicate those leadings, and to weigh the leadings of others.

Friends regard spiritual growth as an essential component of sound education. Such growth occurs when our receptivity to the Inner Light, the Seed of Christ, the Teacher Within is nurtured by studying the Bible and other religious literature. While Friends emphasize spiritual maturation, we do not neglect the acquisition of intellectual and practical skills and of aesthetic appreciation. Whether within the family, monthly meeting, Friends schools and colleges, or the various levels of public education, Friends are committed to an educational experience that balances heart, mind, and hand in spiritual wholeness.

Many Friends today are called to careers in education of every kind and at every level, public and private, and see their service in these vocations as a form of religious witness.

Responsibilities of monthly meetings

Monthly meetings have a special responsibility to bring children and adults under their care into full participation in the life of the Meeting and into an understanding of the beliefs and practices of the Religious Society of Friends. Meetings are expected to offer religious education programs for their members and attenders. Such programs can include special study groups, worship sharing opportunities, service projects, and Meeting libraries, but the cornerstone of religious education for most Meetings is a thriving First Day School program for children, youth, and adults. These efforts will succeed only if members actively support them by full participation, rather than leaving parents to cope alone with the religious education of their children.

While recognizing the limitations of their spiritual, personal, and financial resources, Meetings should actively welcome every opportunity to nurture the spiritual growth of their members and attenders. A Meeting may be asked to assist individuals who seek financial and other practical support in order to attend a Friends school or a college/university. It may be asked to support individuals who are involved in continuing education, whether at a weekend conference or for a term at a Quaker study center. It may be asked to help individuals with special needs to attend public or private schools that have been established with those needs in mind. Occasionally, it may be asked to provide oversight for families that choose to instruct their children at home. A Meeting may consider the challenge

of forming and sustaining its own Friends school, should the children of
its members and attenders not have access to an existing Friends school. In
all of these ways, and in others besides, Meetings may have the opportunity to support the educational needs and objectives of the children and
adults under their care.

A periodic review of these responsibilities may be stimulated and
focused by the following queries:

1. What is our Meeting's vision of Friends witness in the world with
regard to education?

2. In what ways does our Meeting demonstrate support for Friends
education?

3. How do our Meeting and its members support education beyond
Friends schools?

4. If this Meeting has a school under its care, how does it exercise spiritual oversight and governance of the school?

5. How does our Meeting's school define itself as a Friends school?

Friends Schools and Colleges

Friends are the owners and managers of a substantial number of educational institutions. In the region served by Philadelphia Yearly Meeting
there are three colleges, a study/retreat center, and some forty schools
which have been founded and continue to be sustained by Friends and
Friends Meetings. Though the original purpose of most of the schools was
to provide an education for Friends' children that would shelter them from
the temptations of the larger society, they now welcome non-Friends and
seek to engage that society. Indeed, in all of its educational institutions, the
Religious Society of Friends primarily serves not itself, but the larger community. At the same time, these institutions seek to provide a kind of community life and experience that is founded upon and guided by Friends'
beliefs. Ideally, the experience of a Friends school or college, like the experience of a meeting for worship, is a withdrawal from the world into a spirit-led community, followed by a return to everyday life, nourished and
prepared for a more truthful engagement with it. Those who have experienced Friends' concern for simplicity, equality, justice, and compassion in
our educational institutions often have significant and positive influence
in their wider communities.

Friends as individuals and as Meetings have a special responsibility to
support Friends educational institutions. These institutions are an important Quaker outreach to the larger world, insofar as they embody our ways

of worship, our social testimonies, and our commitment to service. Thus, Friends seek to incorporate spiritual values throughout the entire program of our schools and colleges. We acknowledge there the cogency of George Fox's admonition that we "be patterns, be examples...that [our] carriage and life may preach among all sorts of people, and to them," so that both students and staff "will come to walk cheerfully over the earth, answering that of God in everyone." This religious orientation includes meeting for worship and the study of the Bible and other religious literature, and of Quakerism and other faiths. The intent is to deepen the religious awareness and growth of students and staff rather than to proselytize.

A Friends educational institution is more likely to fulfill its mission if there is a solid core of students, parents, and graduates who understand and actively support our Quaker beliefs and practices. The effectiveness of a Quaker witness in our schools and colleges especially depends upon the spiritual depth and commitment to Friends beliefs and practices of the members of the governing body, the administrators, and the staff. That commitment requires careful attention not only to the processes and structures of governance but also to preventing any form of discrimination or disempowerment based on age, gender, race, sexual orientation, economic status, or religion while assuring that prime importance be accorded to the students' welfare and proper education.

Friends schools and colleges today seek to include students and staff from widely varied economic and ethnic backgrounds. Such increasing diversity in our educational communities can both challenge and strengthen them. Bringing different traditions, experiences, and perspectives together in a common search for truth requires time, thought, and a genuine willingness to change, but offers the rewards of deeper understanding and a vital and inclusive community.

Friends and Public Education
Friends have a responsibility, as do all citizens, to be informed, concerned, and active contributors to the public educational system and hence to the quality of life in our communities. Whether as parents, teachers, administrators, school board members, consultants, or taxpayers, Friends can make an important witness.

We should also give informed, active support to those Quaker children who attend public schools and to those Friends who devote themselves as teachers and administrators in the public educational system at whatever level. Such support is of particular importance to those children and adults who, through their commitment to truth and through the quality of their relationships, seek to maintain a Quaker witness in situations where our testimonies are unpopular.

Quaker Marriage Procedure

Marriage is a sacred commitment of two people to love one another in faithful partnership with the expectation that the relationship will mature and be mutually enriching. Friends know that marriage depends on the inner experiences of the couple who marry and not on any external service or words. Thus, the ceremony in which the couple enter into this commitment is performed by the couple alone, in the presence of God, the families, and the worshiping community. Both the solemnity and the joy of the occasion are enhanced by its simplicity.

The Meeting extends its loving care through its oversight of clearness for the couple and, upon approval of the Meeting, through careful attention to a meeting for worship for marriage. In addition, care is given to assure that any applicable legal requirements are addressed.

Securing Meeting approval

The couple intending marriage writes to the Meeting or Meetings under whose care they would be married. Any date the couple is planning for the wedding should be far enough in the future to allow the Meeting time to fulfill its responsibilities.

When the clerk receives the request, the letter is customarily read at meeting for business, often after preliminary consideration by overseers. The Meeting then appoints a committee of clearness. Some Meetings have standing committees for this purpose, chosen from Friends of proven abilities.

The method of securing approval varies with circumstances.

a. When only one Meeting is being asked for the oversight, the couple simply forwards the request to the Meeting, which then appoints the clearness committee.

b. When the two belong to separate Meetings, they must allow time for both Meetings to consider the request. The Meetings may each name committees for clearness, or they may decide to name a joint committee. If one Meeting is at a distance, a correspondent may be assigned to confer with the clearness committee where the marriage will take place. Whatever the process, approval is granted by both Meetings before the couple proceeds with the wedding. A Meeting may offer assistance to Friends wishing to be married under its care, even though they live too far from their home Meeting to be married there.

c. When one of the couple is not a member of the Religious Society of Friends, the clearness committee endeavors through consultation with the couple and the family and friends of the non-member to discover whether obstacles exist.

d. If the Meeting agrees to consider a marriage under its care when neither party is a member of a Meeting, the clearness committee takes the necessary steps to become familiar with the couple and their circumstances before recommending approval. It should encourage the couple to take ample time to attend meetings for worship and offer themselves and the members of the Meeting the opportunity to come to know each other. Only so will non-members feel at home in the Meeting, and only so will the Meeting be able to grant clearness in good conscience. In the case of non-members, the Meeting also assures that any additional applicable legal requirements are met. (See also Marriage not under the care of the Meeting, p. 52)

Clearness: the process
The term clearness referred originally to clearness from other marriage commitments. Today, within a broader sense of clearness, the committee explores areas of understanding with the couple, considering what it takes to achieve the permanence and satisfaction of a committed, loving relationship, and the extent to which the couple is prepared for the dedication and constancy such a relationship requires. Knowledge of available resources for the couple and the committee is essential for any Meeting, including Quaker literature on the subject.

The purpose of clearness is well served when members of the committee ask thoughtful questions and listen attentively, leaving space for worship in the exchange. Potential difficulties—and the role of Divine assistance in this process as well as in the future development of the relationship—can be carefully and openly explored. A committee under the weight of the couple's future success knows that failure to speak truth in kindness is to risk possible suffering. Such truth is best shared from the actual experience of Friends.

The committee can be guided by these suggested queries for the couple:

• How did the couple meet? What values and beliefs do they hold in common? On what matters do they differ? Can they meet differences with humor and respect? Are they open to considering outside help if such guidance seems warranted?

• Do they both see marriage as sacred? Are they open to seeking divine assistance? What are their plans for nurturing the spiritual basis for their marriage?

• Do they each see themselves and their partner as equal and trusted, sharing responsibilities and decisions? Do they communicate feelings, needs, dreams and fears?

• Are they aware of the need for other friendships that contribute to both individual growth and the marriage relationship?

• Have they thought about children, and the joys and the challenges families create, including consideration of how the work is shared?

• If there are children in either relationship to consider, has the couple broached the subject of this change of relationship with them?

• How do they view their relationships to their extended families? to their community? to society as a whole?

• Are there prior obligations—legal or financial or other—that need to be met?

• What are the views of the parents concerning this relationship? (Parents may send a letter.)

• What other questions does the couple have?

The clearness committee does its best to confirm that the intended partners follow a true leading in seeking marriage. Since occasionally obstructions do appear, it is considered wise to treat all applications with the same degree of care. The focus for the committee is the two people being married and attention to their responsibilities to each other and to their families. Particularly with young people, the Meeting seeks from the parents of the couples their expressions of unity with this intention, usually in the form of a letter. When either of the couple brings children to this union, their well-being must be considered; but whether the children should be consulted regarding their feelings about their parent's marriage is a question to which there is no generally accepted answer. If the clearness committee and the couple feel that it would be helpful, it is appropriate to include the children in the clearness process.

While most Friends' marriage ceremonies conform to civil law, couples who do not want, or are not eligible to contract, a legal marriage occasionally ask for a ceremony of commitment or a wedding under the care of the Meeting. The Religious Society of Friends has long asserted its freedom to conduct under divine leading marriage ceremonies not conforming to civil law.

If the clearness committee is satisfied that there is no obstacle to the proposed marriage, it so reports to the monthly meeting at its next business session. If the Meeting finds no objection with the proposed marriage, it will approve holding an appointed meeting for worship for marriage, in accordance with the couple's wishes. Wedding invitations should be sent out only after the Meeting's approval is granted.

Overseeing the preparation

When the Meeting has given its approval for the wedding to take place under its care, it appoints an oversight committee from among its members, usually two men and two women, to oversee the arrangements. The parties to be married should be asked whether there is anyone they would like particularly to serve on this committee. Members of another Meeting may be included if so desired.

The oversight committee provides guidance to the couple as the marriage ceremony is arranged, including the obtaining of the applicable legal license and the Quaker marriage certificate. Oversight continues through the ceremony and afterwards, to assure that details are completed in right order. The oversight committee ordinarily assumes responsibility for the certificate and for the license until it is signed by the couple after the wedding. It keeps track of the process of obtaining and safeguarding the two documents through the completion of the signing, and the transferal to the appropriate parties. It also oversees the presentation of the certificate at the wedding.

Because in some places the proper license form may not be immediately available, it is important to allow enough time for obtaining the license. The Quaker marriage certificate also requires preparation well ahead of time. The couple arranges for the certificate and may need assistance in the details necessary to accomplish this. In addition, any contemplated changes from the traditional text deserve thoughtful and careful consideration, in consultation with the oversight committee.

Conducting a Quaker wedding

A Quaker wedding is a meeting for worship in which a marriage takes place. As the meeting for worship begins, some designated person may rise to explain, for the benefit of those new to Quaker worship, the absence of clergy, the role of the gathered, and the solemnity of the occasion. Printed information also has been found useful.

Following a period of silence, as long or as short as the couple is led to observe, the two rise and, each in turn taking the other by the hand, make their promises to each other, in the words from their marriage certificate, in tones clear enough to be heard throughout the meeting. When they are seated again, the marriage certificate is brought to them for their signatures. The certificate is then read to the meeting by a person asked in advance to do so. The meeting then continues and offers an opportunity to those present to share in the ceremony through prayer, meditation, and other spoken messages. The person chosen to close the meeting may, if desired, first allow the wedding party to withdraw. At the close of the meeting, all those who have been present are asked to sign the certificate as witnesses.

Friends are urged to consider carefully the intrusion into the spirit of worship that recording of any kind can present. Photographing, visible audio taping, and videotaping during the ceremony are often discouraged.

Following the wedding

Both sections of the marriage license obtained from the county or municipality are signed by the couple and by members of the oversight committee as witnesses. The proper section of the license thus signed is then returned within the legal time limit to the office from which it has been obtained.

The marriage certificate is handed to the Meeting's recorder to be entered in the records of the monthly meeting. When this has been done, the recorder sends the certificate to the newly married couple.

At the next business meeting the oversight committee reports to the monthly meeting that the wedding has taken place in accordance with Friends' practice, and that the requirements of the law have been properly observed.

Ongoing care and nurture of Friends married under a Meeting's care continues as long as the couple is in the community of the Meeting. If the couple relocates, the Meeting may maintain an informal relationship with them and stay open to requests for support or help, but the actual nurture is best carried out by the Meeting to which the couple transfers.

Marriage not under the care of the Meeting
Marriage of members apart from the Meeting community
Members who marry outside the Meeting should promptly inform the Meeting of their marriage. It is then the task of the Meeting to assign overseers to visit the newly married couple—or, if they live far away, to write to them—and to express the Meeting's continuing interest and care. Non-member marriage partners should be made welcome and invited to attend meetings for worship and business if they live within reach of the monthly meeting.

Meetings may offer a place of worship and other assistance at the request of Friends from a distance who wish to be married there but under the care of their home meeting. Communication between Meetings assures the proper clearness process and help in the oversight of the wedding.

Marriage of non-members
There are occasions when non-members request marriage with the help of a Meeting, using the Friends marriage ceremony. Since Friends do hold marriage to be under divine guidance, the couple should be fully aware and agreeable to the context of marriage for Friends. Meetings are encouraged to consider in advance what services they can offer, and to look into the legal aspects of marriage of non-members, so that when such requests are made, they can be considered realistically and in a timely fashion.

Review of responsibilities required for the good order of a Quaker marriage ceremony
A review of the duties and responsibilities of those concerned: To promote clarity and understanding, the duties and responsibilities of the persons to be married, of the clerk, and of the committees of the monthly meeting are separately outlined here. These should be reviewed in conjunction with the previous text.

Responsibilities of the persons to be married:
1. To present to the monthly meeting under whose care they wish to be married the following written communications, usually directed to the clerk's attention:
   • a letter signed by both parties stating their intention of marriage and

their desire that the monthly meeting have oversight of the wedding. Whenever possible or appropriate it should be accompanied by letters from parents or guardians assuring the Meeting of their interest in, and approval of, the plans under consideration.

　　• upon approval for marriage, the request for permission to be married in a regular or, the usual practice, a specially appointed meeting for worship. The request should include the date of marriage and the time of day desired.

　　• suggested names of Friends whom the couple would like to have serve as an oversight committee for the wedding.

2. To meet with a clearness committee to explore the leading to marry.

3. To mail out invitations only after approval has been granted by the monthly meeting or Meetings involved.

4. To meet with the oversight committee named to oversee the wedding, at a time and place suggested by the committee, to discuss plans for the wedding, including the choice of persons to read the marriage certificate and to open and close the meeting for worship.

5.　a. To have the certificate prepared in ample time and using words that reflect the contemplated proceedings.

　　b. To arrange for the appropriate license for use where there is no clergy.

6. To inform themselves, with help from the committee overseeing the wedding, of all the applicable legal requirements of the state in which the marriage is to take place and of the forms to be used.

7. To be sure that the license is given to the committee overseeing the wedding before the wedding and that the marriage certificate is ready.

8. To commit to memory the promises to be made vocally, which should be to the following effect:

> In the presence of God and these our friends I __[Name]___ take thee _[Name]___to be my husband/wife/partner, promising with divine assistance to be unto thee a loving and faithful husband/wife/partner so long as we both shall live.

9. To sign the marriage certificate after the promises have been made.

10. To sign both sections of the marriage license after the wedding and before their departure, one section being kept by them and the other returned by a member of the committee overseeing the wedding to the office from which the license was obtained.

Responsibilities of the clerk of the Meeting:

1. To present the letter of intention to marry—and other letters received supporting the request—to the appropriate Meeting body at the earliest opportunity.

2. To see that the request is considered and, if accepted, that a committee for clearness is appointed.

3. To arrange for presentation of the committee's report on clearness to a subsequent session of the monthly meeting.

4. When the report has been accepted and the marriage allowed by the monthly meeting:

    a. to request the Meeting to name an oversight committee for the wedding and to appoint a meeting for worship to be held at the time and place requested for the wedding, if at all possible; and

    b. to inform the parties that they are free to proceed with their plans.

5. To present the report of the oversight committee at the session of monthly meeting following the marriage.

Responsibilities of the committee seeking clearness:

1. To make inquiry and conscientiously satisfy itself that there is nothing to interfere with the accomplishment of the marriage; and in interviews with the couple to explore their leading to marry.

2. To report its findings and recommendations to the next session of the monthly meeting, including any specific plans the couple has as to date and time of day.

3. To make available books and pamphlets on marriage; to have on hand information concerning resources within the yearly meeting, such as the Library and the Committee on Family Relations, as well as organizations within the community which may be helpful and appropriate.

4. To review with the couple the promises they propose to exchange at the marriage and make sure that the words of the certificate are consistent with them.

5. To be informed concerning the applicable legal requirements for obtaining a marriage license.

6. To make sure that the welfare and rights of any children by a former marriage have been properly considered and legally secured.

Responsibilities of the committee to oversee the marriage:

1. To meet with the couple to discuss plans for the wedding, including the choice of a person to read the certificate and one to close the meeting, and

to arrange for the rehearsal.

2. To see in advance that all applicable legal requirements have been met and that the proper license has been obtained; also to see that both sections of the license are dated and signed by the couple following the wedding and by two members of the committee as witnesses and that the proper section of the license thus signed is returned to the office from which it was obtained within the time required by law.

3. To see that the marriage and reception, if any, are accomplished with dignity, reverence, and simplicity.

4. To arrange for the care of the certificate following the meeting for worship and to see that it is signed by those who were present as witnesses.

5. To deliver the certificate to the recorder for copying or duplication for the records of the monthly meeting and to give the recorder an address to which the certificate may be returned.

6. To report to the monthly meeting whether the marriage has been suitably accomplished; whether the applicable legal requirements have been satisfied; whether the certificate has been properly recorded; and to report any name changes that result from the marriage for the recording in the minutes of the monthly meeting, for the quarterly meeting and for the yearly meeting.

The marriage certificate:
This form is the traditional wording of the marriage certificate. The couple reviews the wording of the certificate with the overseers of the marriage, including any desired word changes.

> *Whereas [name] of [address], son of [names of parents: use mother's maiden name], and [name] of [address], daughter of [names of parents: use mother's maiden name], having declared their intentions of marriage with each other to _____monthly meeting of the Religious Society of Friends held at _____, their proposed marriage was allowed by that Meeting.*
>
> *Now this is to certify to whom it may concern, that for the accomplishment of their intention, this _____day of the _____month, in the year of our Lord _____, they, [name] and [name], appeared in a meeting for worship of the Religious Society of Friends, held at _____, and [name],*

taking [name] by the hand, did, on this solemn occasion, declare that he took her, [name], to be his wife, promising with Divine assistance to be unto her a loving and faithful husband so long as they both shall live; and then, in the same assembly [name] did in like manner declare that she took him, [name], to be her husband, promising with Divine assistance to be unto him a loving and faithful wife so long as they both shall live. And moreover, they, [name and name,] did as further confirmation thereof, then and there, to this certificate set their hands.

    name   *name*

And we having been present at the marriage have as witnesses hereunto set our hands.

Intervisitation

From the beginning Quakers have felt a special bond that has overarched geographical and cultural boundaries and has made easy the offer of hospitality to traveling Friends on the one hand and the quiet confidence of welcome on the other. Friendly intervisitation, whether formal or informal, has for more than three hundred years provided an important opening for understanding and cooperation in the affairs of Friends and for mutual ministry and spiritual growth. Friends are encouraged, therefore, as they travel on business or holiday, to allow time for visits with Meetings or with individual Friends and families in the regions they may pass through.

Letters of Introduction
In making such Friendly visits, many have found letters of introduction from home Meetings to be helpful. Such letters, prepared by the Meeting at the request of those planning to travel, usually state the fact of membership, give some indication of participation and witness in the affairs of our Religious Society, and express such greetings as are deemed appropriate. Letters are signed by the clerk and duly noted in the minutes. Since Friends travel for a wide variety of purposes, letters of introduction do not suggest specific obligations either on the visitor or on those visited and

may be issued by the clerk without formal consideration by the Meeting. Such letters are often endorsed by those visited.

Minutes of Travel for Religious Service
As in the past, Friends today find themselves under a sense of divine leading to travel in support of an important cause or to the nurture of the religious life of Friends' families and meetings or of other groups. In carrying out such leadings, they find it supportive to take with them a formal minute for religious service from their monthly meeting.

A Meeting should issue such a minute only after the concern has been laid before its Committee on Worship and Ministry, or such other group as the Meeting may suggest as a clearness committee (see p. 29), and has been favorably recommended to the monthly meeting. A minute of religious service, signed by the clerk, should state clearly the nature, scope, and duration of the proposed service and affirm the Meeting's liberation and support of the Friends concerned.

A Friend who proposes to travel under religious concern may find, as have Friends in the past, that it is a source of strength and comfort to be joined by another Friend who is sympathetic to the concern and able to give counsel and encouragement.

The monthly meeting issuing such a minute should see that insofar as possible the proposed service is not hampered by a lack of funds or other support.

A minute of religious service, especially one that is to be used beyond the bounds of the yearly meeting, after adoption by a monthly meeting, is usually submitted for approval, endorsement, and support by the quarterly or regional meeting and by the Interim Meeting or the yearly meeting Committee on Worship and Ministry.

Friends traveling with such minutes should be welcomed by those among whom they visit and be invited to lay their concerns before appropriate gatherings. It is customary for minutes to be endorsed at the conclusion of the gatherings by the persons presiding.

Under the completion of the service proposed, a minute for religious service should be returned promptly with a verbal or written report to those Meetings who had earlier reviewed the concern and minuted their support.

Death and Bereavement

Responsibilities of the Individual
Friends are advised to prepare for death and for the possibility of incompetence in their last days, to spare their families unnecessary pain and confusion. Provision should be made for the care of dependents and the disposal of real property, financial assets, and personal and household goods. Living wills, or their equivalents, and durable powers of attorney simplify life for survivors, as will recorded wishes relating to the body after death, whether for burial or cremation or donation for medical or scientific purposes. It is also helpful if the locations of any pertinent documents are made known to responsible persons. Any instructions for a memorial meeting under the care of the Meeting should conform to the true simplicity appropriate to a meeting for worship.

Responsibilities of the Meeting
The Meeting should regularly remind its members of their responsibilities as noted above and ask members to share the information that will help the Meeting fulfill its responsibilities. The Meeting should also call its members' attention to sources of information and assistance, and be alert to provide practical, loving care.

Upon the death of a member or of a person in a member's family, either Meeting overseers or a designated committee should visit the family to extend the Meeting's sympathy and support to the bereaved, and gently assist the family as it adjusts to its loss. Such service is most helpful if it is proffered by persons who are well informed and have given prayerful thought to their proper role.

The Meeting may also be of help in many practical ways including hospitality for those from a distance, child care, meals, and housework. It should respond with sensitivity to the family's wishes and be prepared to assist in notifying relatives and friends and the public press.

The Meeting should stand ready to conduct a memorial meeting under its care and to help if the family wishes to arrange for private memorial gatherings. Insofar as possible, members of the Meeting should support the family by attending the memorial meeting.

No Meeting member should slip away unremembered and unmourned. If the family's plans do not include a memorial meeting, it may be rightly ordered for the Meeting to hold one.

Meetings should be especially attentive to the needs of family members during what may be an extended period of mourning. The death of a loved one may leave the survivor alone and unable to cope with unfamiliar financial obligations and difficult decisions about property and arrangements for the future. Emotions surrounding the loss are likely to run very deep for a long time, even where death has come as release from suffering. When sudden death by disease or accident strikes younger couples, especially those with children, the emotional and financial strain upon the survivors can be very heavy. In all these cases, not only the overseers or some comparable group, but all members of a Meeting should feel drawn to provide active, sensitive support that extends well beyond the memorial meeting.

The Meeting may wish to prepare a memorial minute as an expression of its appreciation of the life and service of the deceased member and as a reminder of what we are given time for.

Memorial Meetings for Worship

When Friends experience the death of a member, they gather for a memorial meeting for worship. As the meeting begins, a designated person may describe the nature of the occasion and assure those present that they are free to speak if led to do so. While the worshippers remember the life and service of the deceased and mourn the passing, they also celebrate God's gift of life and the beauty of human character. Members of the family may request that passages of Scripture, poetry, prayer, meditation, or music be shared during the meeting. Those present may be drawn to speak of their memories, poignant, loving, grateful, instructive, even humorous. Yet the occasion should be one in which things temporal are secondary, a time when the mystery of death is deeply felt, and when the presence of God and those gathered in worship bring comfort, hope, and consolation.

Meetings may find it helpful to the bereaved family to hold a simple reception following the memorial meeting. Such an occasion gives an opportunity to express grief and love and thanksgiving, person to person. For many it will also serve as a helpful reentry into everyday life.

If ashes are to be deposited or scattered in some cherished spot or if there is to be an interment, whether done privately or as part of the memorial meeting, the family may ask that someone prepare a brief service of farewell. This can be a particularly poignant moment, and the Meeting needs to be sensitive to these emotions.

Meetings may hold memorial meetings for those not in membership.

Funds, Property, Burial Grounds

MEETINGS AND ECONOMIC RESOURCES

The guidance offered Friends in the disposition of their own economic resources (see pp. 75, 80-85) applies equally to the exercise of economic power by Meetings.

Meetings are encouraged to give heed to the power for good or evil inherent in the money and property in their possession or in the possession of institutions under their care. They should review regularly their policies and practices to ensure the socially responsible investment of endowments and working capital, ecologically responsible management of real property, caring management and equitable compensation of employees, and socially responsible use of the power to purchase and consume.

Meetings as well as individuals can act, in the words of John Woolman, so that "to turn all the treasures we possess into the channel of Universal Love becomes the business of our lives."

Financing yearly meeting activities

The services provided by Philadelphia Yearly Meeting (PYM) to its members and constituent monthly and quarterly meetings, including the operation of its standing committees and working groups, are supported by the covenants of monthly and quarterly meetings, by the voluntary contributions of individual members and others, and by restricted and unrestricted income from bequests and investments.

Making the budget is a cooperative effort. In the spring of the preceding year, the Financial Stewardship Committee (FSC) sends a survey to the monthly and quarterly meetings requesting their discernment on the relative merits of existing and proposed services and projects. The FSC provides this information and financial data to the standing committees, which then evaluate the proposed budgets of the working groups under their oversight. The budgets of approved projects and services are sent by the standing committees to the FSC, which then prepares a preliminary budget for all PYM activities by making adjustments to proposed expenditures to fit the expected income. In the fall of the year, the clerk of PYM convenes a Meeting for Worship and Financial Stewardship to receive the voluntary covenants of the monthly and quarterly meetings. If a discrepancy between income and expenses exists, Friends attending give guidance to the FSC, which then prepares the final draft budget. After Interim Meeting concurrence, the final draft is mailed to monthly and quarterly meetings for their consideration prior to its presentation for approval in March to PYM in session. Implementation begins the following July.

The Financial Stewardship Committee is also responsible for the oversight of income and expenditures during the budget year and for making adjustments as needed. It is accountable to Interim Meeting and Philadelphia Yearly Meeting in session.

Financing monthly and quarterly meeting activities
Monthly and quarterly/regional meetings are expected to forward their conenants of support of the yearly meeting budget in timely fashion. Otherwise, they have broad discretion in the raising, custody, and spending of money. They are encouraged to conduct their affairs so that money for routine operating budgets is raised from the current generation, without undue reliance on the generosity of past members. They are also encouraged to take care that their fund-raising activities spread the burden of financial support suitably. Monthly meetings rely mainly on the contributions of members, but encouragement of contributions from regular attenders is also appropriate.

Broad decisions about the raising, custody, and spending of money are policy matters affecting the welfare of all members. They should be made within the framework of a budgetary process in the monthly or regional meeting for business, rather than a less representative body.

The accounts of all committees and programs of quarterly/regional or monthly meetings should be audited annually--and whenever there is a change of treasurer or other custodian-- by a committee of the Meeting appointed for that purpose. The auditors should report to the meeting for business, and the substance of the audit report should be recorded in the minutes. Monthly and regional meetings may encourage institutions under their care to employ professional auditors, and ask that the audit report be a part of the institution's periodic reporting to the Meeting.

Monthly and quarterly/regional meetings may utilize the investment management services of the Friends Fiduciary Corporation for their endowment funds. Meetings should give thought to the establishment of their own "social responsibility" criteria for the investment of endowment funds not placed in the hands of the Friends Fiduciary Corporation.

Monthly and quarterly/regional meetings holding endowment funds established by gift or bequest should take care that the income is put to the uses specified by the donor. Should that become difficult or impossible, the Meeting may ask Interim Meeting for advice.

Real Property of Meetings

Property endows its possessor with power. Meetings are encouraged to use the power inherent in their real property to enrich the spiritual life of the Meeting and to contribute to the welfare of the surrounding community.

Four options are available for formal ownership of Meeting real property. Legal counsel should be consulted before making a choice. Property may be:

1. Held in the name of an unincorporated Meeting.

2. Held in the name of an unincorporated body of trustees appointed by the Meeting. The Meeting must take care that the board of trustees is kept in existence by the timely replacement of trustees lost through resignation, disability, or death.

3. Held in the name of an incorporated Meeting.

4. Held in the name of an incorporated body of trustees appointed by the Meeting.

Options 3 and 4 require at a minimum the adoption of bylaws, the holding of annual meetings of the corporation, and the election of directors. Those meetings and elections should follow Friends' procedures to the extent possible under the state law. Directors need to be sensitive to the desires of the Meeting as they carry out their statutory responsibilities.

The Friends Fiduciary Corporation of Philadelphia no longer undertakes the role of formal holder of record of properties of active monthly or quarterly meetings.

Burial Grounds

Monthly meetings and their successors have a responsibility in perpetuity to maintain burial grounds and memorial gardens in good order, and to devote to their upkeep any income from perpetual care endowments in the charge of the meeting. A committee of the Meeting should be empowered to authorize interments of bodies or ashes or scatterings of ashes, keep accurate records of the location of the interred, and maintain the grounds. The procedure for recording interment or scatterings of ashes should be consistent with the procedure for recording burials.

Friends have traditionally expressed their commitments to simplicity and the equality of all persons by discouraging the use of elaborate grave markers. Graves should be marked by plain stones that bear only the name of the deceased and dates of birth and death. When opening a new section of a burial ground, Meetings may wish to require that stones be flush with the ground to facilitate maintenance.

Opportunities for Wider
Religious Fellowship and Action

Friends have many openings for giving expression to their faith. From a base in a monthly meeting that is part of a quarterly meeting and a yearly meeting, a Friend may elect to follow a broad range of faith-centered leadings in other settings.

Friends General Conference (FGC) was originally formed in 1900 by seven yearly meetings whose members formally worship in the unprogrammed tradition of Friends. It serves yearly and monthly meetings, and their members and attenders, by providing resources and opportunities for spiritual growth and community building, and by helping to empower Friends and their meetings to live their faith. The FGC Annual Gathering of Friends, held each summer in a different part of North America, is an important opportunity for these services to be provided.

FGC's governing body consists of Friends appointed by affiliated yearly meetings and regional Friends' associations, plus additional co-opted members. The work of Friends General Conference is carried out by a number of program and administrative committees plus staff. Program committees undertake such concerns as advancement and outreach, ministry and nurture, religious education, conference planning, and a meetinghouse loan fund. FGC publishes books and pamphlets, and it distributes a wide variety of publications of interest to Friends through its bookstore.

Friends of Philadelphia Yearly Meeting also work closely on matters of common concern with other associations of Friends such as Friends United Meeting and the Evangelical Friends International, and with unaffiliated yearly meetings here and abroad.

The Friends World Committee for Consultation, through visitation and periodic gatherings, offers opportunity for religious fellowship among Friends throughout the world. It also sponsors the Wider Quaker Fellowship, a support group for Friends and interested others who live at a distance from a local Meeting. It oversees a program for the Right Sharing of World Resources, which offers small grants to community groups in many parts of the world. And it sponsors, in conjunction with the American Friends Service Committee and Friends Service Council of Britain Yearly Meeting, the Quaker United Nations Office (QUNO), in two locations: New York and Geneva.

Friends in Philadelphia Yearly Meeting were among the founders in 1917 of the American Friends Service Committee, whose first mission was the relief of suffering during the First World War. Since then, AFSC has developed programs in the United States and around the world intended, among other things, to encourage improved understanding among different national and ethnic groups, to enable indigenous populations to improve their living conditions, and to relieve suffering caused by economic and social dislocation as well as by war.

The Friends Committee on National Legislation was formed in 1943 to coordinate and enhance the efforts of Friends to lobby for their concerns with the executive and legislative branches of national government. Many members of Philadelphia Yearly Meeting participate in direct lobbying of their senators and representatives with the support of this committee.

Friends also participate in ecumenical bodies. Philadelphia Yearly Meeting is represented in the World Council of Churches through the Christian and Interfaith Relations Committee of Friends General Conference. In addition, Philadelphia Yearly Meeting and its quarterly and monthly meetings maintain formal and informal relationships with the National Council of Churches and with ecumenical bodies of Christian and Jewish leaders in our communities. These affiliations enable the yearly, quarterly, and monthly meetings to engage in ecumenical projects and programs with various Christian denominations and to be reminded of our historic roots in the Christian tradition. Friends also seek opportunities for spiritual fellowship with neighbors from the Moslem, Buddhist, and other religious traditions. Continuing dialogue with such groups and with the various Christian denominations is especially important if Friends are to balance our distinctive witness with a willingness to learn from others. This need is a special concern of the Quaker Universalist Fellowship.

As individuals or small groups, Friends seek opportunities for service with others that also broaden their religious fellowship. Some Friends make their principal religious witness by joining with people of other faiths to address social problems though community organizations with no formal religious identity. Other Friends work with people of other faiths in organizations that were originally founded by Friends, but that have long since acquired an ecumenical character. Friends also find opportunities as volunteers or paid staff in organizations founded by other faiths.

Concerns, Leadings, & Testimonies

Friends are sometimes called "practical mystics" because Quaker worship has been the wellspring for service in the community and world. An old story relates the whispered question asked by someone attending meeting for worship for the first time and puzzled by the absence of overt activity: "When does the service begin?" The response: "When the meeting for worship ends."

CONCERNS AND LEADINGS

The impetus for service is often a concern, which, as Friends use the word, is a quickening sense of the need to do something or to demonstrate sympathetic interest in an individual or group, as a result of what is felt to be a direct intimation of God's will. A concern as an impetus to action arises out of Friends' belief that the realm of God can be realized here and now, not just in another place or time. A concern may emerge as an unexpected insight from prayerful study of a problem or situation, such as a concern to support national policies which promote international peace. It may also grow from an anxious interest in the welfare of a person or group that may result in inquiries or practical support.

When it initially arises, a concern may not yet be linked to a proposed course of action, but may simply be a troubled sense that something is awry. Action, when it follows, is often the result of a leading, a sense of being drawn or called by God in a particular direction or toward a particular course of action. Friends speak of "feeling led" or "being called." The leading may be short-term and specific in its fulfillment, or it may involve transformation of one's life and the life of the Meeting.

Friends have long believed it important that leadings be tested before action is taken. The process of testing is a form of spiritual discipline for Friends. A Friend's concern and consequent leading may be an individual matter—something which one person is called to attend to without requiring assistance. In many cases, however, a Friend may receive guidance, aid, and encouragement from other members of the Meeting. Therefore it has long been the practice of Friends to inform their Meeting when they feel major concerns laid upon them.

Meeting Response

The Meeting should give serious consideration to requests from those seeking unity for a proposed course of action—and may not always approve. It may appoint a clearness committee (see p. 29) to help such persons gain clarity on seeking release to act upon a concern. Such a committee may also provide longer-term support, including ongoing testing and re-evaluation. In cases where Meeting approval is given to a proposed course of action, which may result in allowing Friends to be released to follow such leadings, the Meeting often takes responsibility for providing financial assistance and family support, and continues to give oversight until the leading is fulfilled or laid down.

When a Meeting fails to unite with a member's concern, the member generally reconsiders it very carefully. Sometimes the individual and Meeting agree that the concern should be dropped, and the member feels released from responsibility for action since the concern has been laid on the Meeting. At other times a person may continue to feel led to pursue the matter. Where action by the Meeting is not required, the Meeting may be able to encourage the member to go forward even when the Meeting is unable to reach unity.

Where the concern cannot be furthered without Meeting unity, and a member does not feel right about dropping it, the process of discernment continues. Often this process involves the formation of a small group, which includes Friends who have expressed a diversity of perspectives. The concern, generally with a modified proposal for action, may be brought to the Meeting many times before either unity is reached in support of the concern or a decision is made to lay it down.

Submitting the concern to the judgment of the Meeting is of value. The Meeting may be enlightened by the insights of those who bring concerns, and these Friends may be helped, through the sympathetic consideration of the Meeting, to clarify their leadings. The Meeting's care for its members should cause it to take interest in all concerns felt by its members, even when it cannot unite with them or may feel obliged to admonish members against "running ahead of their Guide."

Depending on the nature and scope of the concern, the monthly meeting may wish to lay it before the regional gathering or quarterly meeting by minute accompanied by personal presentation where possible. In like manner, the regional gathering may lay the concern before Interim Meeting or the yearly meeting. A Meeting may also request that a concern, brought by a member and judged significant by the Meeting, be considered at a threshing session during annual sessions of the yearly meeting.

Individuals also frequently bring concerns to yearly meeting committees. After testing such a concern, a committee may or may not include such concerns in its reports to Philadelphia Yearly Meeting, either through Interim Meeting or at yearly meeting sessions.

When a concern is thus presented, the yearly meeting may reach a decision or may provide for further consideration of the matter. Deep sensitivity to divine leading and to the insights of others is required on the part of both individuals and Meetings when controversial concerns are considered. Concerns involving intensely personal witness or public policy demand a special degree of forbearance, and unity may not always be reached.

TESTIMONIES

For more than three hundred years, Friends have acted upon shared concerns through practices which historically have been distinctive and definitive. While the specifics of Friends' practice have varied as times have changed, Friends today continue to have concerns and underlying beliefs similar to those of past generations. The word testimonies is used to refer to this common set of deeply held, historically rooted attitudes and modes of living in the world.

Testimonies bear witness to the truth as Friends in community perceive it—truth known through relationship with God. The testimonies are expressions of lives turned toward the Light, outward expressions reflective of the inward experience of divine leading, differently described by various Friends and in changing eras. Often in the past they were defined specifically, such as the testimony against taking oaths; recently it has become customary to speak of them more generally, as in the testimony of simplicity. Through the testimonies, with that measure of the Light that is granted, Friends strive for unity and integrity of inner and outer life, both in living with ourselves and others and in living in the world.

The advices that follow concerning how we live our lives seek to avoid rigid definitions of these evolving testimonies. Rather, these testimonies are presented within the areas of our lives where they are likely to emerge, as a reference to actions Friends may be called to take. It is just as likely, however, that we will be challenged in different ways to live out such key Quaker testimonies as equality, peace, simplicity, stewardship, and integrity.

Living with Ourselves and Others: Personal Relationships

OUR MEETING COMMUNITY

Meeting communities are enhanced and enlivened by sharing with those closest to us our relationships and spiritual journeys. Here we have the opportunity to demonstrate our personal commitment to our testimonies. Our private lives and personal relationships can be nurtured and enriched by a shared experience of reliance upon God. Such relationships, both positive and negative, are often intense, and we may have difficulty in finding the way forward as individuals and as a community.

Personal relationships are nurtured through our involvement in meetings for worship and business, worship sharing, retreats, workshops, study groups, reading groups, and social and recreational gatherings. Within most Meetings there are gifted individuals and established procedures that can offer discreet, confidential, loving support to those who may need it. When difficulties arise, shared, prayerful, and determined efforts to seek God's will can help us to gain better understanding. It is important for the Meeting to recognize its limitations and to decide when it is appropriate to seek help and support elsewhere.

It is not easy to live as Friends in today's world—to remain true to our heritage and still be sensitive to new situations. It has never been so. Each generation of Friends has been faced with challenges to our ideas about marriage, family life, the education and discipline of children, and social practices. Living our testimonies helps us confront these challenges.

MARRIAGE

From the beginning, Friends have emphasized the equality of marriage partners. George Fox admonished that Friends should be married "as though they were not, both husband and wife free to do God's work and not possessive of one another." Later, Lucretia Mott wrote that "in the marriage union, the independence of the husband and wife will be equal, their dependence mutual, and their obligations reciprocal." Many modern Friends would add, "and some of their roles interchangeable."

Formal declaration of commitment in the presence of God and Friends under the care of the Meeting sets a foundation for a shared life of spiritual wholeness. Such a religious commitment liberates rather than constricts the couple's natural impulses toward passion and spontaneity and becomes a source of joy, not only for the couple but also for the Meeting and all others in the couple's life. A Meeting's commitment to nurture a marriage continues whether or not that marriage began under its care.

Relationships which were clearly entered into under the covering of the Spirit may nevertheless experience severe strains and difficulties. The Meeting needs to recognize such situations early and be prepared to help with tender understanding and sensitivity. The offering of the services of a clearness committee (see p. 29), which may include members of the couple's own choosing, may be helpful. The Meeting may also help by assisting the couple in finding and paying for professional counseling services such as those associated with the yearly meeting. The couple and those counseling with them may wish to consider together such questions as:

•Have you sought divine guidance for the situation in which you now find yourselves?

•Do commitments to equality, peace, and integrity continue to guide your relationship?

•Have you found it possible to acknowledge that of God in each other as you work through this difficulty?

The Meeting community may not be able to help a couple ameliorate their difficulties. The relationship may have deteriorated beyond the point of reconciliation. Strong feelings may challenge the Meeting community, but should not prevent it from continuing to offer prayerful, sensitive support to all concerned, especially the children, helping them to feel not so much failure as a change in their situation. Among other responses, the Meeting could again offer the services of a clearness committee, to help the couple consider the questions just noted and also such additional ones as:

•Have you been able to make careful and loving efforts to help your children understand what brought about this situation?

•How will you continue to relate with your children to show them that you love them?

•Have you carefully considered equitable ways of handling property and financial matters?

Divorce or the dissolution of any committed relationship is an intimate matter accompanied by strong feelings. The Meeting role is difficult; it should not become intrusive. The need is to be careful and even-handed, keeping in contact with all family members and all parties to the divorce. All concerned need to be encouraged to continue their lives as Friends.

Home and family are both a refuge from the hazards of the world and a path to a better world. In the loving home and family, young and old learn about equality and its limitations, simple forms of stewardship, integrity in its many guises, simplicity in all its complexities, and how hard but how satisfying it is to be peaceable. Family members learn that an enduring spirit of equality underlies apparent differences.

Traditional families once constituted the great majority of a Meeting community. Today's membership reflects societal changes resulting in nontraditional families: single parent households, same gender commitments, blended families. Not all Meetings have accepted new family forms, yet they continue to seek understanding of these situations, extending welcome and loving care to all members. Families remain an inspiring and vital ingredient of our Meeting communities.

As a participant in a Quaker family, a child first becomes aware of the presence of God in our lives. Friends are encouraged to worship as a family. Silent grace at meals, and family and bedtime prayers help children develop a sense of God's presence.

A Quaker home seeks to bind its family members together. Such a home cultivates recognition of authority while at the same time allowing each member appropriate freedom to develop fully. Conflict in a family is natural; when lovingly and constructively dealt with, it is an opportunity for growth and sometimes also an affirmation of individual leadings. The natural give-and-take with one's peers begins at home. Learning to handle disagreements in a calm and fair manner prepares the way for solving differences in school, the neighborhood, and the larger society.

It is within the family that we initially seek to live our testimonies. Two of these, simplicity and stewardship, are especially important. A family that strives to practice simplicity will exercise stewardship in the use of its social and material resources. Considerations of stewardship should include decisions regarding the family's financial commitments to its monthly and quarterly or regional meetings and to the yearly meeting. The importance of other questions such as family witness, service to others, the many ramifications of the peace testimony and equality also need to be recognized. Participation of all family members in discussions and decisions regarding joint family possessions and activities helps children develop judgment not only in their personal decisions and the decision-making process, but also with respect to time values and the worth of the activities themselves. These decisions can be the beginning of one's realization of just how, as a Quaker, one chooses to live out one's life.

Family recreation should promote restoration, solidarity, and spiritual well-being; it should bring balance into life and contribute to wholeness of personality. Such recreation includes reading aloud, gardening, music, and arts and crafts as well as games and sports. All such activities develop fellowship within the family. Both competitive and non-competitive games can teach lessons of fairness, sportsmanship, and self-esteem. Recreational activities should stress cooperation and inclusiveness, and should resist the materialism of our culture.

Fair, loving, and just discipline practiced among all family members brings a sense of security to the children and a sense of order to the adults. The best discipline parents can offer is their own example of conscientious, consistent, Spirit-led conduct day in and day out. Parents have an obligation to be guided by the Inward Teacher in the exercise of their authority. Ideally, the family will unite in seeking such guidance. Assistance in helping each child develop self-discipline is one of a parent's most valuable gifts to children.

The relationship between inward discipline and rules of behavior needs to be continually reviewed with children. Children need to understand that rules are not for them only but that parents too are committed to a disciplined life consistent with the life of the Spirit. Open discussion and the creation of a loving, patient atmosphere in developing rules of behavior is basic to building a Quaker family. If a family has continual problems with rules, a family meeting for clearness may help resolve difficulties. A family should never be embarrassed to seek help from outside the family unit.

SEX AND SEXUALITY

In our personal lives, Friends seek to acknowledge and nurture sexuality as a gift from God for celebrating human love with joy and intimacy. In defining healthy sexuality, Friends are led in part by our testimonies: that sexual relations be equal, not exploitative; that sexual behavior be marked by integrity; and that sex be an act of love, not of aggression. Sexuality is at once an integral and an intricate part of personality. Our understanding of our own sexuality is an essential aspect of our journey toward wholeness. Learning to incorporate sexuality in our lives responsibly, joyfully, and with integrity should be a lifelong process beginning in childhood.

Friends are wary of a preset moral code to govern sexual activity. The unity of the sacred and the secular implies that the sacramental quality of a sexual relationship depends upon the Spirit as well as the intentions of the persons concerned. Our faith can help us to examine relationships honestly, with the strength to reconcile the often conflicting demands of the body, heart, and spirit. Even with its respect for individual leadings, Quakerism does not sanction license in sexual behavior. Precisely because our sexuality is so powerful, seeking the divine will becomes all important. The obedience thus called for is more personal, perhaps more difficult than adherence to an external code. For many Friends, "celibate in singleness, faithful in marriage" has proven consonant with the divine will. Sexual activity, whether or not it includes intercourse, is never without consequence.

Current global population trends and concern for the equitable distribution of resources require us to ask what good stewardship of the earth entails for our decisions about sex and childbearing. Friends approve the concept of family planning and endorse efforts to make pertinent education and services widely available. We are in unity about the value of human life, but not about abortion. We are urged to seek the guidance of the Spirit, to support one another regarding how to end the situations contributing to abortion, and to discern how to act as individuals, family members, and Meetings.

SEX EDUCATION

A Quaker home demands an atmosphere where openness and honesty prevail. It is within the intimate family circle that children establish their identities as persons; an atmosphere which supports their feelings of confidence encourages this development. Children at a very early age develop a sense of their own gender identity and are curious about gender differences. Within a loving and secure family, young children are enabled to ask questions about gender and sex, and parents acquire the confidence to answer these questions.

Sex education needs to begin early with the use of appropriate terms that children understand. The level of understanding is not uniform, and wise parents will judge each child's capacity to absorb answers to questions. Simple, direct answers need be no threat to a child's innocence, and parents do the child no favors by surrounding the subject with fables and mystery. Undramatic introduction of the basic physiological facts of human sexuality is the best preparation for the more sophisticated education needed during the years of puberty and adolescence.

Sex education for children who have come of age sexually should be provided with sympathy and patience. Such education should include clear, direct information regarding sexually transmitted diseases and AIDS. Parents need to remember their own reactions during this confusing and volatile age. Whatever the sexual mores of the time may be, and whatever adolescent peers may do or say, it is important for parents to help their children look past peer pressure toward what contributes to loving, responsible relationships.

In this, as in all facets of education, adults need to remain teachable. Sex education is not necessarily a one-way street. Parents may learn from their children about societal problems of which they have never been aware. Sensitive listening between parents and children will go a long way in establishing mutual understanding.

ADDICTIVE BEHAVIORS:
DRUGS, ALCOHOL, TOBACCO, AND GAMBLING

George Fox and other early Friends contended that drunkenness was incompatible with a life in the Spirit. William Penn wrote in 1678:

> *Drunkenness, or excess in drinking, is not only a violation of God's law, but of our own natures... it fits men for that which they would abhor, if sober.... It renders men unfit for trust or business, it tells secrets, betrays friendship, disposes men to be tricked and cheated; finally it spoils health, weakens the human race, and above all provokes the just God to anger.*
>
> William Penn, *Address to Protestants*

Many other mind-affecting drugs have come to be widely used. Like alcohol, they separate the user from God, family, and friends. Drugs and alcohol easily become the controlling factor of the user's life. Individuals and families are shattered. With the proliferation of some drugs, whole communities have broken down.

The use of tobacco can cause serious illness in both the user and those regularly exposed to second-hand smoke. Smoking deadens the senses; it can come between the user and the Spirit.

Gambling, even in the forms of sweepstakes and lotteries, poses dangers to the individual and the community. It often becomes addictive, bringing ruin to the gambler's family. Gambling harms the community by fostering a get-rich-quick and something-for-nothing attitude that contributes to an unwholesome materialism. Habitual gambling makes undue demands on the gambler's time and attention, leading to a life inconsistent with our testimonies on simplicity and integrity.

Friends should be clear about the negative personal and social effects of gambling, alcohol, drugs, and tobacco. We should also seek to ensure that the children in our meetings and schools are taught about these effects and the relationship of addictive behavior to issues of social justice such as: the marketing of addictive substances; the violence associated with drugs and alcohol; the root causes of some homelessness; and the negative repercussions of gambling and state supported lotteries.

Addictive behavior, whether manifested in gambling or in the use of drugs, tobacco or alcohol, is a symptom of a disease which cannot be controlled by reason or an act of will. It is a terrible, life-destroying trap from which the addict is not easily extricated. Friends urge their members to manifest intelligent compassion toward victims of addiction, to aid and encourage them in seeking appropriate treatment.

Contemporary Friends acknowledge the wisdom of the Advices of our forebears, to:

> *Shun the use of mind-changing drugs and intoxicants, of gambling,*
> *and of other detrimental practices that interpose themselves against*
> *the Inward Light. It is the experience of Friends that these drugs,*
> *intoxicants, and practices lead to a personal willfulness and inability*
> *to listen for the will of God.... Keep your recreations from becoming*
> *occasions for self-intoxication and avoid those conventional amuse-*
> *ments which debase the emotions ....*

Advices, see p. 83

Living in the world

Throughout our history Friends have testified that our lives are not meant to conform to the ways of the world, but that we are meant to live in obedience to the Light of Truth within, and through this witness to contribute to the transformation of the world through the Light of Truth.

> *Let all nations hear the sound by word or writing. Spare no place,*
> *spare no tongue nor pen, but be obedient to the Lord God; go through*
> *the world and be valiant for the truth upon earth; tread and trample*

all that is contrary under.... Be patterns, be examples in all countries,
places, islands, nations, wherever you come, that your carriage and
life may preach among all sorts of people, and to them. Then you will
come to walk cheerfully over the world, answering that of God in
everyone; whereby in them you may be a blessing, and make the wit-
ness of God in them to bless you.

George Fox, 1656

Our testimonies are our guides as we seek to apply George Fox's advice in a world that is beyond his imagining, yet offers myriad opportunities to be valiant for the truth.

Equality
We believe there is that of God in every person, and thus we believe in human equality before God. Friends pioneered in recognizing the gifts and rights of women. Women were ministers and leaders of the early meetings. Friends came more slowly to recognize the evil of slavery and of discrimination in general, and have often been guilty of sharing the prejudices of the broader society. In recent years, Friends have discovered and taken stands against other forms of discrimination and oppression to which they had earlier been insensitive. An element of that insensitivity for some has been a failure to recognize the privileged status many American Friends enjoy. As we continue to seek the Light, ingrained habits and attitudes are subject to searching reexamination.

Social Justice
Enunciation of the principle of equality among human beings in the sight of God is important and necessary, but it is not sufficient. Realization of equality involves such matters as independence and control of one's own life. Therefore Friends aid the nonviolent efforts of the exploited to attain self-determination and social, political, and economic justice, and to change attitudes and practices formerly taken for granted. Friends seek to bring to light structures, institutions, language, and thought processes which subtly support discrimination and exploitation. Beyond their own Society, Friends promote Spirit-led, sense of the meeting decision-making as an instrument of equality. And Friends continue to examine their own attitudes and practices to test whether they contribute as much as they might to social, political, and economic justice.

Friends work with groups that have been victimized by prejudice and exploitation. Too often this work has been difficult because of resistance by the prejudiced and by the exploiters, even within the membership of the Religious Society of Friends. The problem of prejudice is complicated by advantages that have come to some at the expense of others. Exploitation impairs the human quality of the exploiter as well as of the exploited.

Criminal Justice

Many early Friends were victims of an arbitrary and unreasonable criminal justice system. Knowledge of that experience has opened many later Friends to that of God in convicted persons. Friends continue to undertake work in prisons, ministering to the spiritual and material needs of inmates. Believing that the penal system often reflects structural and systemic injustice in our society, Friends seek alternatives. Friends have acted out of the conviction that redemption and restorative justice, not retribution, are the right tasks of the criminal justice system. We strongly oppose capital punishment.

Seeking to heal the wounds of criminal actions, Friends are called to many different kinds of service in the criminal justice system. Prison visiting, victim support services, conflict resolution training for staff of correctional institutions and offenders, and work to abolish the penalty of death are typical of these services. Such service is undertaken in order to restore the victim, the offender, and the community to the greatest extent possible. The healing love, and the trust in divine leading that such disciplined service requires, can greatly assist the rebuilding of broken lives.

Peace

Since all human beings are children of God, Friends are called to love and respect all persons and to overcome evil with good. Friends' peace testimony arises from the power of Christ working in our hearts. Our words and lives should testify to this power and should stand as a positive witness in a world still torn by strife and violence.

The Society of Friends has consistently held that war is contrary to the Spirit of Christ. It stated its position clearly in the Declaration to Charles II in 1660:

> We utterly deny all outward wars and strife, and fightings with outward weapons, for any end, or under any pretense whatsoever; this is our testimony to the whole world.... The Spirit of Christ, by which we

*are guided, is not changeable, so as once to command us from a thing
as evil, and again to move us unto it; and we certainly know, and
testify to the world, that the Spirit of Christ, which leads us into all
truth, will never move us to fight and war against any man with
outward weapons, neither for the Kingdom of Christ nor for the
Kingdoms of this world.... Therefore, we cannot learn war any more."*

Our historic peace testimony must be also a living testimony, as
we work to give concrete expression to our ideals, often in opposition to
prevailing opinion. We recognize that the peace testimony requires us to
honor that of God in every person, and therefore to avoid not only
physical violence but also more subtle forms—psychological, economic, or
systemic.

In explaining his unwillingness to serve in the army, George Fox
records that "I told them...that I lived in the virtue of that life and power
that takes away the occasion of all wars." When we find that life and power
within ourselves, we are strengthened to be valiant for God's truth, to
endure the suffering that may befall our lot.

The Individual and the Peace Testimony
In our individual lives, the peace testimony leads us to accept conflict as an
opportunity for loving engagement with those with whom we disagree.
That love can often be expressed in creative, nonviolent resolution of the
disagreement. When we encounter people of sincere religious conviction
whose views are profoundly different from our own, that love can also be
manifested by acknowledging the sincerity of the other, while forthrightly
expressing our own convictions.

The peace testimony also leads us as individuals to consider seriously
our employment, our investments, our purchases, our payment of taxes,
and our manner of living as they relate to violence. We must become sensitive to the covert as well as the overt violence inherent in some of our
long-established social practices and institutions. We need to avoid, for
example, benefiting not only from the manufacture of arms, but also from
company practices that do violence to employees, consumers, or the
natural world.

Friends and Military Activity
We support those who resist cooperation with conscription and those who
oppose war by performing work as conscientious objectors. While

counseling against military service, we hold in love our members who feel they must undertake it.

We work as we are able to alleviate the suffering caused by war. We acknowledge the contribution that military forces have in some situations made to the relief of suffering, but we are troubled by the use of agents of destruction for such purposes, and by the failure of nations to support the creation of nonviolent legions to undertake humanitarian missions.

Alternatives to War

The almost unimaginable devastation that results from modern war makes ever more urgent its total elimination. We would refrain from participating in all forms of violence and repression. We would make strenuous efforts to secure international agreements for the elimination of armaments and to remove the domination of militarism in our society. We would work for greater understanding at all levels, from the kindergarten to the United Nations, of proven techniques for the nonviolent resolution of conflict. And we would promote and assist programs of conversion to peaceful uses of facilities built for war.

World Order

Friends since William Penn have sought to promote institutions of peace. In this era we promote a vision of a new world order that recognizes the essential unity of a human family sharing a fragile planet.

We prefer governing institutions that work face-to-face, within small communities. But we acknowledge the need for governing institutions at all levels, both as supportive, coordinating bodies, and as courts of appeal from the arbitrary actions of lesser jurisdictions.

We are deeply distressed by a world order dominated by heavily armed nation-states. We apply our gifts—of spirit, of intellect, of time and energy—to work for a new international order under God, within which our communities will be able to redirect their resources from overdependence on the manufacture of arms to human needs and the preservation of the earth.

The Individual and the State

The State, Supportive and Coercive

The attitude of Friends toward the state is conditioned by the fact that the state has many facets. As a necessary instrument for meeting human needs and for maintaining an orderly society with justice under law for all, the state commands respect and cooperation. But when the state acts as a coercive agency resorting to violence, it acts contrary to Quaker principles.

Friends are not opposed to all forms of physical constraint. It is sometimes necessary and proper for peace officers to use minimal forms of physical constraints in dealing with persons who do injury to others or who will not cooperate with just law. But Friends must be watchful for the use of either physical or psychological violence in maintaining public order.

Civic Duties

As a part of their witness to what society may become, Friends are called to participate in public life as voters, public officials, or participants in community groups or professional societies.

As private citizens in the public arena, Friends bear witness by demonstrating respect for others, flexibility, reconciliation, and forgiveness in difficulties, as well as faithful persistence in pursuit of their leadings.

In public office, Friends have an opportunity to bear witness to the power which integrity, courage, respect for others, and careful attention to different points of view can exert in creating a just community. Where there is a conflict between loyalty to God and a seeming necessity for action as a public official, a prayerful search for divine guidance may lead to a suitable resolution of the conflict or to a decision to resign.

Civil Disobedience

From their earliest days Friends have counseled obedience to the state except when the law or ruling involved has appeared to be contrary to divine leading. The state has no claim to moral infallibility. Primary allegiance is to God.

If the state's commands appear to be contrary to divine leading, Friends take prayerful counsel before responding. This usually involves testing one's proposed action by the judgment of the Meeting. When the decision is to refuse obedience to the law or order of the state, in accordance with the dictates of conscience, it is proper for Friends to act openly and to make clear the grounds of their action.

If the decision involves incurring legal penalties, Friends generally have suffered willingly for the sake of their convictions. Friends not personally involved in such actions can strengthen the Meeting community by supporting their fellow members with spiritual encouragement and, when necessary, with material aid.

Stewardship

Stewardship of Economic Resources

All that we have, in our selves and our possessions, are gifts from God, entrusted to us for our responsible use. Jesus reminds us that we must not lay up earthly treasures for ourselves, for where our treasures are, there will our hearts be also. We cannot serve both God and Mammon.

Stewardship is a coming together of our major testimonies. To be good stewards in God's world calls on us to examine and consider the ways in which our testimonies for peace, equality, and simplicity interact to guide our relationships with all life.

> *O that we who declare against wars, and acknowledge our trust to be in God only, may walk in the light, and thereby examine our foundation and motives in holding great estates! May we look upon our treasures, the furniture of our houses, and our garments, and try whether the seeds of war have nourishment in these our possessions.*

> John Woolman, c. 1770

In a world of economic interactions far more complex than John Woolman could have imagined, Friends need to examine their decisions about obtaining, holding, and using money and other assets, to see whether they find in them the seeds, not only of war, but also of self-indulgence, injustice, and ecological disaster. Good stewardship of economic resources consists both in avoidance of those evils and in actions that advance peace, simple living, justice, and a healthy ecosystem. Good stewardship also requires attention to the economic needs of Quaker and other organizations that advance Friends' testimonies.

Right Sharing

Friends worldwide have accepted the idea that the testimony of equality in the economic realm implies a commitment to the right sharing of the world's resources. Friends in comfortable circumstances need to find practical expression of the testimony of simplicity in their earning and spending. They must consider the meaning for their own lives of economic equality and simplicity, and what level of income is consonant with their conclusions. They should consider likewise what portion of that income should be shared beyond the immediate family. That decision entails balancing the social value of self-sufficiency against the social value of greater help for those more needy. It also requires judgments about what expenditures are essential and what are discretionary, and about the values that will underlie discretionary expenditures.

Walking Gently on the Earth

We recognize that the well-being of the earth is a fundamental spiritual concern. From the beginning, it was through the wonders of nature that people saw God. How we treat the earth and its creatures is a basic part of our relationship with God. Our planet as a whole, not just the small parts of it in our immediate custody, requires our responsible attention.

As Friends become aware of the interconnectedness of all life on this planet and the devastation caused by neglect of any part of it, we have become more willing to extend our sense of community to encompass all living things. We must now consider whether we should lay aside the belief that we humans are acting as stewards of the natural world, and instead view human actions as the major threat to the ecosystem.

Friends are indeed called to walk gently on the earth. Wasteful and extravagant consumption is a major cause of destruction of the environment. The right sharing of the world's remaining resources requires that developed nations reduce their present levels of consumption so that people in underdeveloped nations can have more, and the earth's life-sustaining systems can be restored. The world cannot tolerate indefinitely the present rate of consumption by technologically developed nations.

Friends are called to become models and patterns of simple living and concern for the earth. Some may find it difficult to change their accustomed lifestyle; others recognize the need and have begun to adopt ways of life which put the least strain on the world's resources of clean air, water, soil, and energy.

A serious threat to the planet is the population explosion and consequent famine, war and devastation. Called on to make decisions to simplify our lives, we may find that the most difficult to accept will be limiting the number of children we have.

Voluntary simplicity in living and restraint in procreation hold the promise of ecological redemption and spiritual renewal.

Advices

The principal purpose of a book of discipline is to promote discipleship by giving advice on a broad range of aspects of the life of the Society of Friends. In that sense the entire volume, save the quotations from the writings of Friends, is advices, addressed by the yearly meeting to its many individual members and its many constituent bodies.

With that in mind, we have chosen to abandon the practice of recasting to suit our times a set of highly compact advices received from the earlier generations. But rather than drop the compact version entirely, we have, in support of those who cherish them, reprinted the 1972 version. We trust that doing so will not encourage Friends to rely unduly on the compact advices to the neglect of the volume as a whole.

• • •

These advices were paraphrased from materials contained in the Epistles of the Yearly Meeting of Pennsylvania and the Jerseys, 1694 and 1695.

• • •

I

Friends are reminded that our Religious Society took form in times of disturbance, and that its continuing testimony has been the power of God to lead men and women out of the confusions of outward violence, inward sickness, and all other forms of self-will, however upheld by social convention. As death comes to our willfulness, a new life is formed in us, so that we are liberated from distractions and frustrations, from fears, angers, and guilts. Thus we are enabled to sense the Inward Light and to follow its leadings. Friends are advised to place God, not themselves, in the center of the universe and, in all aspects of inward life and outward activity, to keep themselves open to the healing power of the Spirit of Christ.

Take heed, dear Friends, to the promptings of love and truth in your hearts. Seek to live in affection as true Friends in your Meetings, in your families, in all your dealings with others, and in your relationship with outward society. The power of God is not used to compel us to Truth; therefore, let us renounce for ourselves the power of any person over any other and, compelling no one, seek to lead others to Truth through love. Let us teach by being ourselves teachable.

Keep to the simplicity of Truth. Seek for its manifestations in prayer, in reading matter, in the arts, and in all experiences of daily life. Shun the use of mind-changing drugs and intoxicants, of gambling, and of other detrimental practices that interpose themselves against the Inward Light. It is the experience of Friends that these drugs, intoxicants, and practices lead to a personal willfulness and inability to listen for the will of God. Avoid in daily work those involvements and entanglements that separate us from each other and from God. Keep your recreations from becoming occasions for self-intoxication and avoid those conventional amusements which debase the emotions by playing upon them. These, too, lead to self-absorption and to forgetfulness that each person's humanity is shared by all persons. Live and work in the plainness and simplicity of a true follower of Christ.

I I

Our Religious Society endures as a community of friends who take thought for outward society by first taking care of one another. Friends are advised to maintain love and unity, to avoid tale-bearing and detraction, and to settle differences promptly and in a manner free from resentment and all forms of inward violence. Live affectionately as friends, entering with sympathy into the joys and sorrows of one another's daily lives. Visit one another. Be alert to give help and ready to receive it. Bear the burdens of one another's failings; share the buoyancy of one another's strengths.

Remember that to everyone is given a share of responsibility for the meeting for worship, whether through silence or through the spoken word. Be diligent in attendance at meetings and in inward preparation for them. Be ready to speak under the leadings of the Light. Receive the ministry of others in a tender spirit and avoid hurtful criticism. In meetings for business, and in all duties connected with them, seek again the leadings of the Light, keeping from obstinacy and from harshness of tone or manner; admit the possibility of being in error. In all the affairs of the Meeting community, proceed in the peaceable spirit of Pure Wisdom, with forbearance and warm affection for each other.

Use your capabilities and your possessions not as ends in themselves but as God's gifts entrusted to you. Share them with others; use them with humility, courtesy and affection. Guard against contentiousness and love of power; be alert to the personalities and the needs of others. Show loving consideration for all creatures, and cherish the beauty and wonder of God's creation. Attend to Pure Wisdom and be teachable.

I I I

Friends are reminded that it is the experience and testimony of our Society that there is one teacher, namely Christ; and that in that Spirit there are no distinctions between persons, nor any reason of age, sex, or race that elects some to domination. Live in love and learn from one another. Combativeness in family life, whereby one strives to assert a supremacy of will over another, is not compatible with the conviction that there is that of God in everyone. Amid the growing distempers of social existence, Friends are urged to maintain our witness of Truth, simplicity, and nonviolence, and to test our personal lives by them.

The union of two in marriage having a religious basis, any who contemplate it should seek divine guidance, and any who enter into marriage should seek this guidance without ceasing. Within the family, adults and youth, whether formally in membership or not, should instruct one another by example in the way of life which our Religious Society has professed, seeking in all things the Inward Light as the only certain alternative to an unfriendly struggle of wills. Friends are advised to maintain closeness in their family life and, avoiding distractions and contentions, to make their homes places of peace.

The Spirit of Christ can lead parents to wise counsel for their children in education, reading, recreation, and social relationships, while it can also lead children to wise counsel for their parents in these and other aspects of life. If counsel is unwelcome and if difficulties arise, persevere both in prayer and in a sense of humor. Friends are advised in all things to trust in the Light and to witness to it in daily living.

Accept with serenity the approach of each new stage of life. Welcome the approach of old age, both for oneself and for others, as an opportunity for wisdom, for detachment from turmoils, and for greater attachment to the Light. Make provisions for the settlement of all outward affairs while in health, so that others may not be burdened and so that one may be freed to live more fully in the Truth that shall stand against all the entanglements, distractions, and confusions of our times.

I V

Bring the whole of your life under the healing and ordering of the Holy Spirit, remembering that there is no time but this present. Friends are reminded that we are called, as followers of Christ, to help establish the Kingdom of God on earth. In witnessing to the Inward Light, guard against religious intolerance. Strengthen a sense of kinship with everyone and make service, not self-promotion, the chief aim of our outward lives as Friends, as employees or as supervisors, and as citizens.

Let the sense of kinship inspire us to unceasing efforts toward a social order free of violence and oppression, in which no one's development is hindered by meager income, insufficient education, or too little freedom in directing his or her own affairs. Friends are advised not only to minister to those in need, but also to seek to know the facts of social and economic ills so as to work for the removal of those ills. Let the Friendly testimony that there is that of God in everyone lead us to cherish every human being regardless of race or class, and to encourage efforts to overcome prejudices and antagonisms. Friends are advised to cleanse themselves of all prejudice.

Be faithful in maintaining our testimony against all war as contrary to the spirit and teaching of Christ. Every human being is a child of God with a measure of God's Light. War and other instruments of violence and oppression ignore this reality and violate our relation with God. Keep primary our Friends' concern for the elimination of combat in the outward world as in our personal lives. Friends are advised to live in the virtue of that life and power that takes away the occasion of all wars. Friends are further advised to aid in all ways possible the development of international order and understanding.

Dear Friends, keep all your meetings in the authority, wisdom and power of Truth and the unity of the blessed Spirit. Let your conduct and conversation be such as become the Gospel of Christ. Exercise yourselves to have a conscience void of offense toward God and toward all people. Be steadfast and faithful in your allegiance and service to your Lord, and the God of peace be with you.

Elders of Balby, Yorkshire, 1656

Extracts from writings on

Belief

Now faith is the substance of things hoped for, the evidence of things not seen. (Hebrews 11:1).

INTRODUCTION

Quakers have traditionally been wary of creedal statements as limiting our understanding of God. Friends of Philadelphia Yearly Meeting have further avoided prescribed declarations of faith and statements of essential truths as hindrances to communication with the Divine.

The rejection of creeds does not imply the absence of doctrine or statements of belief. From the earliest times of our society, individual Friends, as well as small groups of Friends and Friends' Meetings, have issued written statements of their beliefs to the world. Among the doctrines finding wide acceptance by Friends are a universal saving light and continuing revelation. The selections that follow explore these and other beliefs widely shared among Friends.

· · ·

1   Friends find their essential unity in their profound and exhilarating belief in the pervasive presence of God and in the continuing responsibility of each person and worshiping group to seek the leading of the Spirit in all things. Obedience to the leading of that Spirit rather than to any written statement of belief or conduct is the obligation of their faith.

New England Yearly Meeting, 1985

2   There is a time of preaching faith towards God; and there is a time to be brought to God.

George Fox, 1657

3   What is the Quaker faith? It is not a tidy package of words which you can capture at any given time and then repeat weekly at a worship service. It is an experience of discovery which starts the discoverer on a journey which is life-long. The discovery in itself is not uniquely a property of Quakerism. It is as old as Christianity, and considerably older if you share the belief that many have known Christ who have not known His name. What is unique to the Religious Society of Friends is its insistence that the discovery must be made by each man for himself.

No one is allowed to get it second-hand by accepting a ready-made creed. Furthermore, the discovery points a path and demands a journey, and gives you the power to make the journey.

Elise Boulding, 1954

4   Sing and rejoice, ye children of the day and of the light; for the Lord is at work in this thick night of darkness that may be felt. And truth doth flourish as the rose, and the lilies do grow among the thorns, and the plants atop of the hills, and upon them the lambs do skip and play. And never heed the tempests nor the storms, floods nor rains, for the seed Christ is over all, and doth reign. And so be of good faith and valiant for the truth; for the truth can live in the jails.

George Fox, 1663

5   As Friends we believe that love is the unifying force in human relations. Let us understand what brotherly love is and what it is not. Love is not self-seeking; it is self–giving. Love does not try to make up a deficiency in that of God in another from an overabundance of divinity in ourselves; it opens us to the divine Light in him and rejoices in it. Love does not mean agreeing on all questions of belief, values, or rules of conduct; it means accepting with humility and forbearance such differences as cannot be resolved by open and patient give-and-take. Love does not recreate our brother in our image; it recreates us both in relation to each other, united like limbs of one body yet each distinctly himself.

Philadelphia Yearly Meeting, 1969

6   Now the Lord God opened to me by his invisible power that every man was enlightened by the divine light of Christ, and I saw it shine through all; and they that believed in it came out of condemnation to the light of life, and became the children of it; but they that hated it, and did not believe in it, were condemned by it, though they made a profession of Christ. This I saw in the pure openings of the Light without the help of any man; neither did I then know where

to find it in the Scriptures; though afterwards, searching the Scriptures, I found it. For I saw in that Light and Spirit which was before Scripture was given forth... that all must come to that Spirit, if they would know God, or Christ, or the Scriptures aright.

George Fox, 1648

7   We do not want you to copy or imitate us. We want to be like a ship that has crossed the ocean, leaving a wake of foam which soon fades away. We want you to follow the Spirit, which we have sought to follow, but which must be sought anew in every generation.

Anonymous

8   True godliness don't turn men out of the world, but enables them better to live in it and excites their endeavors to mend it; not hide their candle under a bushel, but set it upon a table in a candlestick.

William Penn, 1668

9   Why gad you abroad? Why trim you yourselves with the saints' words, when you are ignorant of the life? Return, return to Him … who is the Light of the World.... Return home to within, sweep your houses all; the groat is there, the little leaven is there, the grain of mustard-seed you will see, which the Kingdom of God is like;…and here you will see your Teacher not removed into a corner, but present when you are upon your beds and about your labour, convincing, instructing, leading, correcting, judging, and giving peace to all that love and follow Him.

Francis Howgill, 1656

10   If you would know God, and worship and serve God as you should do, you must come to the means He has ordained and given for that purpose. Some seek it in books, some in learned men, but what they look for is in themselves, yet they overlook it. The voice is too still, the Seed too small, and the Light shineth in darkness.... The woman that lost her silver found it at home after she had lighted her candle and swept her house. Do you so too, and you shall find what Pilate wanted to know, viz., Truth. The Light of Christ within, who is the Light of the world, and so a light to you that tells you the truth of your condition, leads all that take heed unto it out of darkness into God's marvelous light; for light grows upon the obedient.

William Penn, 1694

11   The humble, meek, merciful, just, pious, and devout souls are everywhere of one religion; and when death has taken off the mask, they will know one another though the divers liveries they wear here makes them strangers.

William Penn, 1693

12   And, when thy children ask thee any questions of this nature, "What God is; where he dwells; or whether he sees them in the dark"—do not reject it; but wait to feel somewhat of God raised in thee, which is able to judge whether the question be put forth in sensibility or in vanity; and which can give thee an advantage of stirring the good, and reaching to that, which is to be raised both in young and old, to live to the praise of him who raiseth it.

Isaac Penington, 1665

13   We do distinguish betwixt the certain knowledge of God and the uncertain, betwixt the spiritual knowledge and the literal, the saving heart-knowledge and the soaring airy head-knowledge. The last, we confess, may be by divers ways obtained; but the first, by no other way than the inward immediate manifestation and revelation of God's Spirit, shining in and upon the heart, enlightening and opening the understanding.

Robert Barclay, 1678

14   There may be members therefore of this catholic church both among heathen, Turks, Jews, and all the several sorts of Christians, men and women of integrity and simplicity of heart, who, though blinded in some things in their understanding and perhaps burdened with the superstitions and formality of the several sects in which they are engrossed, yet being upright in their hearts before the Lord, chiefly aiming and labouring to be delivered from iniquity, and living to follow righteousness, are by the secret touches of this holy light in their souls enlivened and quickened, thereby secretly united to God and there-through become true members of this catholic church.

Robert Barclay, 1678

15   The Cross as dogma is painless speculation; the Cross as lived suffering is anguish and glory. Yet God, out of the pattern of His own heart, has planted the Cross along the road of holy obedience. And He enacts in the hearts of those He loves the miracle of willingness to welcome suffering and to know it for what is —the final seal of His gracious love.

Thomas R. Kelly, 1939

16   There is a spirit which I feel that delights to do no evil, nor to revenge any wrong, but delights to endure all things, in hope to enjoy its own in the end. Its hope is to outlive all wrath and contention, and to weary out all exaltation and cruelty or whatever is of a nature contrary to itself. It sees to the end of all temptations. As it bears no evil in itself, so it conceives none in thoughts to any other. If it be betrayed, it bears it, for its ground and spring is the mercies and forgiveness of God. Its crown is meekness, its life is everlasting love unfeigned; it takes its kingdom with entreaty and not with contention, and keeps it by lowliness of mind. In God alone it can rejoice, though none else regard it or can own its life. It's conceived in sorrow, and brought forth without any to pity it, nor doth it murmur at grief and oppression. It never rejoiceth but through sufferings; for with the world's joy it is murdered. I found it alone, being forsaken. I have fellowship therein with them who lived in dens and desolate places in the earth, who through death obtained this resurrection and eternal holy life.

James Nayler, 1660

17   There is a principle which is pure, placed in the human mind, which in different places and ages hath had different names. It is, however, pure and proceeds from God. It is deep and inward, confined to no forms of religion nor excluded from any where the heart stands in perfect sincerity. In whomsoever this takes root and grows, of what nation soever, they become brethren in the best sense of the expression. Using ourselves to take ways which appear most easy to us, when inconsistent with that purity which is without beginning, we thereby set up a government of our own and deny obedience to him whose service is true liberty.

John Woolman, 1774

18   We need to guard against under-valuing the material expressions of spiritual things. It is easy to make a form of our very rejection of forms. And in particular we need to ask ourselves whether we are endeavoring to make all the daily happenings and doings of life which we call "secular" minister to the spiritual. It is a bold and colossal claim that we put forward—that the whole of life is sacramental, that there are innumerable "means of grace" by which God is revealed and communicated—through nature and through human fellowship and through a thousand things that may become the "outward and visible sign" of an "inward and spiritual grace."

A. Barrett Brown, 1932

19   Quakerism in spirit and ideal is neither a form of Roman Catholicism nor a form of Protestantism. Protestantism in its original, essential features called for an authoritative creed, specific sacraments, and an authentic form of ordination. Quakerism at its birth was a fresh attempt to recover the way of life revealed in the New Testament, to re-interpret and re-live it in this present world. Its founders intended to revive apostolic Christianity. They did not intend to create a new sect. They carefully avoided calling themselves a "Church." They were content to be a "Society of Friends." George Fox said: "The Quakers are not a sect but are [a people living] in the power of God which was before sects were."

Rufus M. Jones, 1937

20   If God ever spoke, He is still speaking. If He has ever been in mutual and reciprocal communication with the persons He has made, He is still a communicating God as eager as ever to have listening and receptive souls. If there is something of His image and superscription in our inmost structure and being, we ought to expect a continuous revelation of His will and purpose through the ages.... He is the Great I Am, not a Great He Was.

Rufus M. Jones, 1948

21   By ethical mysticism I mean that type of mysticism which first withdraws from the world revealed by the senses to the inward Divine Source of Light, Truth, and Power, and then returns to the world with strength renewed, insight cleared, and desire quickened to bind all life together in the bonds of love. These bonds are discovered by this process of withdrawal and return because the one inward Divine Source is itself the creative unity which seeks to bind all life together. But there is no necessary chronological order in the world of spirit. It may be that the desire to penetrate to the creative unity in the depths of the soul was first aroused by finding it in the outward affairs of daily life.

Howard Brinton, 1967

22   To say that Friends have no creed is not to say that each Friend has no belief. Far otherwise. Each one, and each group, has the responsibility to seek, and seek, and seek again where the Light is leading; to find what the life of God means in the life of man; to wrestle with the great facts and mysteries in the heart of our Christian experience, and to know what we believe about them. It is only when we have formulated our faith for ourselves that we can communicate it to others or know its incisive power in our own day-to-day discipleship.

Hugh L. Doncaster, 1963

23   In this day and age the place where Friends find their unity is in the kind of God they worship. Their apprehension of the relationship of Jesus Christ to God embraces every orthodox and unorthodox shade of theology from unitarian to trinitarian; but whether we regard Jesus…as God himself or as the supreme revealer of God to man, it is the same kind of God: a spirit of peace, truth, love, and redeeming power. We need to feel the influence of this spirit in our lives rather than to argue about our different modes of apprehending Him. Directly we begin to chide each other for orthodoxy or unorthodoxy, we cease to be the catholic body we are; for the logical end of such chiding is sanctions and the excluding of the weaker body by the stronger. Let us keep our different modes of apprehension and remember always that it is the same God we serve, revealing Himself to each according to his faith, his openness, and his need.

Beatrice Saxon Snell, 1961

24   The primary doctrine of the Society of Friends declares that the Presence of God is felt at the apex of the human soul and that man can therefore know and heed God directly, without any intermediary in the form of church, priest, sacrament, or sacred book. As present in man, God is both immanent and transcendent: immanent because He is not mechanically operating on man from without but sharing in his life; transcendent, for the Divine Life extends infinitely out beyond and above all human life. Many figures of speech are used to designate this Divine Presence which as immanent in man is personal, and as transcendent, is super-personal. It is a "Light," a "Power," a "Word," a "Seed of the Kingdom." God dwells in man to guide him and transform him into the likeness of His Son. Man's endeavor should be to merge his will with the Divine Will, as far as he is able to comprehend it, and by obedience to become an instrument through which God's power works upon the world. To seek such a goal is to seek to be an embodiment of the Divine Life through unity with it. In this search man's life acquires unity and purpose.

Howard Brinton, 1940

25   It is easy to misconstrue "Inner Light" as an invitation to individualism and anarchy if one concentrates on the subjective experience known to each one. But it is an equally important part of our faith and practice to recognise that we are not affirming the existence and priority of your light and my light, but the Light of God, and of the God who is made known to us supremely in Jesus.

Hugh L. Doncaster, 1972

26   As a black Quaker, I see the Inner Light as the great liberator and equalizer able to erase the psychological deficits of racism. The internalization of this divine principle has the potential to remove the sense of powerlessness that so often characterizes the thinking of the downtrodden. For if the Divine Light is the Seed of God planted in the souls of human beings, in that Seed lies all the characteristics of its source. Consequently, the Light within is also the Divine Power within. It is the indestructible power in us that is able to create from nothing, able to make ways out of no way, able to change what appears to be the natural order of things. It is the power in us that can never be overcome by the darkness of fear and hatred or altered by the might or money of people. It is the power in us in which lies unfathomable capacity to love and forgive even the most heinous of crimes.

Ayesha Clark-Halkin Imani, 1988

27   As a teenager I looked for proof of the existence of God, but soon realised that there would be none. I chose to adopt as a working hypothesis a belief in God, and to go on from there. I have not felt the need to revise that hypothesis – yet. I believe in a powerful, all-knowing God, but a caring and a forgiving God. I believe he says to us: "All right, you've got life, get on with it, live it! I am there behind to guide you, to help you live it; but don't expect me to interfere to make life smooth for you—you are old enough to stand on your own two feet."

From what I have learnt as an astronomer I believe that the Universe evolved itself without any active participation from God, and it seems reasonable to me that the world continues, at least on a grand scale, to evolve by itself—that God does not directly interfere with the running of the world; but that he does through people and their attitudes....

I believe that we are God's agents in this world and that he may require things of us. A lot of my effort goes into trying to understand what God expects of me. I do this by trying to maintain an orientation towards God—to live my life in the spirit—to bring my whole life under the ordering of the spirit of Christ—to acknowledge my discipleship.

S. Jocelyn Burnell, 1976

28   The word "sacrament" has been defined as meaning "the outward and visible sign of an inward and spiritual grace," and according to the Quaker belief, that "outward and visible sign" is a life lived in absolute obedience to God, a revelation of His indwelling Spirit in the heart. This, of course, is an integral part of the Christian faith, the eternal truth behind all symbols and observances. But every section of the Christian Church has some special witness to uphold, and for over three hundred years the Society of Friends has testified to this sacramental conception of the whole of life.

Elfrida Vipont Foulds, 1962

29   Each of us can be a theologian. We can enrich our spiritual lives and those of people around us by articulating our spiritual experiences. In drawing on theological writings from the past, we can find continuity and wipe out feelings of isolation. We can divine answers to our toughest concerns.... We can dare to find out what God is saying to us.

Shirley Dodson, 1980

30   We are called to obedient love even though we may not be feeling very loving. Often it is through the performance of loving acts that loving feelings can be built up in us. We may start with small, perhaps very tiny steps. It is only as we begin to allow Christ's love to act in and through us that it can become a part of us.

Sandra Cronk, c. 1983

31   The mystical accent in Quakerism does not lessen its Christian rootage even though it does break down barriers and contains within it a strong ecumenical current. In the years immediately following the First World War, the Quakers worked in Poland distributing food and clothing. A woman worker who served a cluster of villages became ill with typhus and in twenty–four hours she was dead. In this village there was only a Roman Catholic cemetery, and by canonical law it was quite impossible to bury one not of that confession in its consecrated ground. They laid their cherished friend in a grave dug just outside the fence of the Roman Catholic cemetery and the next morning they discovered that in the night the villagers had moved the fence so that it embraced the grave. This moving outward of every type of fence so that it may embrace but not erase the unique and very special witness of the different religious groups comes close to the core of the meaning of this ecumenical current.

Douglas Steere, 1984

32   I come back again and again in my own mind to this word Truth. "Promptings of love and truth" — these two sometimes seem to be in conflict, but in fact they are inseparable. If we are to know the truth, we must be able to see with unclouded eyes, and then we will love what is real and not what is duty or fancy. Once when I was in the middle of a difficult exercise of Quaker decision-making, I wailed to an older and wiser Friend, "How can I speak the truth in love when I feel no love?" Her reply was, "Unless you speak the truth there never will be love."

Alison Sharman, 1986

33   The life of a religious society consists in something more than the body of principles it professes and the outer garments of organisation which it wears. These things have their own importance: they embody the society to the world, and protect it from the chance and change of circumstance; but the springs of life lie deeper, and often escape recognition. They are to be found in the vital union of the members of the society with God and with one another, a union which allows the free flowing through the society of the spiritual life which is its strength.

William Charles Braithwaite, 1905

34   Does anything unite this diverse group beyond our common love and humanity? Does anything make us distinctively Quaker? I say yes. Each of us has different emphases and special insights, but wherever Friends are affirming each other's authentic experience of God, rather than demanding creedal statements, we are being God's faithful Quakers. Wherever we are seeking God's will rather than human wisdom, especially when conflict might arise, we are being faithful Quakers. Wherever we are affirming the total equality of men and women, we are being God's faithful Quakers. Wherever there is no division between our words and our actions, we are being faithful. Whenever we affirm that no one—priest, pastor, clerk, elder—stands between us and the glorious and mystical experience of God in our lives, we are faithful Friends. Whether we sing or whether we wait in silence, as long as we are listening with the whole of our being and seeking the baptism and communion of living water, we will be one in the Spirit.

Val Ferguson, 1991

35   We are an instrument in this world. No matter which way we look, no matter where we go, we know we have a world filled with injustice, inequality, racism, thousands of problems, whether out in the open or hidden.... We are told that the light that comes from God to us, comes to everyone to light the world—this is what we call the Inner Light.... That Light has to illuminate our problems, but we must not live only for resolving our internal problems and nothing else.

                                                            Heredio Santos, 1991

36   We can actually rejoice in...diversity; we do not always need a formula which will iron out differences. That seems to me to be Quakerism in practice. When I talk about the content of the Quaker treasure chest, I often refer to that wonderful epistle sent out to Friends everywhere written by Young Friends from all parts of the Quaker family in Greensboro in 1985. Here, after many tears and misunderstandings and strong disagreements, a group of Young Friends sat down together and, respecting each other, wrote out what for them was the essence of the Quaker good news. They came up with the four sources of authority: The Light or voice in the heart, the discernment of the worshiping group, Christ speaking in the heart, and the words of the Bible. These four elements are in tension in the world family of Friends. We do not all agree on them, but the Quaker treasure chest offers these diverse heirlooms. Some parts of the family are happier with some of the jewels than others. But the greatest disservice we can do is to keep the chest shut. By sharing the jewels with our guests, our guests may actually begin to feel as if the home belongs to them as well. And who knows, our guests may even become the next generation of hosts and show off the jewels in a new light.

                                                            Harvey Gillman, 1993

37   Let us recognize that while spiritual life in its externals often presents us with a bewildering diversity, the saints of each spiritual tradition are practically indistinguishable from each other in their lives, their way of being. Though their theological concepts may be different, their feelings and conduct are amazingly similar. They dwell in love, and God dwells in them because God is love. Increasingly in this modern age, the capacity to apprehend the One in the many constitutes the special responsibility of those who would dwell in love. May this capacity to apprehend the One in the many, and the love it expresses, be the special gift of the friends of Jesus to people of faith everywhere!

                                                            Daniel A. Seeger, 1994

38   Someone in worship today gave a brief summary of the naturalistic interpretation of religion. How rational, judicious, and powerless seemed our intellectual expressions and how little they met the need of a young attender, obviously in need of deeper ministry, who left, overcome by emotion, in the middle of meeting. The real ministry of our meeting came from the concern of several who followed him out to give him comfort. I saw that such lovingkindness, call it love or agape, is the manifestation in the natural world of that which transcends it. Love does have power—not the political or mechanical power the world seems to covet, but a basic power that works in another way, not by overcoming but by reunion. Such a working, when it points to its source, can be called a miracle—not a breach of nature, but an inbreak of love....

Going home, I mused on the occasional tensions in our meeting between its rational–academic and its quietly religious tendencies. Sometimes the balance tips one way, sometimes the other. At times, a few members have fallen away to worship in more congenial, more "spiritual" meetings; this is a pity, for a secularized meeting needs a religious few to leaven the lump, just as a more religiously enthusiastic meeting needs a few good agnostics as burrs under its saddle.

Carol Murphy, 1989

39   I was under great temptations sometimes, and my inward sufferings were heavy; but I could find none to open my condition to but the Lord alone, unto whom I cried night and day. And I went back into Nottinghamshire, and there the Lord showed me that the natures of those things, which were hurtful without were within, in the hearts and minds of wicked men. The natures of dogs, swine, vipers, of Sodom and Egypt, Pharoah, Cain, Esau, etc. The natures of these I saw within, though people had been looking without. And I cried to the Lord, saying, "Why should I be thus, seeing I was never addicted to commit those evils?" And the Lord answered that it was needful I should have a sense of all conditions, how else should I speak to all conditions. And in this I saw the infinite love of God. I saw also that there was an ocean of darkness and death, but an infinite ocean of light and love, which flowed over the ocean of darkness. And in that also I saw the infinite love of God and I had great openings.

George Fox, 1647

40   The word we have is not a purse of gold bestowed unilaterally on us, which we in turn may dole out unilaterally upon others. It is a living spring which may well up alike in others as in ourselves.

Ferner Nühn, 1967

41   This much is clear: Christians and Universalists need each other. Our culture is grounded in ancient Christian symbols, which, if we listen, still quiver with dense ineffable meanings. In an effort to persuade us to listen to those meanings, Christians try to find words for them. The danger is that the words may become idols: creeds graven in stone.

Universalists, alive to this danger, remind us that other cultures have other symbols which—could we but attune ourselves to their resonance—are just as fraught as ours. There are other ways of seeing. Here the danger is that we may abandon particularity altogether and find ourselves adrift on an ocean of light without stars, landmarks, or anchorage.

Christians would call us back to terra firma lest we dissolve. Universalists would have us venture forth lest we petrify. The interplay of universal and particular must be as old as religion itself. Each has dangers which the other counteracts.

The Church Universal needs both its seafarers and its stay-at-homes. Why is that so difficult? Why have I myself never understood it until now?

Esther Murer, 1986

42   We see that the teachings of [the] divine spirit have been the same in all ages. It has led to truth, to goodness, to justice, to love. Love was as much held up among [the] old [Testament] writers, [the] old religious teachers, and as clearly set forth, as in the later days. Their testimony fell upon ears that heard not, upon eyes that saw not, because they had closed their eyes, shut their ears, and hardened their hearts. They had substituted something else for this divine light; this word, which...Moses declared to his people was "nigh unto them, in the mouth, and in the heart."...Believe not, then, that all these great principles were only known in the day of the advent of the Messiah to the Jews – those beautiful effects of doing right.

Lucretia Mott, 1858

43   Quaker theology and the Biblical precedents supporting it show that both man and woman are to share in the oversight of the creation, as well as other roles in the Church. Neither man nor woman is to dominate the creation or each other, but all are to live under God's guidance. The power to be used by both man and woman is God's power, and not human power.

Virginia Schurman, 1990

44   Quakers from the whole world await a message of hope. But how shall they hear? The presence and work of the Spirit is much more important than our words and forms of worship. That within us should also be transformed outward.

Some of us place special emphasis on the historical Jesus Christ as our personal Savior; others on the Light within everyone, which is interpreted by some of us as the Holy Spirit, and by some as the Christ principle; while others emphasize the universal spirit of God. We see these as three aspects of the one God and rejoice in our unity.

As we love one another, we find unity and become peacemakers. The barriers that separate us are broken, as Jesus broke the barrier between the Samaritans and the Jews through the conversation between him and the Samaritan woman. We should support each other in the diversity of our witness. We are one world trying to live our lives as Christ did.

Mable Lugalya, 1991

Extracts from writings on

Worship

INTRODUCTION

Worship is the foundation for spiritual life and renewal in the Religious Society of Friends. The selections that follow address the distinctive character of Friends communal worship and the forms of ministry to which it gives rise. These selections include practical advice regarding how to prepare for and settle into worship as well as broader statements regarding the meaning and significance of our form of worship. Selections have been gathered into four groups: Worship; Prayer; the Scriptures, Jesus, Inward Teacher; Discernment and Guidance.

• • •

Worship

45   The first that enters into the place of your meeting...turn in thy mind to the light, and wait upon God singly, as if none were present but the Lord; and here thou art strong. Then the next that comes in, let them in simplicity of heart sit down and turn in to the same light, and wait in the spirit; and so all the rest coming in, in the fear of the Lord, sit down in pure stillness and silence of all flesh, and wait in the light.... Those who are brought to a pure still waiting upon God in the spirit, are come nearer to the Lord than words are; for God is a spirit, and in the spirit is he worshiped.... In such a meeting there will be an unwillingness to part asunder, being ready to say in yourselves, it is good to be here; and this is the end of all words and writings—to bring people to the eternal living Word.

                                                        Alexander Parker, 1660

46   We earnestly advise all who attend our meetings to lift their hearts to God immediately on taking their seats. The avoidance of distracting conversation beforehand is a great help to this end, and the walk to meeting may often prove a true preparation for divine worship....

The meeting affects the ministry quite as truly as the ministry affects the meeting. If those who come together do so in expectant faith, and in genuine love and sympathy with one another, striving to put far from them thoughts of criticism and fault-finding, and praying earnestly that the right persons may be led to speak and the right messages be given, they will not go away unhelped. It is in such an atmosphere that the Holy Spirit can work effectively to bring forth the utterances that are needed, and to check those that are not required. On the other hand, the spirit of indifference or of cold and unfriendly criticism injures the whole life of the meeting, and we need not wonder if in such an atmosphere speakers mistake their guidance.

Revision Committee, London Yearly Meeting, 1911

47   Observance of special days and times and use of special places for worship serve a helpful purpose in calling attention at regular intervals to our need for spiritual communion. They cannot, however, take the place of daily and hourly looking to God for guidance. Nor can any custom of fasting or abstaining from bodily comforts take the place of constant refraining from everything which has a tendency to unfit mind and body for being the temple of the Divine Spirit. The foundation for all our personal life and social relations should be the sufficient and irreplaceable consciousness of God.

Philadelphia Yearly Meeting (Race Street), 1927

48   There are times of dryness in our individual lives, when meeting may seem difficult or even worthless. At such times one may be tempted not to go to meeting; but it may be better to go, prepared to offer as our contribution to the worship simply a sense of need. In such a meeting one may not at the time realise what one has gained, but one will nevertheless come away helped.

Ministry and Extension Committee, Berks
and Oxon Quarterly Meeting, London Yearly Meeting, 1958

49   For, when I came into the silent assemblies of God's people I felt a secret power among them which touched my heart; and as I gave way unto it I found the evil weakening in me and the good raised up; and so I became thus knit and united unto them, hungering more and more after the increase of this power and life, whereby I might feel myself perfectly redeemed....

Robert Barclay, 1678

50   And as many candles lighted, and put in one place, do greatly augment the light and make it more to shine forth; so when many are gathered together into the same life, there is more of the glory of God, and his power

appears, to the refreshment of each individual, for that he partakes not only of the light and life raised in himself, but in all the rest.

Robert Barclay, 1678

51   Yea, though there be not a word spoken, yet is the true spiritual worship performed, and the body of Christ edified; yea, it may, and hath often fallen out among us, that divers meetings have passed without one word; and yet our souls have been greatly edified and refreshed, and our hearts wonderfully overcome with the secret sense of God's power and Spirit, which without words hath been ministered from one vessel to another.

Robert Barclay, 1677

52   When you come to your meetings...what do you do? Do you then gather together bodily only, and kindle a fire, compassing yourselves about with the sparks of your own kindling, and so please yourselves, and walk in the light of your own fire, and in the sparks which you have kindled...? Or rather, do you sit down in True Silence, resting from your own Will and Workings, and waiting upon the Lord, with your minds fixed in that Light wherewith Christ has enlightened you, until the Lord breathes life in you, refresheth you, and prepares you, and your spirits and souls, to make you fit for his service, that you may offer unto him a pure and spiritual sacrifice?

William Penn, 1677

53   On one never-to-be-forgotten Sunday morning, I found myself one of a small company of silent worshipers, who were content to sit down together without words, that each one might feel after and draw near to the Divine Presence, unhindered at least, if not helped, by any human utterance. Utterance I knew was free, should the words be given; and before the meeting was over, a sentence or two were uttered in great simplicity by an old and apparently untaught man, rising in his place amongst the rest of us. I did not pay much attention to the words he spoke, and I have no recollection of their import. My whole soul was filled with the unutterable peace of the undisturbed opportunity for communion with God, with the sense that at last I had found a place where I might, without the faintest suspicion of insincerity, join with others in simply seeking His presence. To sit down in silence could at least pledge me to nothing; it might open to me (as it did that morning) the very gate of heaven.

Caroline E. Stephen, 1890

54   Our worship is a deep exercise of our spirits before the Lord, which doth not consist in exercising the natural part or natural mind, either to hear or speak words, or in praying according to what we, of ourselves, can apprehend or comprehend concerning our needs; but we wait, in silence of the fleshly part, to hear with the new ear what God shall please to speak inwardly in our own hearts, or outwardly through others, who speak with the new tongue which he

unlooseth and teacheth to speak; and we pray in the spirit, and with a new understanding, as God pleaseth to quicken, draw forth, and open our hearts towards himself.

Isaac Penington, 1661

55   He that lets his mind be ungoverned out of meeting, cannot set it so right as it should be when he comes into one; and such as get not forward in their spiritual journey when in meeting, it's certain they will go backwards when out of them.

John Bellers, 1703

56   True worship may be experienced at any time; in any place—alone on the hills or in the busy daily life – we may find God, in whom we live and move and have our being. But this individual experience is not sufficient, and in a meeting held in the Spirit there is a giving and receiving between its members, one helping another with or without words. So there may come a wider vision and a deeper experience.

Revision Committees, London Yearly Meeting, 1925 and 1994

57   The whole fellowship of disciples without distinction of sex or of official position are called to be priests, and to each one may be given some work of ministry. Our common worship must give opportunities for this, and in our experience we have found that in waiting upon God in silence we have the freedom and opportunity for such ministry and also for a deep experience of communion.

T. Edmund Harvey, 1937

58   Meeting for worship can be more than just an occasion on which one's private religious needs are satisfied. Silent devotion should lead to an awareness that the meeting is less and less a place we choose ourselves, and more and more a place to which, out of love, God has called us. To understand this is to sense the meaning of those lovely phrases about the community of faith being the body of Christ.

John Punshon, 1987

59   In a truly covered meeting an individual who speaks takes no credit to himself for the part he played in the unfolding of the worship.... For the feeling of being a pliant instrument of the Divine Will characterizes true speaking "in the Life." Under such a covering an individual emerges into vocal utterance, frequently without fear and trembling, and subsides without self–consciousness into silence when his part is played. For One who is greater than all individuals has become the meeting place of the group, and He becomes the leader and director of worship. With wonder one hears the next speaker, if there be more, take up another aspect of the theme of the meeting. No jealousy, no regrets that he didn't

think of saying that, but only gratitude that the angel has come and troubled the waters and that many are finding healing through the one Life. A gathered meeting is no place for the enhancement of private reputations, but for self–effacing pliancy and obedience to the whispers of the Leader.

Thomas Kelly, 1945

60   How does a Quaker Meeting work? Its foundation is the conviction that God is not a distant remote being but a living presence to be discovered in the deep centre of every human being....

The Quaker experience is that, in the silence, as we are open to one another in love, we help each other by sharing our strengths and weaknesses. The Quaker conviction is that as we go deeper into ourselves we shall eventually reach a still, quiet centre. At this point two things happen simultaneously. Each of us is aware of our unique value as an individual human being, and each of us is aware of our utter interdependence on one another.

George Gorman, 1982

61   As Catholic worship is centered in the altar and Protestant worship in the sermon, worship for the Society of Friends attempts to realize as its center the divine Presence revealed within. In a Catholic church the altar is placed so as to become the focus of adoration; in a typical Protestant church the pulpit localizes attention; while in a Friends Meeting House there is no visible point of concentration, worship being here directed neither toward the actions nor the words of others, but toward the inward experience of the gathered group.

Howard Brinton, 1952

62   A concern for the fellow–worshipers of our meetings which leads us to find the necessary time to know them, to visit them, to have them in our homes, and to make their needs our concern is a tested preparation for ministry of the highest importance. A person who throughout the week thinks of the approaching meeting for worship and holds up inwardly some of the needs of those who attend, is being prepared for that kind of participation in the meeting for worship that may open the way for helpful ministry. Ministry is often deepened by our natural exposure to those in greatest need, whether it be physical need, as in a constant visiting of the poor, of those in prison, of those whom group prejudice segregates; or to the poor in spirit, those who face mental turmoil and inner problems. Few who feel this kind of responsible love for the meeting do not in the course of the week find some experience, some insight, something they have read that has helped them, some crushing burden they know some member or some group is bearing which they have held up to the Light, without these things appearing as seeds out of which ministry could grow.

Douglas Steere, 1955

63   The Society of Friends can make its greatest contribution to community by continuing to be a religious society—I mean by centering on the practice of a corporate worship which opens itself to continuing revelation. Again, community is simply too difficult to be sustained by our social impulses. It can be sustained only as we return time and again to the religious experience of the unity of all life. To put it in the language of Friends, community happens as that of God in you responds to that of God in me. And the affirmation that there is that of God in every person must mean more than "I'm okay, you're okay."

The silence of the Quaker meeting for worship can be an experience of unity. I am an orthodox, garden variety Christian; I find the image of God first in Jesus the Christ. But it is my joy in the silent meeting to seek with those who find different ways to express the inexpressible truths of religious experience. Words can divide us, but the silence can bring us together. Whatever kinds of community the world needs, it surely needs the kind that embraces human diversity.

Parker J. Palmer, 1977

64   Worship is a hunger of the human soul for God. When it really occurs, it is as compelling as the hunger for food. It is as spontaneous as the love of boy for girl. If we feel it, no one needs to tell us we should worship. No one has to try to make us do it. If we do not feel it, or have no desire to feel it, no amount of urging or forcing will do any good. We simply cannot be forced from the outside to worship. Only the power within us, the life within, can move us to it.

N. Jean Toomer, 1947

65   I have never lost the enjoyment of sitting in silence at the beginning of meeting, knowing that everything can happen, knowing the joy of utmost surprise; feeling that nothing is preordained, nothing is set, all is open. The light can come from all sides. The joy of experiencing the Light in a completely different way than one has thought it would come is one of the greatest gifts that Friends' meeting for worship has brought me.

Ursula Franklin, 1979

66   As I silence myself I become more sensitive to the sounds around me, and I do not block them out. The songs of the birds, the rustle of the wind, children in the playground, the roar of an airplane overhead are all taken into my worship. I regulate my breathing as taught me by my Zen friends, and through this exercise I feel the flow of life within me from my toes right through my whole body. I think of myself like the tree planted by the "rivers of water'" in Psalm 1, sucking up God's gift of life and being restored. Sometimes I come to meeting for worship tired and weary, and I hear the words of Jesus, '"Come unto me, all that labour and are weary, and I will give you rest." And having laid down my burden, I feel refreshed both physically and spiritually. This leads me on to whole-hearted adoration and thanksgiving for all God's blessings. My own name, Tayeko, means "child of many blessings" and God has surely poured them upon me. My heart overflows with a desire to give Him something in return. I have nothing to give but my own being, and I offer Him my thoughts, words, and actions of each day, and whisper, "Please take me as I am."

Tayeko Yamanouchi, 1980

67   I think it's extremely important that we learn to listen. Listening is a lost art. And when I say learn to listen I mean listen to our spouses, listen to our children, listen to our fellow believers in our communities of faith. But I also want us to learn to listen to God. I know from personal experience that God speaks through the Scriptures. He speaks through preaching. He speaks through friends. But He also speaks directly. We can know that, but we must make time and space and silence in our lives if we are to learn this in real ways and be the beneficiaries of His leading and His guidance directly. We are told in the 46th Psalm, "Be still and know that I am God." In another translation it says, "Stop fighting and know that I am God." Let's take time to listen to God.

Kara Cole Newell, 1982

68   It is unfortunate that much formal training in ministry does not even recognize that... inward preparation exists. In our world of degrees, exams, and training programs, it is easy to forget that ministry is not primarily a task; it is a way of being in the world. It is living in relationship with God and being a witness to God. Ministry is being able to listen to the Word of God and thereby have a word of life to share with others. Fundamentally, we do not do ministry. We are ministers.

Sandra Cronk, 1991

69   Meeting for worship—which includes troubled silences, pompous speechifying, and uncertain searchings, as well as clear leadings—has taught me that the difficult things are often the most fruitful. Reading the Bible is fruitful for me precisely because it challenges me to a deeper level of compassion, commitment, and understanding....

Once, for instance, I was reading the section on the woman at the well, which I had previously dismissed as being one more miracle story. Jesus, I thought, was being credited with knowing the woman's whole life story through mysterious means. But as I reread the passage it became clear to me that Jesus was not showing off—he was explaining to her that God could be worshiped anywhere, that there was Living Water which quenched the deep thirsts we have....

With this new understanding of reading, and this return to my cultural roots, I can carry meeting for worship with me throughout the week and practice the concentration and love which I have found there.

Molly Bishop, 1994

Prayer

70   The silence gives me time to center, sometimes using a few simple words, sometimes watching the play of sunlight on the floor. In the silence, I may simply go over what needs to be done for the week, or focus on concerns for friends, or worry through a problem. In the silent worship, space is there to hold these all up to God. Other times I am drawn into a sense of awareness of Presence, a place of comfort, or instruction, or prayer, or awe.

Margery Post Abbott, 1995

71   Let none allow the rush of engagements or the hurry of business to crowd their opportunities for private retirement and waiting upon God. The more our engagements multiply, the greater is the call to watch unto prayer. He who is a stranger to prayer enters upon them in his own strength, and finds, to his unspeakable loss, that a life without prayer is a life practically without God.

London Yearly Meeting, 1877

72   [Dig] deep, ...carefully cast forth the loose matter and get down to the rock, the sure foundation, and there hearken to the divine voice which gives a clear and certain sound.

John Woolman, c. 1770

73   It came into my mind to write a prayer of my own composing, to use in the mornings. So I wrote a prayer, though I then could scarcely join my letters, I had so little a time learned to write....

The next prayer I wrote was for an assurance of pardon for my sins.... I felt how desirable a thing to be assured of the pardon of one's sins; so I wrote a pretty large prayer concerning it.

I felt a fear of being puffed up with praise, as several persons had praised me for the greatness of my memory, so I wrote a prayer of thanks for the gift of memory and expressed my desires to use it to the Lord.

Mary Proude Springett Penington, c. 1635

74   The place of prayer is a precious habitation....I saw this habitation to be safe, to be inwardly quiet, when there was great stirrings and commotions in the world.

John Woolman, 1770

75   In intercession we share with God our deepest desires for others.... We need constantly to remind ourselves that we can have no right desire for others in which God has not forestalled us. It was His desire before it was ours.... All intercession is self-offering, a self-giving, a longing that what we ask for others may be done, if need be, through ourselves.

Edgar G. Dunstan, 1946

76   Do not let us be discouraged because we find the path of silent prayer difficult or because we do not experience that joy of conscious communion which is given to some. The sunlight shines through the cloud; even when the cloud is so thick that we cannot see the sun at all, its rays carry on their healing work, and it does us good to go out into the open, even on a grey day. The experience of many of the greatest saints points to the traversing of a dark night of the soul before the light of full communion dawns, and to times of dryness of spirit coming at intervals to test the faith and perseverance of the seeker.

T. Edmund Harvey, 1929

77   The habit of turning instinctively to God at any moment of life is of immeasurable benefit to the mind and spirit. The entreaty of the moment may be for one's own strength, forgiveness, courage, or power to endure. It may be a petition for the wellbeing of another. It may be an involuntary expression of gratitude for joy or peace in one's own or another's life. Whatever the need, longing, or aspiration, this instinctive prayer may take the form of silent communion, of petition in words, or something akin to intimate conversation.

Agnes L. Tierney, c. 1930

78   There is a way of living in prayer at the same time that one is busy with the outward affairs of daily living. This practice of continuous prayer in the presence of God involves developing the habit of carrying on the mental life at two levels. At one level we are immersed in this world of time, of daily affairs. At the same time but at a deeper level of our minds, we are in active relation with the Eternal Life.

Thomas Kelly, 1942

79   The highest purpose of prayer is to lift the soul into close companionship with God. Such prayer is not an attitude of the body; is not a formula of words. It is an impulse of the soul that often cannot express itself in words. In the midst of our busiest occupations, when hands and mind and heart are bent upon accomplishing the purpose of the hour, there may come a flash of divine illumination, flooding our souls with light, showing us how God is the center of all things, the life of all that lives. In that moment's deep revealing comes to us the secret of faith that need not question; of hope that foresees its own fulfilling; of strength that wearies not in the walk with God; of love whose beneficent impulses go out to all the needy, and sweeten all life's relationships; of peace that bears the soul upward to the regions of perpetual calm.

Elizabeth Powell Bond, 1895

80   We would do well as Friends to acknowledge our indebtedness to the great religions other than Christianity as we search through the world's treasury for resources to sustain our prayer life.

Elsie Landstrom, 1970

81   In prayer, the seeds of concern have a way of appearing. Often enough, a concern begins in a feeling of being personally liable, personally responsible, for someone or some event. With it there may come an intimation that one should do some little thing: speak to some person, make an inquiry into a certain situation, write a letter, send some money, send a book. Or it may be a stop in our minds about some pending decision, or a clear directive that now is not the time to rest, or an urge to stay home when we had been meaning to be away; it may be that no more than this will be given us. But this seed is given us to follow, and if we do not follow it, we cannot expect to see what may grow from it. Seeds, not fruit, are given in prayer, but they are given for planting.

Douglas V. Steere, 1962

82   It is helpful to think that God is waiting for us to offer ourselves to him in the ministry of healing. Just as the remedies for many diseases had to wait on the development of medical science (through which we must believe that his Spirit is working), so in this service of intercession, results are waiting upon our obedience and readiness to do our part. Thus we shall come to know what it is to share in the fellowship of the Spirit, and become 'workers together with God.'

Frederick J. Tritton, 1958

83   When I read that I was supposed to make 'a place for inward retirement and waiting upon God' in my daily life, as the Queries in those days expressed it, I thought: "Oh, those stuffy old Friends, they don't understand! Do they think I'm going to be able to sit for an hour, or half an hour, or a quarter of an hour, or for any time at all, in my very busy life, just to have some kind of feeling of 'inward retirement'?" I felt irritated and misunderstood, and I tried to put the whole thing out of my mind. At last I began to realise…that I needed some kind of inner peace, or inward retirement, or whatever name it might be called by.… I began to realize that prayer was not a formality or an obligation; it was a place which was there all the time and always available.

Elfrida Vipont Foulds, 1983

84   Prayer would be an evil rather than a blessing if it were only a way of getting God to do what we ourselves will not make the effort to do. God does not do things for us—he enables us to do them for ourselves.

Elisabeth Holmgaard, 1984

85   Obviously, then, all the activities of a meeting—the prayer of worship, the vocal prayer of a gathered meeting, the prayer which sustains and nourishes its cells or prayer groups, family prayer, the ministry of love which expresses itself in counseling, the impact of a meeting on the outside community— all of these should be grounded in the prayer life of the individual. If prayer has not been a reality through the week for at least a core of its members, participants

in the Sunday meeting cannot reach high levels of worship. Vocal prayer flows when the cup is already full before we come to meeting. Activity which is meaningful results from insights gained in prayer. Counseling which is helpful comes from the bringing of divine perspective to human confusion. Prayer, then, is a necessity in our lives. It must be at the center of them.

Helen Hole, 1962

86   There were three separate occasions when heart-felt disturbances called me back to prayer. One was entirely joyful: sitting up in bed early one summer morning nursing my week-old first child, looking out on the sunshine and being swept into a feeling of miraculous oneness with all creation and able to thank a real God with the whole of my being.

The second was in great contrast. The winter after my husband's death, when I was physically stretched to the limit caring singlehanded for six young children and emotionally in a state of bleak torpor, I came across Simone Weil's *Waiting on God* and in a chapter called 'The love of God and affliction' recognised my own condition. I could not claim that I knew the worst that she, in her utterly clear and ruthless style, was describing, but it was near enough; and knowing that someone else recognised it brought a certain comfort. But most important, she showed a place for God in the shape of the crucified Christ, and part of my misery for some time had been the blank absence of any sense of the presence of God....

The third experience, some years later, concerned a friend who was extremely ill. She was one of the few really good people I had ever known, and I saw her in great distress. When I reached home from the hospital I went to my room and tried to lay myself alongside her suffering and bring us both before God. In the depth of affliction I had sometimes felt like Job; now I found myself wrestling like Jacob. This last episode began the process of break-up which led on by slow degrees to a time when I knew I had to try to pray again; not just in dire immediate need but as a basis for daily living.

Joan Fitch, 1980

87   Now as the Father teacheth to pray, so he giveth desires or words (if he please) according to the present need. Sometimes he gives but ability to sigh or groan (if he gives no more he accepts that).... Now, if the prayer be in words, for there is praying without words, then it must be in those words which he pleaseth to give, from the sense which he kindleth, and not in the words which man's wisdom teacheth, or would choose.

Isaac Penington, c. 1665

88   The way to [submerge the individual self in the one eternal Self] ...is through prayer. Some Friends use a short and oft-repeated prayer or a mantra as an aid to concentration. Prayer often involves adoration, gratitude, and love. Passages from the Psalms, incidents in the life of Jesus, or sayings of spiritual leaders may be brought to mind, pondered and related to your life. Sometimes

prayer takes the form of petition, not to tell God of your desires for He knows already nor to seek special favors for that would be impossible, but to set your deepest longings in the Light to see if they are pure. In this silence comes a deep peace beyond words and thoughts, as natural as breathing. The native American chief Papunehang, who had attended a meeting with Woolman, said, "I love to feel where words come from."

George Peck, 1988

89   Lord, baptize us again and again with the pure water of life, the life of Thy love for us. Touch our hearts with brands from Thine altar, to destroy those things in our lives that keep us from being authentic examples of the work of Thy transforming power. Open our eyes, that we may see the work which Thou wouldst have us do for Thee. With grateful hearts we come with assurance unto Thee.

Charles Warner Palmer, c.1940

90   Oh God, our Father, spirit of the universe, I am old in years and in the sight of others, but I do not feel old within myself. I have hopes and purposes, things I wish to do before I die. A surging of life within me cries, "Not yet! Not yet!" more strongly than it did ten years ago, perhaps because the nearer approach of death arouses the defensive strength of the instinct to cling to life.

Help me to loosen, fiber by fiber, the instinctive strings that bind me to the life I know. Infuse me with Thy spirit so that it is Thee I turn to, not the old ropes of habit and thought. Make me poised and free, ready when the intimation comes to go forward eagerly and joyfully, into the new phase of life that we call death.

Help me to bring my work each day to an orderly state so that it will not be a burden to those who must fold it up and put it away when I am gone. Keep me ever aware and ever prepared for the summons.

If pain comes before the end help me not to fear it or struggle against it but to welcome it as a hastening of the process by which the strings that bind me to life are untied. Give me joy in awaiting the great change that comes after this life of many changes, let my self be merged in Thy Self as a candle's wavering light is caught up into the sun.

Elizabeth Gray Vining, 1978

91   So much of life is just going on and going on, long after the excitement and stimulus has faded...there is so much to ask for that I get very lost. And then I just come back to the simple longings, the simplest prayers of all; that Christ may be in those we love, that our love may be more Christ-like, more unmoveable, that we may be kept sinless by some immense miracle, and by God's side whatever happens. We must give up trying to hold His hand, and just stretch out our hands—even if they are just fists—for God to hold. There is all the difference...between holding and being held.

George Lloyd Hodgkin, 1912

92   A friend tells me that when she prays for someone she does not so much pray to God for them as for God for them. This seems to me a vital clue about prayer. It is God that the troubled person needs, not our advice and instructions. As we learn more about worship we learn to listen more deeply so that we can be channels through which God's love reaches the other person. It is God at work, not we ourselves; we are simply used.

Diana Lampen, 1979

93   Be still and cool in thy own mind and spirit from thy own thoughts, and then thou wilt feel the principle of God to turn thy mind to the Lord God, whereby thou wilt receive his strength and power from whence life comes, to allay all tempests against blusterings and storms. That is it which moulds up into patience, into innocency, into soberness, into stillness, into stayedness, into quietness, up to God, with his power.

George Fox, 1658

The Scriptures, Jesus, Inward Teacher

94   And the scriptures—some of them are history done in their times when they were written, and some of them are shadows and figurative and typical of things in their times—of which Christ is the substance and end.

So the scriptures of truth is the best book upon the earth to be read, believed, fulfilled, and practiced. And Christ, the substance of them, is to be enjoyed and walked in....
Holy men of God spake them forth as they were moved by the Holy Ghost. So it is the Holy Ghost that leads into all the truth of them, in both the old and the new testaments.

George Fox, 1689

95   We find many renowned women recorded in the Old Testament, who had received a talent of wisdom and spiritual understanding from the Lord. As good stewards thereof they improved and employed the same to the praise and glory of God...as male and female are made one in Christ Jesus, so women receive an office in account of their stewardship to their Lord, as well as the men. Therefore they ought to be faithful to God and valiant for his Truth upon the earth, that so they may receive the reward of righteousness.

Elizabeth Bathurst, 1683

96   [The scriptures] are only a declaration of the fountain and not the fountain itself, therefore they are not to be esteemed the principal ground of all truth and knowledge, nor yet the adequate, primary rule of faith and man-

ners. Yet, because they give a true and faithful testimony of the first foundation, they are and may be esteemed a secondary rule, subordinate to the Spirit, from which they have all their excellency and certainty: for, as by the inward testimony of the Spirit we do alone truly know them, so they testify that the Spirit is that Guide by which the saints are led into all truth: therefore, according to the Scriptures the Spirit is the first and principal Leader.

Robert Barclay, 1678

97   The case of David hath often been before me of late years. He longed for some water in a well beyond an army of Philistines who were at war with Israel, and some of his men, to please him, ventured their lives in passing through this army and brought that water. It doth not appear that the Israelites were then scarce of water, but rather that David gave way to delicacy of taste; but having thought on the danger these men were exposed to, he considered this water as their blood, and his heart smote him [so], that he could not drink it, but poured it out to the Lord. And the oppression of the slaves which I have seen in several journeys southward on this continent and the report of their treatment in the West Indies hath deeply affected me, and a care to live in the spirit of peace and minister just cause of offence to none of my fellow creatures hath from time to time livingly revived in my mind, and under this exercise I for some years past declined to gratify my palate with those sugars.

John Woolman, 1769

98   Wait on the Lord, that thou mayst, from him, feel the right limit to thy mind, in reading the Scriptures. For the mind of man is busy and active, willing to be running beyond its bounds, guessing at the meaning of God's Spirit and imagining of itself, unless the Lord limit it. Therefore, read in fear; and wait understandingly to distinguish between God's opening to these words concerning the kingdom and the things of the kingdom, and thy own apprehensions about them; that the one may be always cast by, and the other always embraced by thee. And always wait God's season; do not presume to understand a thing, before he give thee the understanding of it: and know also, that he alone is able to preserve the true sense and knowledge in thee; that thou mayst live dependently upon him for thy knowledge, and never "lean to thy own understanding."

It is one thing to understand words, testimonies, and descriptions; and it is another matter to understand, know, enjoy, possess, and live in that which the words relate to, describe, and bear witness of.

Isaac Penington, c. 1670

99   And the end of words is to bring men to the knowledge of things beyond what words can utter. So learn of the Lord to make a right use of the Scriptures: which is by esteeming them in their place, and prizing that above them which is above them.

Isaac Penington, c. 1670

100   No sincere Quaker can entertain a doubt that the immediate influence of the Spirit was the moving cause which gathered our forefathers in the truth; and that it is the root of our peculiar Christian testimonies.... Here, however, I must observe in passing that our early Friends were not led into their spiritual views of the Gospel independently of Scripture, but in connection with the diligent searching of that blessed book. While they renounced all dependence on human wisdom and learning, it was their privilege to maintain a firm, unshaken hold on scriptural Christianity. The Bible, in their view, was not one of the "appendages" of religion; much less did they regard it as "'the letter" which "veiled the mysteries of the kingdom." On the contrary they hailed it as the divine record by which these mysteries are plainly declared to us; it was their treasure of knowledge, their storehouse of materials for the Redeemer's service.

Joseph John Gurney, c.1840

101   As to John's revelations, they are some of that apostle's last writings, written at a time when he was far advanced in deep experience; and we find that the most deep and mysterious writings of the prophets and apostles are often couched in allegorical similes; therefore, it requires our coming to the same experience, rightly to comprehend or understand them; and hence, when I meet with parts or passages of scripture that I do not understand, I leave them until I may arrive at a state of deeper experience, by which means I have come clearly to comprehend and understand some things that, at a previous time, seemed mysterious to me.

Elias Hicks, 1820

102   In making a comparison of the blessed spirit of the gospel with the Scriptures of truth, there is nothing lost to them; for placing it above them is no diminution of their excellency, nor of their character; nor can there be any dishonor brought to the sacred writings, by placing the all-manifesting spirit, and light, and grace of God, through our Lord Jesus Christ, over and above them in the rightful order of God's manifestations and provisions for the children of men. Nay! truly, it cannot be derogatory to the Scriptures, nor to any other creature here below, to place the second Adam, the Lord from heaven, the quickening spirit above them.

John Wilbur, c.1850

103   I absorbed a great deal about Jesus and the Bible in my upbringing. But I was late in coming to a personal sense of the reality of God and later still in coming to a personal sense of Jesus. I believe it was a combination of the difficult Christian ethic I had absorbed together with the strong scientific temper of the twentieth century that led me to put the demands of truth very high and made an affirmation of belief in something ultimate not easy for me to make.

So, in my thirties, with the spiritual world beginning to open in a surprising way, I was trying, with my twentieth century mind, to understand the role of Jesus in truth and reality. The Jesus of the Sermon on the Mount had been a hero of mine right along. But I was troubled about much that was claimed concerning the Jesus of Christian tradition and also, in some respects, the biblical records. I was particularly puzzled, at this time, by the image of Jesus which comes through in the last part of Matthew 25. Was this merciless judge and dictator—the "Son of Man" now come into a strangely asserted personal power and glory—the same as the Jesus of the Sermon on the Mount, of the prayer shared with his disciples ("thine be the power and the glory"), of the prayer made on his very cross for those who "know not what they do"?

Whatever the merit of my puzzlement – and I believe it had merit – it was at this time that I received an impression of Jesus as a personality as distinguished from a figure fixed in the records. I could elaborate on the details of the occasion. Suffice it to say, this living Being seemed to be asking me – somewhat humorously, I thought – whether I imagined that he was any less humble and earnest in seeking truth than I was. He himself – so I understood him to be telling me – is a living Being and need not be thought of as fixed, like a dead specimen, within certain pages of a book.

From that time on I have not been troubled about the credibility of the figure of Jesus, whose meaning in my own life has grown steadily more vivid and present now than ever.

Ferner Nühn, 1974

104   Perhaps you, like me, have had trouble with the ancient laws handed down by Moses. I accepted the Ten–Commandment–core with a Sunday School deference which could never quite make the laws of Moses as real or as important as the laws of science. For me, this began to change when I began to read the Bible in what I sometimes call the Quaker way—that is, reading with both the analytical mind and the intuitive mind leaving plenty of space for the Holy Spirit. On the one hand Biblical scholarship and all the light science can provide; on the other hand, savoring and resting in the meaning, pausing from time to time to stare off into space....

As I reread the Old Testament laws in this more meditative way, two recognitions helped open my understanding. First, I realized, as did George Fox, that most of the laws of Moses were designed for a specific culture of long ago....　Then I began to face the cultural trappings or rubbish with which I had surrounded the concept of law; I realized that I had connected "law" with fallible legislators, judges, policemen, and childhood memories of adults who ruled my life. Even so there is a living core of the Law of Moses which remains as vital as it ever was.

Moses like all true prophets was a seer, for like Newton and Einstein he saw or felt the law as a vital force, not merely as a string of words. I have little doubt that he actually heard the words of the Commandments on Sinai. I also believe that he could not have done what he did if he had not also seen how these laws were an indispensable part of the fabric of the new age fellowship he was to build.

William Taber, 1984

105   What kind of approach to the Bible leads to ... discovery? An intelligent analytical and critical approach has its rightful place. We then stand over the Bible as subjects investigating an object. An inversion of this subject-object relationship is, however, possible. We then approach the Bible not mainly to criticise, but to listen; not merely to question, but to be challenged, and to open our lives penitentially both to its judgments and to its liberating gospel.

Pathways to God are many and varied. Friends, however, along with a great company of other seekers, have been able to testify that this receptive personal response to the biblical message, and especially to the call of Jesus, leads to joyous self-fulfilling life, and to a redemptive awareness of the love and glory of God.

George Boobyer, 1988

106   How much the Bible has to teach when taken as a whole, that cannot be done by snippets! There is its range over more than a thousand years giving us the perspective of religion in time, growing, and changing, and leading from grace to grace. There is its clear evidence of the variety of religious experience, not the kind of strait-jacket that nearly every church, even Friends, have sometimes been tempted to substitute for the diversity in the Bible. To select from it but a single strand is to miss something of its richness. Even the uncongenial and the alien to us is happily abundant in the Bible. The needs of men today are partly to be measured by their difficulty in understanding that with which they differ. At this point the Bible has no little service to render. It requires patient insight into the unfamiliar and provides a discipline for the imagination, ... a crying need of our time.

Further the Bible is a training school in discrimination among alternatives. One of the most sobering facts is that it is not on the whole a peaceful book – I mean a book of peace of mind. The Bible is the deposit of a long series of controversies between rival views of religion. The sobering thing is that in nearly every case the people shown by the Bible to be wrong had every reason to think they were in the right, and like us they did so. Complacent orthodoxy is the recurrent villain in the story from first to last, and the hero is the challenger, like Job, the prophets, Jesus, and Paul.

Henry J. Cadbury, 1953

107   I think that we suffer from lack of biblical study both individually and in groups; I do not urge that this should be done in the regular gatherings for worship, but rather in groups during the week. To restrict our fellowship to the single hour on Sunday mornings is, under ordinary conditions, to impoverish our times of worship. The over-busyness resulting from the changed and difficult home conditions has, I fear, told on this side of our lives and does need distinct attention.

Joan Mary Fry, 1947

108   Though I am not an assiduous reader of the Bible, its wisdom and its cadences are bred in my bones and deep in the fibers of my mind. "The days of our years are threescore years and ten; and if by reason of strength they be fourscore years, yet is their strength labour and sorrow; for it is soon cut off, and we fly away." I can write the words without hesitation, but must look in the Concordance to see where they come from. (Psalm 90, that wonderful one, which begins, "Lord, thou hast been our dwelling place in all generations," and ends, "And let the beauty of the Lord our God be upon us; and establish thou the work of our hands upon us; yea, the work of our hands establish thou it.")

                                                   Elizabeth Gray Vining, 1978

109   It makes me sad when I hear discussions about not introducing children to "God" until they're old enough to understand. I grew into the Lord's Prayer, and am still growing into it. All religious language, all devotional books, and particularly the Bible, provide growing room for young minds and spirits. Because they have sometimes been used as straitjackets by adults who did not understand, does not mean that they are straitjackets.

                                                   Elise Boulding, 1975

110   My own vital relation to the Bible actually began during my early association with Quakerism. One elderly and wise Friend habitually used sections from Psalms in his messages. Some of these fragments began singing through me, and I started using them in my daily meditations. Their value for me then as now is that they address the Divine directly rather than talk about Him. At their best, they gather the depth and breadth of Person into an interplay of I and Thou. During one of my early Meetings, a woman, describing Jacob wrestling with an angel, equated this to her own struggle, and pleaded with this angel not to let her go until it blessed her. She lent imagery to a nebulous, inarticulate process going on within me, and her image became permanent equipment of my religious life.

                                                   Dorothea Blom, 1967

111   But as I had forsaken all the priests, so I left the separate preachers also, and those called the most experienced people; for I saw there was not one among them all that could speak to my condition. And when all my hopes in them and in all men were gone, so that I had nothing outwardly to help me, nor could tell what to do, then, Oh then, I heard a voice which said, "There is one, even Christ Jesus, that can speak to thy condition," and when I heard it my heart did leap for joy. Then the Lord did let me see why there was none upon the earth that could speak to my condition, namely, that I might give him all the glory; for all are concluded under sin, and shut up in unbelief as I had been, that Jesus Christ might have the pre-eminence, who enlightens, and gives grace and faith and power. Thus, when God doth work who shall [prevent] it. And this I knew experimentally.

                                                   George Fox, 1647

112   My health now in a measure restored, I felt that I should do something for others. No way seemed open that met my desires. I searched my Bible and soon settled it in my own mind, that if I followed Christ I must of necessity live as He lived, and as I traced His life, I learned that it was in doing good, helping the poor, visiting the sick, comforting those in sorrow, lightening the burdens, and increasing the joys of the world. There were at that time few poor families in Richmond (Indiana). These I sought out and aided.

Rhoda Coffin, c. 1850

113   I cannot see the life of Jesus as other than God trying to disclose his love for us and his attempt, at any price, to show us that the cosmos is grounded in love. All hate, all sin, all discord, all clefts, all ignorance, all confusion will finally give way to love. But this love, like a strip of wood, has its grain which must be followed. If we follow this grain we will find that we must change the patterns in which we have previously cast our lives. And I do not see how God could have made this disclosure more effectively than by placing his love in the body of a child who was to become a man, and letting this cosmic message shine through the material envelope of a human life.

Douglas Steere, 1965

114   Fox is not interested in drawing people into an assent to a set of propositions about the life of Jesus sixteen hundred years before. That was the cultural norm of seventeenth century England. His mission is to bring people into a possession of what they profess – to help them incarnate the life of Christ as well as to speak of it. That was far from the cultural norm.

Douglas Gwyn, 1986

115   Our growing, mystical consciousness shall transform us into evangelical Christians, bursting to share what we have learned about living in the Kingdom from Jesus of Nazareth, through the gospels, and from our personal discovery of the Christ within – a Christ who is not limited to Jesus and can therefore be good news to men and women of other living religions and to countless humanists who, in being true to themselves and their own sense of honesty and wholeness, will never be able to accept the Christ myth in its traditional form.

John Yungblut, 1974

116   Thousands [are] now mistaken as to the dignity and origin of God's Spirit in them; they think it is of man, a part of his nature and being; whereas it is of the very life, power, and substance of God. Its descent is as truly from heaven as was that of the Lord Jesus. He came in that low, mean, and ordinary appearance as to outward show and accommodations, teaching us thereby not to despise the day of small things, nor to overlook the littleness of the motions of divine life in our own souls. And when he compares the kingdom of heaven, which he expressly says is within, to outward things, he very instructively

inculcates to us that the beginnings of it are small—"a little leaven ... a grain of mustard seed ... least of all seeds"(Matt. 13:31-32). This is true in the inward, whatever it may be in the outward, for the seed of the kingdom is the least of all the seeds in the field or garden of the heart.

Job Scott, 1765

117   Jesus's question in the Sermon on the Mount: "If ye salute your brethren only, what do ye to excess?" What do ye to excess? How often he showed his approval of extravagant generosity when it arose from a simple and pure impulse of the heart. He defended the act of the woman who broke the alabaster box of precious ointment so that she might pour it over his feet. "If thy brother ask of thee thy coat, give him thy cloak also" — in other words, more than he expects to receive. In his parable of the Prodigal Son, the father does not wait to welcome his son at the door of the house; he runs to meet him, and it is the best robe which he puts on him. It is this excess, this extravagance, which we find in God's love for us, that for me shows the meaning of the word "Grace".

Phyllis Richards, 1948

118   Perhaps a shortcoming of modern Quakerism can be traced to the great revelation of early Quakers who acted to replace outward cult and ceremony in religious worship with inward spiritual relationships. As the concrete manifestations of inward spirit, i.e. water baptism, laying-on-of-hands, taking communion in bread and wine, were eliminated, an outward, physically present and actively manifested spiritual energy was called for as a replacement. That alternative replacement was, as Jesus described, the baptism and spirit of fire. He called for a physical witness, a continuous entry in the Temple to upset the ongoing corruptions of the money changers, the on-going rebuilding of the institutional secular structures of wealth and power, political domination, sexism, and the other demons which interfere with a life of love in practice. A physical, spiritual activization of the inward Light was imperative. Without it we would simply be left with a passive, inward spirit with no function but to nourish our own individual idiosyncrasies. Without the outward expressions of the inward spirit, the fire would be truly only a moderate one, if a fire at all. The loss of the outward witness in turn reduces the flame which kindles the inward spirit as well. Inward revelation cries out for the outward spiritual witness of pacifism and nonviolence, which leads to courtrooms and prisons when practiced before the bastions of power. It cries out for corporate radical community, which characterized the first meetings.

William Durland, 1988

119   To allow [the] inward work to take place is to allow the universal Light of the eternal Christ to reveal our sundered and separate individualism, our own areas of darkness and sin, and then to cooperate with this Light as it seeks to transform, guide, gift, and empower us....

This inward work takes time and may cause us to make painful changes in our life as we become more and more sensitive and obedient to the inward guide....

It is this inward work of Christ, and not our verbal statements about Christ, that can produce that amazing unity in a gathered meeting for worship, a gathered meeting for business, or a gathered opportunity between two people. And finally, it is this inward work of Christ that leads inevitably to the important outwardness of Quakerism; to a life able to behave in all those ways which Jesus taught and in which he led the way, to a living equality of men and women, to a radiant and supple pacifism that comes not merely from books or movements or anger but that wells up from deep inner springs.

William Taber, 1984

120   It is not enough to hear of Christ, or read of Christ; but this is the thing —to feel him my root, my life, my foundation; and my soul ingrafted into him, by him who hath power to ingraft. To feel repentance given me by him, faith given me by him, the Father revealed and made known to me by him, by the pure shinings of his light in my heart; God, who caused the light to shine out of darkness, causing it to shine there; so that in and through him, I come to know, not the Son himself only, but the Father also.

Isaac Penington, 1670

121   Perhaps what we are now considering is the question: What was the central concern of Jesus? I may say quite simply, The answer to that question is: human conduct.... [For Jesus there] are not primarily questions of religious ritual...[nor] questions of philosophy, or theology or belief. There are rather questions of how you should behave.... Jesus, in his teaching, would not be asked … abstract questions nearly as much as … questions about the will of God for our conduct.

Henry J. Cadbury, 1961

122   Consider now the prayer-life of Jesus. It comes out most clearly in the record of St. Luke, who leaves us with the impression that prayer was the most vital element in our Lord's life. He rises a great while before day that he may have some hours alone with His Father. He continues all night in prayer to God. Incident after incident is introduced by the statement that Jesus was praying. Are we so much nearer God that we can afford to dispense with that which to Him was of such vital moment? But apart from this, it seems to me that this prayer-habit of Jesus throws light upon the purpose of prayer.... We pray, not to change God's will, but to bring our wills into correspondence with His.

William Littleboy, c.1937

123   I do not know if Jesus is God, or the divine son of God, or the only mediator, or a saint among other saints. I don't claim to understand those things which only God can know, but I sense the reality of this Christian mystery that makes God's promise and requirements more than words. This Jesus offers his life as a ransom for many. He dies for the multitudes. He gives himself to draw all into salvation. In his life and death we sense the love and power of God. We are called to follow. We are called to do the same for the sake of all.

Carol Reilley Urner, 1994

124   Pain isolates one. It pervades everything; blackens the sky, pushes other humans away, reduces music and poetry and the outside world to dullness; grinds on and on endlessly.

Some say Christianity is a morbid religion, over-emphasizing a Christ tormented on a cross. I can only say that even as a child I could sometimes comfort myself in pain by remembering his suffering…. It was Jesus the man, enduring agonising pain in terrible loneliness, who spoke to my condition and brought me sometimes much needed consolation.

Joan Fitch, 1988

125   The resurrection, however literally or otherwise we interpret it, demonstrates the power of God to bring life out of brokenness; not just to take the hurt out of brokenness but to add something to the world. It helps us to sense the usefulness, the possible meaning in our suffering, and to turn it into a gift. The resurrection affirms me with my pain and my anger at what has happened. It does not take away my pain; it still hurts. But I sense that I am being transfigured; I am being enabled to begin again to love confidently and to remake the spirit of my world.

S. Jocelyn Burnell, 1989

Discernment and Guidance

126   [You are] not to spend time with needless, unnecessary, and fruitless discourses, but to proceed in the wisdom of God: not in the way of the world, as a worldly assembly of men, by hot contests, by seeking to outspeak and overreach one another in discourse, as if it were controversy between party and party of men, or two sides violently striving for dominion… not deciding affairs by the greater vote… but in the wisdom, love, and fellowship of God, in gravity, patience, meekness, in unity and concord, submitting one to another in lowliness of heart, and in the holy Spirit of truth and righteousness, all things [are] to be carried on by hearing and determining every matter coming before you in love,

coolness, gentleness, and dear unity — I say, as one only party, all for the Truth of Christ and for the carrying on the work of the Lord, and assisting one another in whatsoever ability God hath given; and to determine of things by a general mutual concord, in assenting together as one man in the spirit of truth and equity, and by the authority thereof.

Edward Burrough, 1662

127   The Quaker way of trying to invite and be open to divine guidance is to begin with a time of silence. This is not the "moment of silence" which is a mere nod in passing to the Divine. Nor is it a time for organizing one's thoughts. This is a time for what has been called recollection: for an intentional return to the Center to give over one's own firm views, to place the outcome in the hands of God, to ask for a mind and heart as truly sensitive to and accepting of nuanced intimations of God's will as of overwhelming evidences of it. It is possible that someone designated or undesignated may offer vocal prayer for the joint undertaking. Spoken or not, it is understood that each person present will be holding the undertaking in the Light in his own way.

Patricia Loring, 1992

128   Even if Friends are careful to attend Meetings for Business and to assemble promptly, they may nevertheless fritter away God's opportunity, perhaps because the business has been poorly prepared and presented, or because Friends do not apply themselves promptly and earnestly, or because Friends are self-indulgent, or simply because Friends do not wait upon the Lord.

The Query whether Friends are careful to come to Meetings for Worship "with hearts and minds prepared" should be extended to include our Meetings for Business as well. It is essential that the period of worship prior to the undertaking of business be long enough to permit Friends to put aside the heat and tumult of the day's anxieties and to enter into the quietness that comes from trust in God and in God's concern for the affairs of men and women.

Thomas Shipley Brown, 1963

129   Each of these Quarterly Meetings were large and sat near eight hours. Here I had occasion to consider that it is a weighty thing to speak much in large meetings for business. First, except our minds are rightly prepared and we clearly understand the case we speak to, instead of forwarding, we hinder business and make more labour for those on whom the burden of the work is laid.

If selfish views or a partial spirit have any room in our minds, we are unfit for the Lord's work. If we have a clear prospect of the business and proper weight on our minds to speak, it behooves us to avoid useless apologies and repetitions. Where people are gathered from far, and adjourning a meeting of business is attended with great difficulty, it behooves all to be cautious how they detain a meeting, especially when they have sat six or seven hours and [have] a great distance to ride home.

In three hundred minutes are five hours, and he that improperly detains three hundred people one minute, besides other evils that attend it, does an injury like that of imprisoning one man five hours without cause.

John Woolman, 1758

130   In meeting for business, Friends are seeking to discover and to implement the will of God. Aware that they meet in the presence of God, Friends try to conduct their business reverently, in the wisdom and peaceable spirit of Jesus. Insofar as a divine-human meeting takes place, there is order, unity, and power. The Quaker way of conducting business is of central importance. It is the way Friends have found of living and working together. It can create and preserve the sense of fellowship in the meeting, and from there it can spread to other groups and decisions in which individual Friends or meetings have a part. Thus it contributes to the way of peace in the world.

Faith and Practice, New England Yearly Meeting, 1985

131   We recognize a variety of ministries. In our worship these include those who speak under the guidance of the Spirit and those who receive and uphold the work of the Spirit in silence and prayer. We also recognise as ministry service on our many committees, hospitality and childcare, the care of finance and premises, and many other tasks. We value those whose ministry is not in an appointed task but is in teaching, counselling, listening, prayer, enabling the service of others, or other service in the meeting or the world. The purpose of all our ministry is to lead us and other people into closer communion with God and to enable us to carry out those tasks which the Spirit lays upon us.

London Yearly Meeting, 1986

132   Few of us, by our efforts alone, can activate our spiritual natures in a vital and creative way. We need God's help. We need the help of one another. But God's help may not come at once. Our help to each other, even though we are gathered in a meeting for worship or actively serving our fellow men outside the meeting, may be and often is delayed as regards our kindling one another spiritually. What are we to do in this case? There is only one thing we can do--wait. Having done our part to overcome the separated self, we can but wait for the spiritual self to arise and take command of our lives. Having brought ourselves as close as we can to God, we can but hold ourselves in an attitude of waiting for Him to work His will in us, to draw us fully into His presence.

N. Jean Toomer, 1947

133   A common misconception about Quaker business process is that a decision can never go forward if one person decides to "stand in the way." Inactive members, new attenders and non–Friends trying to imitate Quaker process often interpret our principle of unity to mean that each individual has veto power over any decision of the community. Nothing could be further from the truth.

"Standing in the way" is not a right which inheres in paper membership or attendance at meeting for business. It is rather a privilege granted by the community because it believes that the dissent is grounded in spiritual integrity and not in ego or a power trip. We acknowledge that the Friend may have light which the rest of us don't yet see; we wait in love for the Friend to see our light. We are willing to remain teachable in the trust that the dissenting Friend is also teachable....

Difficulty arises when some show themselves not to be teachable, as for instance when they attach themselves to an external "party line" which precludes submission to the Spirit. The Meeting may rightly decline to trust such persons. Trust is something which must be earned. Perhaps that is a central meaning of the term "weighty Friend": one whom the community trusts to "attend to pure wisdom and be teachable."

Esther Murer, 1989

134   In our meetings for church affairs an effective continuing life can be secured only if there is at least a strong nucleus of Friends attending with regularity, willing to accept responsibility and to give judgments based on informed minds as well as spiritual wisdom. There are few things which tend to destroy interest and loyalty in any business so easily as prolonged and unnecessary discussions on trivia: such discussions are very often provoked and kept up by those who do not trouble to inform themselves adequately of the facts, or who use their occasional attendance to re-open matters already decided. The meeting should expect and encourage its clerk to take firm action in such circumstances.

Quaker Faith and Practice, Britain Yearly Meeting, 1995

135   At monthly meeting there was a strong sense of unity on the matter—except for one person. (How easy to have ignored this one dissenting voice.) But in view of it, it was agreed to hold a second monthly meeting to reconsider the matter. Because the venue was different (our meetings are not normally "monthly") a different group of Friends was present, although three of the first meeting were there. The sense of unity was equally strong in the other direction— except for two Friends. It was therefore decided to hold a third "monthly" meeting. By this time feelings were running high and we were each convinced of the rightness of our own viewpoints. Then suddenly Christ's presence moved in, and in my own case I remembered his words to his disciples, "By this shall all men know that ye are my disciples, that ye have love one for another." And quite suddenly it seemed more important to love than to be right.

Rosemary M. Elliott, 1967

136   Many Friends of all ages need the training provided by a good meeting for business: one that starts with real worship, that respects the insights of all its members; one that remembers it does God's work, that God is in no hurry, and that, in the vast pattern of God's universe, even man may not be very important—no matter how wonderful a creation he is.

Martin Cobin, 1964

137   As a structure to facilitate discernment of the will of God, the clearness committee partakes of many of the features of a meeting for worship for the conduct of business. Where meetings for business have been assimilated to more secular models, with emphasis on getting through agendas within time constraints, on decision–making rather than discernment, consensus rather than unity, it is helpful to incorporate in the model some aspects of worship sharing.

The crucial element is the establishment of a context of prayerful attentiveness, not just for the beginning and end of the time together but for the entire meeting. Liberal amounts of silence between utterances permits them to be heard with all their resonances and taken below the surface mind. The space between can remove the temptation to revert to discussion or conversation. It can help reinforce disciplined speaking and listening. It can allow what does come forth to arise spontaneously from the Center.

Patricia Loring, 1992

138   A great deal of charity is needed about messages that come in the meeting. No message is likely to be meant for every one of the worshipers. What may not affect me may open out life for another, and this consciousness must always be there.

Douglas Steere, 1972

139   Perhaps one in worship senses ... that he is only going round and round in his mind about a problem, to no good point. He will and must take these things up again later, perhaps with new energy and insight. For the moment, however, it seems right simply to be in the quiet. The worshiper does not try to do anything, but simply to be in that which is eternal.

Sandra Cronk, 1991

140   If worship does not change us, it has not been worship. To stand before the Holy One of eternity is to change. Resentments cannot be held with the same tenacity when we enter His gracious light. As Jesus said, we will need to leave our gift at the altar and go set the matter straight (Matthew 5:23). In worship an increased power steals its way into the heart sanctuary, an increased compassion grows in the soul. To worship is to change.

Richard Foster, 1978

141   To love and be loved is a universal human urge. Is it any wonder, then, that we are moved to seek God's love?...It is to this divine love that we are called. This is the high promise of man's life. We are called away from indifference, from meanness, malice, prejudice, and hate. We are called above the earthly loves that come and go and are unsure. We are called into the deep enduring love of God and man and all creation. Worship is a door into that love. Once we have entered it, our every act is a prayer, our whole life a continuous worship.

N. Jean Toomer, 1947

142   Feeling the spring of Divine love opened, and a concern to speak, I said a few words in a meeting, in which I found peace. Being thus humbled and disciplined under the cross, my understanding became more strengthened to distinguish the pure spirit which inwardly moves upon the heart, and which taught me to wait in silence sometimes many weeks together, until I felt that rise which prepares the creature to stand like a trumpet, through which the Lord speaks to his flock.... All the faithful are not called to the public ministry; but whoever are, are called to minister of that which they have tasted and handled spiritually. The outward modes of worship are various; but whenever any are true ministers of Jesus Christ, it is from the operation of his Spirit upon their hearts.

John Woolman, 1741

143   One characteristic institution among Friends of the "quietist" period was the traveling ministry.... The call to this ministry came often in a childhood sense of the presence of God when alone and out-of-doors. It was reinforced by powerful examples of local and traveling ministers and tested by the trials of learning to respond to the Spirit's moving to speak in meeting. After sufficient testing, the minister would become more sensitive to the spiritual condition of others. He or she would not only speak at various meetings, often at wearisome distances from home, but would hold "religious opportunities" with families or individuals, giving them spiritual counsel. Though much of this ministry was among Friends and designed to maintain the spiritual health of the Society, it was not uncommon to call special meetings for Blacks, Indians, or apprentices, as well as to visit jails or mines. The Quaker leaven in the world owes much to these "active contemplatives" of the past, whose central message was that the living presence of the Spirit is here and now.

Carol Murphy, 1983

144   It is our earnest desire that ministers and elders may be as nursing fathers and mothers to those that are young in the ministry, and with all care and diligence advise, admonish, and if they see occasion, reprove them in a tender and Christian spirit, according to the rules of our Discipline and counsel of Friends in that respect; also exhort them frequently to read the Holy Scriptures, and reverently seek the mind of the Spirit of Truth to open the mysteries thereof, that, abiding in simple and patient submission to the will of God, and keeping down to the openings of Divine love in themselves, they may witness a gradual growth in their gifts, and be preserved from extending their declarations further than they find the life and power of Truth to bear them up.

Philadelphia Yearly Meeting, 1723

145   When men and women come to this pass that they have nothing to rely on but the Lord, then they will meet together to wait upon the Lord: and this was the first ground and motive of our setting up meetings; and I would to God that that was the use that everyone would make of them, then they would be justly and properly used according to the institution of them at first; we should use them as poor desolate helpless people that are broken off from all their own confidence and trust and have nothing to rely on but the mercy and goodness of God.

Stephen Crisp, 1663

146   [Some] need to share their pain and have found no other way of being heard than during the silent Meeting. They come for the healing of their hurts, but they come with only an incomplete acceptance that the mystery of God's presence is at the heart of Meeting for Worship. Because their audience does not include God they don't listen for an answer, they don't allow the power of the Holy Spirit in a gathered Meeting to overshadow them as a hen gathers her chicks under her wings. If you don't believe God is present, what answer are you expecting and from whom?

Brenda Clifft Heales and Chris Cook, 1992

147   There can be complete unity of worship without a single word being said. I have known a few such meetings and shall never forget them. It was their silence, not their words, that was memorable. And even one short sentence, spoken nervously at the spirit's prompting, is better than a well-phrased five-minute talk prepared beforehand.

Clive Sansom, 1962

148   And thou, faithful babe, though thou stutter and stammer forth a few words in the dread of the Lord, they are accepted.

William Dewsbury, 1660

149   It has been my experience that if I come to meeting in a state of strong emotion and follow an easy impulse to talk about it, I—and the meeting?—are left with a sense of emptiness. But if I trust that there's a reason why I'm here, now, in this state, but that it's God's reason, not mine, and my part is to wait in holy expectancy—strange things happen. Messages which speak to my condition are given by people who couldn't possibly know of it. The meeting ministers to my need and uses my state to minister to others—quite without my willing it.

I believe that there's an explanation for this phenomenon. Strong emotion can make us what the early Friends called tender: vulnerable to the workings of the Spirit. I suspect that the presence of one such person in our midst can cause the meeting to gather.

Esther Murer, 1988

150   On First-days I frequented meetings and the greater part of my time I slept, but took no account of preaching nor received any other benefit, than being there kept me out of bad company which indeed is a very great service to youth...but one First-day, being at meeting, a young woman named Anne Wilson was there and preached; she was very zealous and fixing my eye upon her, she with a great zeal pointed her finger at me uttering these words with much power: "A traditional Quaker, thou comest to meeting as thou went from it, and goes from it as thou came to it but art no better for thy coming; what wilt thou do in the end?" This was so pat to my then condition that like Saul I was smitten to the ground as it might be said, but turning my thoughts inwards, in secret I cried, "Lord, what shall I do to help it?" And a voice as it were spoke in my heart, saying "Look unto me, and I will help thee."

Samuel Bownas, 1696

Extracts from writings on

Experience

INTRODUCTION

Margaret Fell records that in the year 1652 George Fox arrived at Swarthmoor Hall for the first time. The hall was a place of hospitality for visiting preachers. He spent the night and on the following day went to Ulverston steeplehouse where, when the congregation had assembled, he asked if he might speak. He was told he might, and Margaret Fell remembered his words for the rest of her life.

Fox spoke of the inwardness of true religion and of how the prophets, Christ, and the apostles "enjoyed and possessed" that which the Lord had given them. And then he continued: "You will say, Christ saith this, and the apostles say this; but what canst thou say? Art thou a child of Light and has walked in the Light, and what thou speakest is it inwardly from God?"

As a religious society we value the process by which we find the words to describe the inward experience of being a child of Light and of the myriad ways in which we learn to trust that Light.

The selections that follow tell of what we can say; they also declare that which we have come to enjoy and possess. Some passages that more directly address issues of living and dying have been gathered under that heading.

• • •

151   [F]or some time I took no notice of any religion, but minded recreation, as it is called; and went after it into many excesses and vanities—as foolish mirth, carding, dancing, and singing. I frequented music assemblies, and made vain visits where there were jovial feastings. But in the midst of all this my heart was often sad and pained beyond expression. I was not hurried into those follies by being captivated by them, but from not having found in religion what I had sought and longed after. I would often say within myself, what are they all to me? I could easily leave all this; for it hath not my heart, it is not my delight, it hath not power over me. I had rather serve the Lord, if I could indeed feel and know that which would be acceptable to Him.

O Lord, suffer me no more to fall in with any false way, but show me the Truth.

Mary Proude Springett Penington, c. 1650

152   In the condition I have mentioned, of weary seeking and not finding, I married my dear husband Isaac Penington. My love was drawn to him because I found he saw the deceit of all mere notions about religion; he lay as one that refused to be comforted until he came to His temple, who is truth and no lie. All things that had only the appearance of religion were very manifest to him, so that he was sick and weary of show, and in this my heart united with him, and a desire was in me to be serviceable to him. I gave up much to be a companion to him.

I resolved never to go back into those formal things I had left, having found death and darkness in them; but would rather be without a religion, until the Lord manifestly taught me one....

Whilst I was in this state, I heard of a new people called Quakers, but I resolved not to inquire after them, nor their principles. I heard nothing of their ways except that they used thee and thou to every one; and I saw a book written about plain language by George Fox.

Mary Proude Springett Penington, c. 1655

153   [I]n consequence of my decided resolution to attend the meetings of Friends, my dear father (no doubt in faithfulness to his own religious views, and from the desire to rescue a poor child from apprehended error) requested me not to return to the paternal roof, unless I could be satisfied to conform to the religious education which he had conscientiously given me. This, with a tender, heart-piercing remonstrance from my dear, dear mother, was far more deeply felt than I can describe; and marvelous in my view, even to this day, was the settled, firm belief that I must follow on, to know the soul's salvation for myself; truly in a way that I knew not!

Mary Capper, c.1830

154   Today I have felt all my old irreligious feelings. My object shall be to search, try to do right, and if I am mistaken, it is not my fault; but the state I am now in makes it difficult to act. What little religion I have felt has been owing to my giving way quietly and humbly to my feelings; but the more I reason upon it, the more I get into a labyrinth of uncertainty, and my mind is so much inclined to both scepticism and enthusiasm, that if I argue and doubt, I shall be a total sceptic; if, on the contrary, I give way to my feeling, and as it were, wait for religion, I may be led away.

But I hope that will not be the case; at all events, religion, true and uncorrupted, is all that comforts the greatest; it is the first stimulus to virtue; it is a support under every affliction. I am sure it is better to be so in an enthusiastic degree than not to be so at all, for it is a delightful enthusiasm.

Elizabeth Gurney Fry, 1798

155   The first gleam of light, "the first cold light of morning" which gave promise of day with its noontide glories, dawned on me one day at meeting, when I had been meditating on my state in great depression. I seemed to hear the words articulated in my spirit, "Live up to the light thou hast, and more will be granted thee." Then I believed that God speaks…by His spirit. I strove to lead a more Christian life, in unison with what I knew to be right, and looked for brighter days, not forgetting the blessings that are granted to prayer.

Caroline Fox, 1841

156   I have been tried with the applause of the world, and none know how great a trial that has been, and the deep humiliations of it; and yet I fully believe it is not nearly so dangerous as being made much of in religious society. There is a snare even in religious unity, if we are not on the watch. I have sometimes felt that it was not so dangerous to be made much of in the world, as by those whom we think highly of in our own Society: the more I have been made much of by the world, the more I have been inwardly humbled. I could often adopt the words of Sir Francis Bacon— "When I have ascended before men, I have descended in humiliation before God."

Elizabeth Gurney Fry, 1844

157   Hope, peace, and encouragement is not enough to depict my religion. When my spirit is animated by my religion and is aware of the inviolable Truth prevailing, my heart dances for joy and gratitude and sings the praise of God! Every moment is a mystery. Even this body of mine, what a mystery it is, whose heart is beating incessantly without my knowing, and whose lungs breathe ceaselessly without my knowing! This air is God's, the light is God's, we are his. I am living with all the universe, and all the universe is living with me, in God.

Yukio Irie, 1957

158   Some time ago I was in Germany, visiting isolated Friends throughout that country. One man I met was a factory worker. He spoke ungrammatical German. His teeth were discoloured, his shoulders were stooped. He spoke the Swabian dialect. But he was a radiant soul, a quiet, reticent saint of God. He knew the inner secrets of the life that is clothed in God. We were drawn together by invisible currents. We knew each other immediately, more deeply than if we had been neighbours for twenty years. I called at his simple home near Stuttgart. He motioned me to escape from the rest of the visitors and come into the bedroom. There, leaning on the window sills, we talked together. Immediately we gravitated to the wonders of prayer and of God's dealing with the soul. I told him of some new insights that had recently come to me. He listened and nodded confirmation, for he already knew those secrets. He understood and could tell me of things of the Spirit of which I had only begun to guess. I feel sure that I knew more history and mathematics and literature and philosophy than did he. And the social gulf in Germany between a professor and a factory man is infinitely wide. But that afternoon I was taught by him, and nourished by him, and we looked at each other eye to eye and knew a common love of Christ. Then as the afternoon shadows fell and dissolved with twilight, our words became less frequent, until they ceased altogether. And we mingled our lives in the silence, for we needed no words to convey our thoughts. I have only had one letter from him in the year, but we are as near to each other now, every day, as we were that afternoon.

Thomas Kelly, 1942

159   I have sometimes been asked what were my reasons for deciding on that refusal to register for war duties that sent me to Holloway Jail twenty-two years ago. I can only answer that my reason told me that I was a fool, that I was risking my job and my career, that an isolated example could do no good, that it was a futile gesture since even if I did register my three small children would exempt me. But reason was fighting a losing battle. I had wrestled in prayer and I knew beyond all doubt that I must refuse to register, that those who believed that war was the wrong way to fight evil must stand out against it however much they stood alone, and that I and mine must take the consequences. The "and mine" made it more difficult, but I question whether children ever really suffer loss in the long run through having parents who are willing to stand by principles; many a soldier had to leave his family and thought it his duty to do so. When you have to make a vital decision about behaviour, you cannot sit on the fence. To decide to do nothing is still a decision, and it means that you remain on the station platform or the airstrip when the train or plane has left.

Kathleen Lonsdale, 1964

160   The field of my religious training presupposed a clear definite call to a particular kind of service. I must confess that this has never happened to me.... I have never aspired to a particular job or asked for one; nor have I been "stricken on the road to Damascus" as was Paul and had my way clearly dictated to me from the heavens. The entire course has been a maturing of family and personal decisions. In perspective I should say in all humility that my life has been characterized by an inadequate, persistent effort to try to find a workable harmony between religious profession and daily practice.

Clarence E. Pickett, 1966

161   By day I sat in the Gandhi library reading the writings that had poured from Gandhi's pen in his life. As I read his passionate words about sarvodaya (welfare) I knew that these [people] were my brothers and sisters too, and that I also could not want what they could not have. I wrote long letters home about stripping ourselves of what we did not need....

I saw how we all had chained ourselves to daily rhythms that were bound to defeat us. Day after day we recapitulated the old cycle of effort, irritation, impatience and anger—softened by small epiphanies of love and remorse. The spirit had to break through from time to time, because spirit is our very nature, but...how heavy-handed our daily behavior. For how many millennia had this gone on? Was the human race never to discover its self-forged chains?

The snapping of my chains was my signal that the human race was indeed to be freed—in theological language—from the bondage of sin and death. My experience is one of the simplest and oldest religious experiences that come to humans.... Was the leap an act of the will or an invasion of grace?

Elise Boulding, 1975

162   For me the certain realisation of God came at the time of the breakdown of my marriage. The unthinkable had happened and I seemed to be at my lowest state physically and mentally. There seemed to be no present and no future but only a nightmare of dark uncertainty. One distinct message reached me: to "go under" was out of the question, I could only start again, learn from my mistakes and take this second chance at life that I had been given. I found a strength within I did not know I had and I believe now that it came from the prayers and loving support of so many people round me.

This rebirth was for me a peak experience, the memory of which is a constant reassurance in times of emptiness and doubt. Facing the future, even with a sure faith, is not easy. I am cautious at every step forward, taking time and believing I shall be told where to go and what to do. Waiting patiently and creatively is at times unbearably difficult, but I know it must be so.

Jennifer Morris, 1980

163   About a dozen years ago I became critically ill and I have a vivid memory of looking down on my self on the bed; doctors and nurses worked on that body, and I felt held in such secureness, joy, and contentment, a sense of the utter rightness of things.... The crisis passed and I was filled with wonder at the newness of life....

Soon after, I had radical surgery followed by many months of slow recovery with repeated setbacks and further operations. There were times when truly out of the depths I cried; I had no reserves of strength left, either physical, emotional, or spiritual, but I never completely lost the memory of being held and the wonder at being alive. Gradually the wounds healed: old griefs as well as disease and operations.

Jenifer Faulkner, 1982

164   When I was a child, the man who lived next door and who was our landlord, tried to rape me. He then frightened me into silence, threatening to make us homeless again if I were to tell. My mother used to say, "I can't think why you have changed so much." Well of course I knew, but I couldn't tell, so I withdrew into a shell. People used to say how serious I had become. Where was all my former sparkle?

Thirty years later, his wife visited my father after my mother's death. I happened to be there at the time. She told me that her husband whom we had called Uncle Sid, was dying. I knew at once from the sudden lurch of my stomach what I had to do. I had to go and see him. I was terrified.

The next day I drove to the hospital. I parked outside, and then I became paralysed with fear. I simply could not get out of the car. "God," I prayed urgently, "you'll have to take over. I can't do this myself." I was able to get out of the car and go and find Uncle Sid. He was very shocked to see me and looked frightened. But God had taken over, and I was given just the right gentle words to say, and Uncle Sid said to me, "I can't thank you enough for coming. Now I can die at peace."

Diana Lampen, 1991

165   God's love is ministered to most people through the love of our fellow human beings. Sometimes that love is expressed physically or sexually. For me and my lover, John, God's love is given through our homosexual relationship. In common with other people who do not have children to raise, we are free from those demands to nurture other vital things. This includes our meeting and the wider Society of Friends.

We both draw on our love a great deal to give us the strength and courage to do the things to which God calls us.... Our spiritual journey is a shared one. Sometimes the pitcher needs to be taken back to the fountain. In order to grow, I need my church to bless and uphold not just me as an individual, but also our relationship.

Gordon Macphail, c.1985

166   Several years ago I had the experience of feeling called to go speak in love and friendship to an old friend who had shunned me. I was very nervous. He might reject my friendship. I might make a fool of myself. But as I walked to his house, I felt that I was carried by something bigger than myself. Afterwards, I felt elated. I had answered the call. Clearly God had been with me, directing and supporting.

Patience Schenck, 1988

167   About 50 years ago, the Second World War began and I was sent away from London, the city of my birth, into the country to avoid the bombing. My father was in the war in North Africa, and my mother was a cook for the Royal Air Force. I lived in a small cottage with my grandparents. Food was scarce and strictly rationed. The house was lit by oil lamps and heated with wood and coal, and my jobs included gathering wood in the nearby forest, and fetching water from the spring in a pail every morning.

When the war was over, we went back to London, and the only place we could find to live in was a converted warehouse that was wet and unsanitary, where in due course I caught a disease and became completely paralysed.

Happily, I recovered the use of most of my limbs, but I never recovered my health. To this day, I cannot lift, or run, ride a bicycle or dance, and I have never been able to romp with my children in the way other people take for granted.

That might sound a fairly unhappy story of deprivation, illness, and disability, but in fact it is not. As time has gone by, I have seen with increasing clarity that these things are a blessing, and were the gifts of God to me. I know this to be the truth, and I know it through the Spirit.

John Punshon, 1991

168   Following the operation all sense of God disappeared, and anyone who came to my bedside (and the love and visiting I received was one of the great treasures of my life) I asked to take my hand and mediate God's love to me. In fact healing and prayer surrounded me on every hand, although I myself felt cut off in complete inner aridity except when actually held in the inner place by someone taking my hand and praying.

Damaris Parker–Rhodes, 1985

169   We all know about the traditional antagonism between Quakerism and the Arts. At Swarthmore College, when I was there in the forties, there was no studio art offered. The Quaker emphasis was definitely on the social sciences, and the feeling was strong that one would be expected to contribute to society in a social-activist kind of way. Nevertheless, I aspired to be an artist; I also joined the Quaker meeting there. That these two avenues were incompatible was obvious by the clichés that were then available concerning Art and Quakerism.

The artist was a proverbially selfish person, bound to do his or her own thing at the expense, if necessary, of society. He or she was given to exhibitionist promotion and passionate emotional extremes, and offered a product that was suspiciously commercial or superfluously decorative.

The Quaker, on the other hand, was geared to the needs of society and ready to offer his or her own life for the good of others; was not going to waste time in trivial pursuits, and was solidly grounded, with an emotional and productive life very much under control.

Well, my ideas have come a long way since then. This was all a very exterior view of the outside from the outside. What I missed at that stage of my life was that the artist and the Quaker are on the same internal journey. Each is seeking a relationship with the Divine, and each is seeking a way to express that relationship. There are just many different ways of expressing it. For many, the path to the Self has to be entered by way of the arts, whether or not we are gifted in that field. That doesn't seem to matter. As St. Paul says: If we have not love, we are as sounding brass or a tinkling cymbal. And for many of us, the pathway to love is through the arts.... The process of working with and forming material things can lead beyond them to the spiritual, and shape of clay or colors of paint can be a window into another world.

Janet Mustin, 1992

170   My first experience of healing came when I was very ill for many weeks with lung and respiratory problems and in an extremely physically weak condition. Whilst fighting for each very painful breath I began to think I might not recover and lay in a twilight world of sleep, pain, and exhaustion but yet knowing "Thy will be done." It would have been so easy to let life slip at this point, but it was exactly then that I felt a surge of energy go through my body and I knew that it was right for me to be given more time on earth and that I would recover. It felt as if I was being "ticked off" for lacking faith. As that energy passed through me I remembered clearly and strongly a very dear member of my Meeting and wondered if she was praying for my recovery. I continued to hold on to her image in my mind and began to feel the strength returning to my body. She later told me she had indeed prayed for me daily and had sometimes been joined by other Friends for intercession. I knew experientially I had been upheld in God's healing light and power, and it is this experience which has made me so convinced of the healing ministry. I know there may be more mundane, matter-of-fact explanations for my recovery but in extremis and in great need I was reaching for far more than the mundane.

Joolz Saunders, 1994

171   [An] unforgettable experience occurred while I was a student nurse in a city hospital. I was on night duty in the infants ward. When the doctor made his rounds I went with him. As we came to Peter's cot, the doctor said:

"He will not live through the night. Don't even call me for him. I can write out his death certificate tomorrow morning. But if you find spare time, carry him around." That night I carried Peter around for several hours, and mine was an unforeseen reward: a glance into a human soul. Here I was, a young student nurse, an agnostic who did not believe in the existence of a soul, in the value of religion. That night I saw a human life unfolding in front of my eyes. It covered the whole cycle of life—from beginning to end.

When I picked him up, Peter was an infant with the face and expression of an infant. While I held him he passed through all stages of life. His face and expression changed from a young child to an adult and then to an old wise man. There was no pain in his face—no doubt—no fear. He did not fight death. He seemed to know his way. He was very serene. He looked straight at me. It seemed that he wanted me to know what he knew. He understood, and he wanted me to understand, too. Peter died in my arms. I closed his eyes and put him in his cot. "Yes", I thought, "This is not a broken–off life, nipped off in the beginning. It is a fulfilled life. Peter has lived his whole life."

Ilse Karger, 1995

172   I was by now high up on the moraine. The lazy clouds, that had hung all day as a light veiling about the snow-powdered rock peaks were just breaking up in the clear splendour of sunset. The dazzling mantles of Combin and Courbassiere caught the last rays. It was no moment for reasoning. Too often my spiritual life runs shamefully shallow, lamentably in need of more living water from the eternal springs. May I be pardoned—I was utterly unworthy— but at that moment there swept over me unbidden, the experience of Christ. No more tiresome ratiocination, interpretations or mis-interpretations, dogmas and differences. Just the fact that, in Christ, God was and is sharing the tragedy and sorrow, and the joy of the world. And—most glorious assurance—in his death and resurrection he faced the worst the world can do, faced these same problems and perplexities with all their mental anguish, which so often beat us till we cry inwardly for quarter—Christ faced them and triumphed over them and through them, with and for man in his struggle after righteousness, for all time.

Corder Catchpool, 1956

173   My sunrise meditation means more to me now than ever. At dawn it is easier to feel the universe is one organic whole, held together by that Radiating Power of Love which flows through everything—including thee and me....

By using the power of mature, redemptive love we can show each individual that we need his or her uniqueness to make us whole. We will then see that we have something to give others and that others have something to give us.

Rachel Davis DuBois, c. 1978

174   (5 a.m.) Something is happening around me: the dark is less dark, the silence is less deep. Even the air is changing. It is damper, sweeter. Morning is at hand. Light will soon come flowing over the edge of the world, bringing with it the day. What a gift! Whether wrapped in streamers of color or folded in tissues of mist, it will be mine to use in ways that I can foresee and in those that are unexpected. The day will make its own revelation, bring its own challenge; my part will be to respond with joy and gladness.

                                                 Elizabeth Yates, 1976

175   It may seem paradoxical for me to say that I would not have missed the experiences of those two years of my life in a Nazi prison for anything. But it is so. When one's existence, which has seemed quite secure, suddenly melts away, when one is cut off…from the circle of one's family and friends, and must rely entirely on one's self in an indifferent, hostile world; when the ground is taken from under one's feet and the air one breathes is taken away, when every security fails and every support gives way — then one stands face to face with the Eternal, and confronts Him without protection and with fearful directness.

                                                 Eva Hermann, c. 1947

176   At home when I was a small child there had been little to suggest to me the restriction placed upon women in the outside world. Our family sitting room was presided over by a large steel engraving of Elizabeth Fry in Quaker cap and flowing Quaker dress. When I joined the family group around the fire after supper there she hung, an imposing figure on the wall above me. We all honored her because she had visited the cruel British prisons of her day and reformed them. According to Quaker theory women were the equals of men, the two sexes facing each other "with level–fronting eyelids," a phrase I often heard. And in practice twice a week at the Sunday and Thursday morning meetings for worship I saw my mother sit opposite, even though a little below, my father in the raised gallery for ministers and elders. On the one occasion when I attended a joint business session of the Men's and Women's Monthly Meeting, as I pushed open the door at the far end of the room I saw my mother and my father seated side by side in solitary state before a long table littered with papers. They performed respectively the duties of the clerk of the Men's and clerk of the Women's meeting. I remember the sharp stab of pride I felt as I stood in the doorway to look at my parents.

                                              Helen Thomas Flexner, 1940

177   It happened in the night. I was at a very low point. I was sleeping out of doors on the porch close to the hill. A light breeze rustled through the overhanging branches of a great walnut tree. I was very tired. I looked up at the stars edging over the hill in my mood of great despondency. I said to God, "It's no use. I've tried all I can. I can't do anything more." All of a sudden I seemed to be swept

bodily out of my bed, carried above the trees and held poised in mid–air, surrounded by light—a light so bright that I could hardly look at it. Even when I closed my eyes I could feel it. A fragrance as of innumerable orange blossoms inundated my senses. And there was an echo of far–off music. All was ecstasy. I have no idea whether it lasted a minute or several hours. But for the rest of the night I lay in a state of peace and indescribable joy. How impossible it is to explain such a phenomenon in everyday language, but whatever it was changed my life. It was not a passing illusion. I never was the same again. For days I was terribly happy. The whole world seemed to be illumined, the flower colors were brighter, bird songs gayer, and people were kind, friendly and loving. This exaggerated brilliance faded somewhat with time and the intense sense of communion fluctuated. Later on there were, of course, low moments amidst the high peaks, and there were failures, dry seasons, and the recurring need for patience and perseverance. But I never lost the clarification of mind and spirit that was revealed to me on that night.

Josephine Duvenek, 1978

178   In my younger days I felt unsure and afraid of life, but the experience of God through Quakerism has created an inner ground of harmony and deep security, something not originating from my own power, not grasped by my intellect, yet with roots within myself. God is in life itself, in silence, in fellowship, in nature, in absorption in service for others.

I experience God unexpectedly, without premeditated device or plan; I "happen" to meet those who just then and there need help or contact, and I experience God in action. Something guides me without my knowing. Praying for others is to me a kind of telepathy with God geared in.

Elsa Cedergren, 20th Century

Living and Dying

179   Now is where we live, now is where the past must be overcome, now is where we meet others, now is where we must find the presence of God.

Carol Murphy, c.1993

180   To many people throughout history, God has been intensely real because they have found that they can experience communion with God. But such experience is not gained without persistence. We must listen; we must make time to step aside, even from good works, in order to talk with God. Sometimes a physical withdrawal is not possible, but when communion has become a constant attitude of mind it is deeply satisfying because it fulfills our need for the companionship of someone who loves us in spite of our failings.

Kathleen Lonsdale, 1962

181   This relatedness of all life, as it binds us to all that has passed, surely binds us to the future as well. So the divine spark kindled in us can never really be extinguished, for it is part of a universal flame.

Once we have squarely faced the inescapable fact of our own death, we need never fear it, but turn and live life to the hilt, as we have seen that it should be lived. Then, whether that life be long or short, it will have been a full one.

Life is a gift so precious that we would accept it on any terms rather than never to have had it. Even among the poorest and most deprived—and especially among them, as I often thought in India—you see this zest for, this clinging to life. But we get more than the gift itself. We get life with the guarantee that it does conform to universal laws which affect and control every scrap of living matter. How much this gives us!—minds that can work in harmony with others, skills we can learn and transmit, health, zest for food and love, the absolute assurance that the laws are fixed, and not things that alter with a flippant changefulness from day to day.

Bradford Smith, 1965

182   There are clearly-marked signposts which, if followed, lead the way to recovery. First there has to be the wish, however transient, to find the way to better things. It is the beginning of hope, that basic ingredient for all life. From there, confidence and belief develop, and the certainty that in spite of all evidence to the contrary, good is in us and around us offering support. In such a situation of positive thinking we cease to be dreamers and accept fully our present lot. It is the material from which we are to build our future, whether long or short in time.... The remarkable discovery we can make is that love has not deserted us, and that it is available to us now in a new way. Our own willingness to love and to give in the world about us is the secret of recovery and the new beginning.

Margaret Torrie, 1975

183   I am convinced it is a great art to know how to grow old gracefully, and I am determined to practice it.... I always thought I should love to grow old, and I find it is even more delightful than I thought. It is so delicious to be done with things and to feel no need any longer to concern myself much about earthly affairs.... . I am tremendously content to let one activity after another go, and to wait quietly and happily the opening of the door at the end of the passageway that will let me into my real abiding place.

Hannah Whitall Smith, 1903

184   I have been learning…that when we accept our finiteness realistically and without bitterness, each day is a gift to be cherished and savored. Each day becomes a miracle. I am learning to offer to God my days and my nights, my joy, my work, my pain, and my grief. I am striving to keep my house in order, and my relationships intact. I am learning to use the time I have more wisely....

And I am learning to forget at times my puritan conscience which prods me to work without ceasing, and instead, to take time for joy.

Elizabeth Watson, 1979

185   One of life's hardest lessons is that there is no justification for expecting that our neighbour is to traverse precisely the same path as that which we ourselves have followed…. The difficulty a man has in grasping this truth is increased in proportion as his own experience has been vivid and clearly defined. One who has been lifted out of the horrible pit, has had his feet set upon a rock, and a new song put into his mouth, finds it hard to believe that another who has arrived quietly and without crisis, with no strong consciousness of guilt and no corresponding ecstasy of deliverance, can really be a disciple at all.

William Littleboy, 1916

186   Those of us known as "activists" have sometimes been hurt by the written or spoken implication that we must be spending too little time on our spiritual contemplative lives. I do know many atheists who are active in improving the lot of humankind; but, for those of us who are Friends, our attendance at meeting for worship and our silent prayerful times are what make our outer activity viable and effective—if it is effective.

I have similarly seen quieter Friends hurt by the implication that they do not care enough, because they are not seen to be "politically active". Some worry unnecessarily that they may be doing things of a "less important" nature, as if to be seen doing things by the eyes of the world is the same thing as to be seen doing things by the eyes of God…. I suggest that we refrain from judging each other, or belittling what each is doing; and that we should not feel belittled. We cannot know the prayers that others make or do not make in their own times of silent aloneness. We cannot know the letters others may be writing to governments…. We were made differently, in order to perform different tasks. Let us rejoice in our differences.

Margaret Glover, 1989

187   The practice of journal keeping is … a way of becoming aware of the patterns of our inner life, of growing in self-knowledge and discovering our own gifts and possibilities…. Keeping a journal is just one way … of beginning to re-create your life. At its most basic it is a decision that your life has value and meaning and deserves the effort of recollection and reflection. It is also a decision that what you are living and learning is worth recording. That decision has its roots in a very deep layer of gospel truth.

Jo Farrow, 1986

188   The secret of finding joy after sorrow, or through sorrow, lies, I think, in the way we meet sorrow itself. We cannot fight against it and overcome it, though often we try and may seem at first successful. We try to be stoical, to suppress our memories…to kill [the pain] with strenuous activity so that we may be too tired to think. But that is just the time when it returns to us in overwhelming power. Or we try to escape from it…. But when the trip is over, the book closed…the research accomplished, there is our sorrow waiting for us, disguised, perhaps, but determined….

What we must do,…with God's help, is to accept sorrow as a friend, if possible. If not, as a companion with whom we will live for an indeterminate period, for whom we have to make room as one makes room for a guest in one's house, a companion of whom we shall always be aware, from whom we can learn and whose strength will become our strength. Together we can create beauty from ashes and find ourselves in the process.

Elizabeth Gray Vining, 1952

189   Sometimes religion appears to be presented as offering easy cures for pain: have faith and God will mend your hurts; reach out to God and your woundedness will be healed. The Beatitude "Blessed are they who mourn, for they shall be comforted" can be interpreted this way too, but the Latin root of the word "comfort" means "with strength" rather than "at ease." The Beatitude is not promising to take away our pain; indeed the inference is that the pain will remain with us. It does promise that God will cherish us and our wound, and help us draw a blessing from our distressed state.

S. Jocelyn Burnell, 1989

190   I've gone to many kinds of schools, but of all the courses in the university of life, the course in old age is the hardest; the one with the most lessons to learn. Your own generation is gone. You can no longer count on your intellect or your memory. Your hearing lets you down. You can't keep track of things and you're constantly misplacing them. But you learn so much. You learn to accept help and to remember with your heart. To live always with the generations that went before, with those alive now, and with the generations to come—all that we must surely learn. In one way life is like a mountain climb, and we keep going steadily upward toward our death. And when we meet it, when Brother Death comes and gives us permission to go on across the frontier, then we must meet him with thankfulness, only with thankfulness.

Emilia Fogelklou, 1985

191   Friends do not take readily to being cared for. "Caring matters most" has been quoted to us when seeking direction during our active years. But many of us will find that we ourselves are in need of full care in our old age. This will not be easy. It calls for "a different kind of living", as one Friend commented when answering questions about experience in a home for the elderly. Uprooted from familiar well-loved things, of house and neighbours, released from stabilising responsibilities (however small), there will be adjustments to be made.

But there are compensations and opportunities. Loss of physical well-being can bring a new experience of the strength of the Spirit which can overcome pain and suffering. A new and fuller understanding of prayer can come, given the time to study and practise how to pray. And in the experience of living in a Home with others, a deep sense of sharing the darkness and the light can lead to a sense of community not known before. Finally, living close to physical death (our own and that of others), we come to recognise death as a natural and often welcome event. Yet another movement of growth into the fullness of the knowledge of God.

Margaret McNeill, 1990

192   A moral code, even when accepted for the best of reasons, necessarily tends to be negative rather than positive, to be concerned with "Thou shalt not" rather than with what an individual should give to his fellows. We are much concerned about the whole content of human relationship, about the meaning of "Thou shalt love thy neighbour as thyself" in the full range and depth of its implications. Loving does not merely mean doing good works; it goes further than feeding the hungry and clothing the naked. It means warmth and intimacy, open-heartedness and overwhelming generosity of hand and spirit. It means a desire to know and a courageous willingness to be known. Loving implies commitment to the other person, involvement in that person's life, whatever it may cost in suffering, whether that suffering comes through being repudiated or through identification and sharing.

The life of society desperately needs this warmth of giving and receiving. Everywhere we see sociabiltiy without commitment or intimacy and, especially in our towns, intense isolation and loneliness. We see human energy that should be creative and loving deflected into activities that are coldly power-seeking; we see love inhibited, frustrated, or denied, turning into its opposite—into ruthlessness and aggression.

A Group of Friends, London Yearly Meeting, 1963

193   People so often talk of someone "getting over" a death. How could you ever fully get over a deep loss? Life has been changed profoundly and irrevocably. You don't get over sorrow; you work your way right to the centre of it.

Diana Lampen, 1979

194   As I grow older, I seem to need more time for inner stillness.... This can happen in the midst of daily chores or when walking in a crowd or riding in a train. It means being still, open, reflective, holding within myself the crucible of joy and pain of all the world, and lifting it up to God. Praise comes into it, and thankfulness for all the love I have known and shared, the realization of how much of the time I am carried, supported, upheld by others and the love of God. [During this process] comes the deep sense of the unity of all being, the intermeshing of the animate and inanimate, the secular and the sacred, the tangible and the intangible....it means just waiting, or just lifting the heart.

Dorothy Steere, 1995

Extracts from writings on

Concerns, Leadings, Testimonies

INTRODUCTION

Out of worship come Friends' service and witness—actions that stem from personal leadings and concerns which both arise from and cause evolution of our corporate testimonies. The selections here include corporate statements and individual observations, and begin with statements about service, testimonies, concerns, and leadings in general, followed by selections specific to peace, simplicity, equality and community, and integrity.

· · ·

195   A Quaker testimony is a belief that stems from our fundamental understanding of religious truth. It is a corporately held belief about how we should individually act. In practicing them, we witness to our understanding of the very nature of God's spirit of love and truth.

Jonathan Dale, 1996

196   Our testimonies arise from our way of worship. Our way of worship evokes from deep within us at once an affirmation and a celebration, an affirmation of the reality of that Light which illumines the spiritual longing of humanity, and a celebration of the continual resurrection within us of the springs of hope and love; a sense that each of us is, if we will, a channel for a power that is both within and beyond us.

Lorna M. Marsden, 1986

197   Ever since I first came among Friends, I was attracted to the testimonies as an ideal. I wanted to belong to a church which made the rejection of warfare a collective commitment and not just a personal option. I admired a simplicity, a devotion to equality, and a respect for others which reflected what I already knew of Christ. In a deceitful world I warmed to those who did not swear oaths and strove to tell the truth in all circumstances. But this was a beginning in the spiritual life. The seed that was sown in my mind and my politics struck root in my soul and my faith.

The choice of the word "testimony" is instructive. The testimonies are ways of behaving but are not ethical rules. They are matters of practice but imply doctrines. They refer to human society but are about God. Though often talked about, they lack an authoritative formulation....

A "testimony" is a declaration of truth or fact.... It is not an ejaculation, a way of letting off steam, or baring one's soul. It has a purpose, and that is to get other people to change, to turn to God. Such an enterprise, be it in words or by conduct and example, is in essence prophetic and evangelical.

                                                              John Punshon, 1987

198   Leading and being led: the words are simple enough. But for Quakers they have their most profound resonance as defining religious experience. Friends speak variously of being drawn to an action, feeling under the weight of a concern, being called or led to act in specific ways. We speak of being open to the leadings of the Light, of being taught by the Spirit or the Inward Christ. Extraordinary claims lie embedded in those phrases. They say that it is not only possible but essential to our nature for human beings to hear and obey the voice of God; that we can be directed, daily, in what we do, the jobs we hold, the very words we say; and that our obedience may draw us to become leaders in all spheres of human life—in the professions, arts, and sciences, but also in discovering the ethical, political, social, and economic consequences of following the will of God.

                                                              Paul Lacey, 1985

199   "Concern" is a word which has tended to become debased by excessively common usage among Friends, so that too often it is used to cover merely a strong desire. The true "concern" [emerges as] a gift from God, a leading of his spirit which may not be denied. Its sanction is not that on investigation it proves to be the intelligent thing to do—though it usually is; it is that the individual...knows, as a matter of inward experience, that there is something that the Lord would have done, however obscure the way, however uncertain the means to human observation. Often proposals for action are made which have every appearance of good sense, but as the meeting waits before God it becomes clear that the proposition falls short of "concern."

                                                              Roger Wilson, 1949

200   Our disciplines are not unalterable documents like the laws of the Medes and Persians, but represent a manifest development in full harmony with the growth of things in the world of life. In studying the discipline ... we must consider the conditions of thought and life at the time when the disciplinary provisions were first formulated ... we must look at all our testimonies and requirements from the standpoint of the present, in connection with right social standards and general need. While a forced disciplinary morality may be better than none at all, the function of the discipline is not to dominate the conscience in an arbitrary way, but to lead to that constant self-examination and genuine concern, which shall make the individual conduct right from choice, and not because of fear or compulsion.

Henry W. Wilbur, 1908

201   A concern is God-initiated, often surprising, always holy, for the life of God is breaking through into the world. Its execution is in peace and power and astounding faith and joy, for in unhurried serenity the Eternal is at work in the midst of time, triumphantly bringing all things unto Himself.

Thomas Kelly, 1941

202   A Quaker social concern seems characteristically to arise in a sensitive individual or very small group.... The concern arises as a revelation to an individual that there is a painful discrepancy between existing social conditions and what God wills for society and that this discrepancy is not being adequately dealt with. The next step is the determination of the individual to do something about it—not because he is particularly well fitted to tackle the problem, but simply because no one else seems to be doing it.

Dorothy H. Hutchinson, 1961

203   I expect to pass through this world but once; any good thing therefore that I can do, or any kindness that I can show to any fellow creature, let me do it now; let me not defer or neglect it, for I shall not pass this way again.

Attributed to Stephen Grellet, c. 1800

204   In all our fervor–in all my fervor–to be doing, have I paid too little attention to the power that lies in being? Do we remember that it is the spirit of our service, the aura that surrounds it, the gentleness and the patience that marks it, the love made visible that compels it, that is the truly distinctive quality that lifts Quaker service above lobbying, above pressure, above coercion, that inspires the doubtful, and reaches the heart of the adversary?

Stephen Cary, 1979

205	Whether the experience of Divine companionship comes soon or late, whether it is a sudden realisation of the Indwelling Spirit, the Divine Presence, the Eternal Light Within, the Seed of God in the heart, it becomes increasingly the mainspring of our life on earth and our hope for the life to come. We recognize this as an element of the Divine in every human heart, however denied and stifled and concealed; it is something to which we can appeal from the innermost depths of our being; an inward experience of God in which we ourselves must live.

From that inward relationship, the testimonies which generations of Friends have been challenged to maintain take on a deeper meaning. One of the most revealing passages in George Fox's Journal is that in which he records his answer to the officials who offered him his liberty, if he would accept a commission and "take up arms for the Commonwealth against the King." He did not say that he believed war to be wrong, or that in his opinion brute force never settled anything; he went straight to the heart of the matter and said that he "lived in the virtue of that life and power that took away the occasion of all wars." To uphold such a testimony involved a dedicated life. The Quaker peace testimony is more than a repudiation of war, and more than a denial of the use of force; it is a way of life to which we must be faithful in small things as well as in great, in our human relationships, our business and social activities, and in the life and witness of our meetings.

Elfrida Vipont Foulds, 1981

206	If a concerned Quaker (or any man or woman committed to an absolute religious ethic) decides to enter practical politics in order to translate his principles into actuality, he may achieve a relative success: he may be able to raise the level of political life in his time, as John Bright did, or maintain a comparatively happy and just and peaceful society, as the Quaker legislators of Pennsylvania did. But he can apparently do it only at a price—the price of compromise, of partial betrayal of his ideals. If, on the other hand, he decides to preserve his ideals intact, to maintain his religious testimonies unsullied and pure, he may be able to do that, but again at a price—the price of isolation, of withdrawal from the mainstream of life in his time, of renouncing the opportunity directly and immediately to influence history.

Let me call the two positions the relativist and the absolutist. And let me suggest that perhaps each one needs the other. The relativist needs the absolutist to keep alive and clear the vision of the City of God while he struggles in some measure to realize it in the City of Earth. And conversely, the absolutist needs the relativist, lest the vision remain the possession of a few only, untranslated into any degree of reality for the world as a whole.

Frederick B. Tolles, 1956

207   We wish we could say that our response to God's calling was immediate and unequivocal, but in fact there followed several months of indecision, as we struggled with our leading. We initiated, in a tentative way, the application process through Friends United Meeting, and were encouraged by them to schedule a trip to Indiana for an interview. Finally, five months after Yearly Meeting, we reached clarity, together as a couple: if FUM offered us the position (and we were the only serious candidates), we were prepared to accept. The final moment of decision stands out in our minds, because it came on Liz's birthday, when we were out cross-country skiing together.

That very evening, as we basked in the warm glow of our newly found clearness, we received a phone call...there was no opening, and no need for an interview.

The word "disappointment" does not adequately describe how we felt. Our process of discernment had been slow and gradual but, we felt, genuine. We were left feeling empty, as though we were somehow "in transition"—but transition to what? We had now given up our expectations for the future not once, but twice. Our lives were outwardly the same as before, but we were empty, waiting for a further leading, and not entirely sure when or if it would come.

It took several difficult months, but eventually, reluctantly, we were able to give up the idea that Lugulu was in our future. Then one day, about a year later, a letter came in the mail.... The mission board was asking, almost apologetically, if we would still consider going to Lugulu.

Suddenly, we could see the bumpy and circuitous road that we had been traveling for those eighteen months in a larger perspective. God had been asking, "Whom shall I send? Who will go for me?" Now, and only now, were we prepared to answer unequivocally with the prophet Isaiah, "Here we are, Lord. Send us."

Tom and Liz Gates, 1995

208   There is that near you which will guide you. O wait for it and be sure you keep to it.

Isaac Penington, 1678

209   To most of us are given some common little jobs every day of our lives. To a very few comes the call to do something extraordinary, some great task. The world abounds in men and women who find happiness and opportunities for self-expression in being faithful in the humble stations of life which are theirs at a given time. If we are loyal to the truth as we see it, and respond with our might in the "common" situations in day-to-day living as we face them, the glow of the grace of God deepens and nurtures our faculties for insight and for recognition of the true worth of things and of men.

Ranjit Chetsingh, 1975

210   Friends are conservative radicals. They are conservative because they are religious, and religion, as the origin of the word indicates, suggests binding together. Religion binds the present with the past and it binds diverse people into communities. Quakers, because of their deep Christian roots, are bound into the past history of man. The words and actions attributed to Isaiah, to Jesus, to Saint Francis, to George Fox, and to John Woolman, come down through the centuries and are bound into the life and witness of today. In the meeting for worship Friends seek to break through the here-and-now into that which is eternal. Here that which is beyond time and in every time becomes part of the present.

With all this conservatism, however, Friends are also radical. Their authority is the light within, the present and personal experience by which past undoubted authority must be tested. "Thou sayest Christ said this and the apostles saith that, but what canst thou say," says George Fox.... This "What canst thou say" is the key to a religion in which we have "No time but this present" and in which there is a constant hunger to apply the eternal principles of love, justice, and redemptive suffering to this present world.

Kenneth Boulding, 1988

211   After a great war there is and will continue to be intense physical need. If we meet that we shall have some insight into deeper issues. At any rate our choice is today clear as it was on the Jerusalem-Jericho road years ago. Either we shall be among the good Samaritans, or we shall be among those that pass by on the other side. As the gospel suggests elsewhere, when food, clothing, and care are concerned it is either "Inasmuch as ye did" or "Inasmuch as ye did not." Beginning from there, we may expect further insight.

Henry J. Cadbury, 1947

212   No one dreamed in the sharp crisis of 1917, when the first steps of faith were taken, that we should feed more than a million German children, drive dray loads of cod-liver oil into Russia, plough the fields of the peasants and fight typhus in Poland, rebuild the houses and replant the wastes in Serbia, administer a longtime service of love in Austria, become foster parents to tens of thousands of children in the coal fields in West Virginia, Kentucky, Pennsylvania, and Ohio, inaugurate plans for the rehabiliation of the stranded soft coal miners, carry relief to the children on both sides of the warring forces in Spain and create new types of peace activity which have brought this supreme issue of these times vitally home to the minds and consciences of people in all parts of America.

We verily went out in those days of low visibility not knowing whither we were going; but, like the early patriarch, we were conscious of a divine leading, and we were aware, even if only dimly, that we were "fellow-laborers with God" in the rugged furrows of the somewhat brambly fields of the world.

Rufus Jones, 1937

213   I think I have wasted a great deal of my life waiting to be called to some great mission which would change the world. I have looked for important social movements. I have wanted to make a big and important contribution to the causes I believe in. I think I have been too ready to reject the genuine leadings I have been given as being matters of little consequence. It has taken me a long time to learn that obedience means doing what we are called to do even if it seems pointless or unimportant or even silly. The great social movements of our time may well be part of our calling. The ideals of peace and justice and equality which are part of our religious tradition are often the focus of debate. But we cannot simply immerse ourselves in these activities. We need to develop our own unique social witness, in obedience to God. We need to listen to the gentle whispers which will tell us how we can bring our lives into greater harmony with heaven.

Deborah Haines, 1978

214   If we are faithful followers of Jesus, we may expect at times to differ from the practice of others. Having in mind that truth in all ages has been advanced by the courageous example of spiritual leaders, Friends are earnestly advised to be faithful to those leadings of the Divine Spirit which they feel fully assured after mature meditation and consideration they have interpreted truly.

Book of Discipline, Philadelphia Yearly Meeting (Race Street), 1927

Peace

215   [After Fox had been in Darby jail for several months]...they filled the House of Corrections with persons that they had taken up to be soldiers and then they would have had me to be captain of them to go forth to Worcester fight and the soldiers cried they would have none but me. So the keeper of the House of Correction was commanded to bring me up before the Commissioners and soldiers in the market place; and there they proffered me that preferment because of my virtue [valor]...and asked me if I would not take up arms for the Commonwealth against the King. But I told them I lived in the virtue of that life and power that took away the occasion of all wars, and I knew from whence all wars did rise, from the lust according to James's doctrine...I told them I was come into the covenant of peace which was before wars....

George Fox, 1651

216   There is no security except in creating situations in which people do not want to harm you. This is a difficult truth for most people to face, but the difficulty is more emotional than rational or scientific. "If thine enemy hunger, feed him," is not only Christian teaching, but it is profound wisdom, for the best way of getting rid of an enemy is to convert him into a friend. Feeding in this sense does not mean, necessarily, shipping food; it may mean applying science to create local production that he may have both subsistence and self-respect. Whence come the qualities which enable men to tackle so hard and bold a task? We know that they are latent in all men, that they have been manifest in the pursuit of science, and that they respond to cultivation. We know too that religion, in the universal sense of human aspiration that is above sect or creed or any other dividing influence, constitutes a fertile soil in which the best that is in men may grow. It is expressed in many ways, but those who feel a deep loyalty as citizens of the Kingdom of God have an impelling reason to serve their fellow men.

James G. Vail, 1953

217   The foundations of Quaker pacifism are religious. We fully recognize the value of the intuitive recognition of the evil of coercive violence in the individual and national life. The sense of the contrast between the way of war and the way of love shown us in the life of Jesus Christ has compelling force. It is also enlightening to think of pacifism as a corollary of the fundamental Quaker postulate of the Divine Spark in every human being. This fundamental Quaker postulate lays on us the obligation to consider and cherish every human being. It follows, for those who accept the postulate, that they cannot do to human beings the things that war involves. It may follow that they become aware that other sorts of human relations are also evil, such as slavery, economic injustice, inferior status for women, and the results of the traffic in narcotics....

Quaker pacifism is an obligation, not a promise. We are not guaranteed that it will be safe. We are sure that it is right. We desire to make our individual decisions in harmony with it, and to help our fellows to do so.

Friends Peace Committee,
Philadelphia Yearly Meeting (Race Street), 1940

218   We have to take responsibility in our own countries for the trade in weapons, which will continue unless we intensify our actions against it. Let us do this together as an international body. Let us picture where Jesus Christ would be in this matter. What would he be saying about the trade in weapons?...

Quakers have often taken on a prophetic role in the past. We should be glad of the example of the slave abolitionists and remember their strength, their courage, their witness, and do likewise now.

Jo Vallentine, 1991

219   Once the horrible inhuman and ungodly war had started, the consequences could not be avoided. That is why I'm writing to you so seriously tonight. I believe that my generation can keep peace for awhile, if we work at it hard enough; but your generation must not forget the capacity for destruction that exists in man, and must somehow see that neither you nor your children face this again. I don't want your sons, if you have any, to look upon the sight that I saw today, or on even worse sights which another war may bring with improved technical means of killing and maiming the bodies and souls of other men.

In order to accomplish that, you, I, and everyone else who believes in the Christian ideals by which we supposedly live must get into the political race and fight for right, even though it inconveniences each of us and interferes with the things we want to do.

Walter C. Michaels, 1945

220   To become a nonviolent society, a basic change we need to make is in the way we think. We need to stop dividing people, ideas, situations, countries, etc. into separate categories while failing to recognize their interconnectedness. We need to seek resolutions of conflict that result in all sides "winning" rather than in one side winning and the other losing. The changes needed are fundamental, and all of us need to reflect on how we might be contributing to a violent culture....

Deb Sawyer, 1987

221   We gladly pay the civilian part of our taxes, but many have reached a point in their conscience which prevents or makes difficult the payment of the military portion.

We warmly approve of people following their conscience, and openly approve civil disobedience in this matter under Divine compulsion. We ask all to consider carefully the implications of paying taxes that relate to war-making.

Philadelphia Yearly Meeting, 1970

222   In a world which desires the fruit but does not understand the root of the peace testimony, we who would live this witness must take care not to succumb to the notion that the fruit can exist independent of the root.

Sandra Cronk, c.1983

223   This meeting fervently recommends to the deep attention of all our members, that they be religiously guarded against approving or showing the least connivance at war, either by attending at or viewing military operations, or in any wise encouraging the unstable deceitful spirit of party, by joining with political devices or associations, however speciously disguised under the ensnaring subtleties commonly attendant thereon; but that they sincerely labour to experience a settlement on the alone sure foundation of the pure unchangeable truth, whereby, through the prevalence of unfeigned Christian love and good will to men, we may convincingly demonstrate that the kingdom we seek is not of this world: A kingdom and government whose subjects are free indeed, redeemed from those captivating lusts from whence come wars and fightings.

As we are called out of wars and fightings, so let them be as seldom as possible the subjects of our conversations; but let an holy care rest upon us, to abide in that power which gives dominion over the hopes and fears that arise from the concerns of an unstable world, which tend, as they are admitted into the mind, to lessen the trust on that rock which is immovable.

Philadelphia Yearly Meeting, 1806

224   We totally oppose all wars, all preparation for war, all use of weapons and coercion by force, and all military alliances: no end could ever justify such means.

We equally and actively oppose all that leads to violence among people and nations, and violence to other species and to our planet.

This has been our testimony to the whole world for over three centuries.

We are not naïve or ignorant about the complexity of our modern world and the impact of sophisticated technologies—but we see no reason whatsoever to change or weaken our vision of the peace that everyone needs in order to survive and flourish on a healthy, abundant earth.

The primary reason for this stand is our conviction that there is that of God in every one which makes each person too precious to damage or destroy.

While someone lives, there is always the hope of reaching that of God within them: such hope motivates our search to find nonviolent resolution of conflict....

There is no guarantee that our resistance will be any more successful or any less risky than military tactics. At least our means will be suited to our end.

If we seemed to fail finally, we would still rather suffer and die than inflict evil in order to save ourselves and what we hold dear.

If we succeed, there is no loser or winner, for the problem that led to conflict will have been resolved in a spirit of justice and tolerance.

Such a resolution is the only guarantee that there will be no further outbreak of war when each side has regained strength....

The places to begin acquiring the skills and maturity and generosity to avoid or to resolve conflicts are in our own homes, our personal relationships, our schools, our workplaces, and wherever decisions are made.

We must relinquish the desire to own other people, to have power over them, and to force our views on to them. We must own up to our own negative side and not look for scapegoats to blame, punish, or exclude. We must resist the urge towards waste and the accumulation of possessions.

Conflicts are inevitable and must not be repressed or ignored but worked through painfully and carefully. We must develop the skills of being sensitive to oppression and grievances, sharing power in decision making, creating consensus, and making reparation.

In speaking out, we acknowledge that we ourselves are as limited and as erring as anyone else. When put to the test, we each may fall short.

We do not have a blueprint for peace…. In any particular situation, a variety of personal decisions could be made with integrity.

We may disagree with the views and actions of the politician or the soldier who opts for a military solution, but we still respect and cherish that person.

What we call for in this statement is a commitment to make the building of peace a priority and to make opposition to war absolute.

What we advocate is not uniquely Quaker but human and, we believe, the will of God. Our stand does not belong to Friends alone—it is yours by birthright….

[L]et us reject the clamour of fear and listen to the whisperings of hope.

Aotearoa/New Zealand Yearly Meeting, 1987

Simplicity

225   It may surprise some of us to hear that the first generation of Friends did not have a testimony for simplicity. They came upon a faith which cut to the root of the way they saw life, radically reorienting it. They saw that all they did must flow directly from what they experienced as true, and that if it did not, both the knowing and the doing became false. In order to keep the knowledge clear and the doing true, they stripped away anything which seemed to get in the way. They called those things superfluities, and it is this radical process of stripping for clear-seeing which we now term simplicity.

Frances Irene Taber, 1985

226   The Spirit of Truth which led our early Friends to lay aside things unbecoming the Gospel of Christ still leads in the same path all who submit to its guidance; we therefore earnestly encourage all Friends to watch over themselves in this respect, and seriously to consider the plainness and simplicity which the Gospel enjoins, manifest it in their conversation, apparel, furniture, buildings, salutation, and manner of living, exercising plainness of speech without respect of persons in all their converse among men, not balking their testimony by varying their language according to their company.

Philadelphia Yearly Meeting (Race Street), 1894

227   Has Quakerism anything to tell the world about simplicity in religion? It has. This is the main secret of its remarkable success in its early days. It was as simple as the Galilean's Gospel. It made no compromise with the interminable mass of scholastic theology. It cut loose from it all. One sentence from George Fox announces its whole program— "Let nothing come between your souls and God but Jesus Christ."

Rufus Jones, 1906

228   We have a testimony about simplicity and we need to think about what that means in the world we're living in right now. What does it mean to be lean and disciplined and not dependent upon our things?

Kara Cole Newell, 1982

229   The important thing about worldly possessions, in fact, is whether or not we are tied to them. Some, by an undue love of the things of this world, have so dulled their hearing that a divine call to a different way of life would pass unheard. Others are unduly self–conscious about things which are of no eternal significance, and because they worry too much about them, fail to give of their best. The essence of worldliness is to judge of things by an outward and temporary, and not an inward and eternal standard, to care more about appearances than about reality, to let the senses prevail over the reason and the affections.

London Yearly Meeting, 1958

230   Wealth is attended with power, by which bargains and proceedings contrary to universal righteousness are supported; and here oppression, carried on with worldly policy and order, clothes itself with the name of justice and becomes like a seed of discord in the soil. And as this spirit which wanders from the pure habitation prevails, so the seeds of war swell and sprout and grow and become strong until much fruit is ripened. Thus cometh the harvest.... Spoken of by the prophet Isaiah, which is "a heap in the day of grief, and of desparate sorrow." O that we who declare against wars, and acknowledge our trust to be in God only, may walk in the Light and therein examine our... motives in holding great estates! May we look upon our treasures... and try whether the seeds of war have any nourishment in these our possessions.

John Woolman, c. 1764

231   Frugality is good, if liberality be join'd with it. The first is leaving off superfluous expenses; the last bestowing them to the benefit of others that need. The first without the last begins covetousness; the last without the first begins prodigality: Both together make an excellent temper. Happy the place wherever that is found.

William Penn, 1698

232   Perhaps it is this integrity, the concept of the wholeness of creation, that will jolt humanity onto a course of sustainability, which people may see as threatening at first. Of course change is often uncomfortable, but change is a must. We need to nurture ourselves and each other, but ultimately we need to nurture the earth—our mother.

Jo Vallentine, 1991

233   Is our concern for simplicity relevant to our concern for the national economic situation? If we think of simplicity in terms of doing without certain things, of voluntarily reducing our standard of living, I believe this is almost irrelevant at the economic level in view of the scale of the world's need. If we think of simplicity as a spiritual quality which incidentally simplifies life styles then I believe it has relevance. This kind of simplicity goes straight to the heart of things and puts first things first....

Anonymous, c. 1995

234   But at the first convincement, when Friends could not put off their hats to people nor say 'you' to a [single person], but 'thee' and 'thou'; and could not bow nor use the world's salutations, nor fashions, nor customs; many Friends, being tradesmen of several sorts lost their custom at the first; for the people would not trade with them nor trust them, and for a time Friends that were tradesmen could hardly get enough money to buy bread. But afterwards people came to see Friends' honesty and truthfulness and 'yea' and 'nay' at a word in their dealing, and their lives and conversations did preach and reach to the witness of God in all people, and they knew and saw that, for conscience sake towards God, they would not cozen and cheat them, and at last that they might send any child and be as well used as [if they had come] themselves, at any of their shops.

George Fox, 1653

235   My mind through the power of Truth was in a good degree weaned from the desire of outward greatness, and I was learning to be content with real conveniences that were not costly; so that a way of life free from much entanglements appeared best for me, though the income was small. I had several offers of business that appeared profitable, but saw not my way clear to accept of them, as believing the business proposed would be attended with more outward care and cumber than was required of me to engage in.

I saw that a humble man with the blessing of the Lord might live on a little, and that where the heart was set on greatness, success in business did not satisfy the craving; but that in common with an increase of wealth, the desire of wealth increased. There was a care on my mind so to pass my time as to things outward that nothing might hinder me from the most steady attention to the voice of the True Shepherd.

John Woolman, 1743

236   Undue luxury often creates a false sense of superiority, causes unnecessary burdens upon both ourselves and others, and leads to the neglect of the spiritual life.

Philadelphia Yearly Meeting (Race Street), 1927

237   Poverty does not mean scorn for goods and property. It means the strict limitation of goods that are for personal use.... It means a horror of war, first because it ruins human life and health and the beauty of the earth, but second because it destroys goods that could be used to relieve misery and hardship and to give joy. It means a distaste even for the small carelessnesses that we see prevalent, so that beautiful and useful things are allowed to become dirty and battered through lack of respect for them.

Mildred Binns Young, 1956

238   Love silence, even in the mind.... Much speaking, as much thinking, spends; and in many thoughts, as well as words, there is sin. True silence is the rest of the mind; and is to the spirit, what sleep is to the body, nourishment and refreshment.

William Penn, 1699

239   I wish I might emphasize how a life becomes simplified when dominated by faithfulness to a few concerns. Too many of us have too many irons in the fire. We get distracted by the intellectual claim to our interest in a thousand and one good things, and before we know it we are pulled and hauled breathlessly along by an over-burdened program of good committees and good undertakings. I am persuaded that this fevered life of church workers is not wholesome.... The concern-oriented life is ordered and organized from within. And we learn to say *No* as well as *Yes* by attending to the guidance of inner responsibility. Quaker simplicity needs to be expressed not merely in dress and architecture and the height of tombstones but also in the structure of a relatively simplified and coordinated life-program of social responsibilities. And I am persuaded that *concerns* introduce that simplification, and along with it that intensification which we need in opposition to the hurried, superficial tendencies of our age.

Thomas Kelly, 1941

240   The testimony of outward simplicity began as a protest against the extravagance and snobbery which marked English society in the 1600s. In whatever forms this protest is maintained today, it must still be seen as a testimony against involvement with things which tend to dilute our energies and scatter our thoughts, reducing us to lives of triviality and mediocrity.

Simplicity does not mean drabness or narrowness but is essentially positive, being the capacity for selectivity in one who holds attention on the goal. Thus simplicity is an appreciation of all that is helpful towards living as children of the Living God.

North Carolina Yearly Meeting (Conservative), 1983

Equality-Community

241   Dear Friends, With my love to you all, in God's holy peaceable Truth, and my desires are that you may all be kept careful of God's glory. Now in your settling of plantations and provinces, and especially in woody countries, you may have many trials and troubles, but if you keep in the wisdom of God, that will keep you both gentle, and kind, and easy to be entreated one of another, and that will preserve you out of heats, or extremes, or passions.

And I desire that you may be very kind and courteous to all in necessity, in the love of God; for there are many people [going] over to your countries, some poor and some rich; and so, many eyes are upon you. And therefore my desire is that you may all be careful in the love of God, and in his truth and righteousness, as the family of God, and be careful and tender to all your servants in all respects.

And dear Friends, I desire that you would send over an account by the next ship how many Meetings you have, and let us know how Truth spreads and prospers amongst you; which you would do well to write every year, to the Yearly Meeting at London.

                                                            George Fox, 1682

242   We know ourselves as individuals but only because we live in community. Love, trust, fellowship, selflessness are all mediated to us through our interdependence. Just as we could not live physically without each other, we cannot live spiritually in isolation. We are individually free but also communally bound. We cannot act without affecting others and others cannot act without affecting us. We know ourselves as we are reflected in the faces, action and attitudes of each other.

                                                            Janet Scott, 1980

243   How many…women or men have come to Quakerism for its historic and contemporary support of the equality of all persons is hard to judge. The Quaker stress on individual responsibility and individual faithfulness makes it a demanding religious path. Friends do not expect to become a mass movement in the foreseeable future.… [There is] a long parade of Quaker women who have acted on the basis of the Light, sure that more light will come. It is a strengthening and liberating belief. From Margaret Fell to Mary Fisher, Mary Dyer, Elizabeth Haddon, Susanna Morris, Charity Cook, Rebecca Jones, Angelina and Sara Grimke, Sarah Douglass, Abby Kelley Foster, Lucretia Mott, Elizabeth Comstock, Hannah Bean, Rhoda Coffin, Emma Malone, Susan B. Anthony, Ann Branson, Mary Meredith Hobbs, Sybil Jones, Hannah Whitall Smith, Alice Paul, Emily Green Balch, Kay Camp, Elise Boulding, Kara Cole, and Mary Ann Beall, the parade continues, bringing to each generation the same message, that in Christ there is neither male nor female, and in souls there is no sex.

                                                            Margaret Hope Bacon, 1986

244   Friends recognize that much of the misunderstanding, fear, and hatred in the world stems from the common tendency to see national, religious, and racial groups as blocks, forgetting the varied and precious individuals who compose them. Differences between individuals, and between groups, are to be prized as part of the variety of divine creation. Every person should be free to cultivate his individual characteristics and his sense of belonging to a racial or cultural group as long as by so doing he does no violence to any one in the human family. Only when differences are the basis for feelings of superiority do they become barriers of hate and fear.

Philadelphia Yearly Meeting, 1969

245   [A participant in a survey on the stewardship of wealth] saw a broader concern—the contrast between our pretensions to universal brother– and sisterhood and the embarrassing fact that we have signally failed to attract into membership the wealthy, the working class, ethnic minorities, and a lot of others. There is a sad irony in our continually reaching out to fellow human beings in other countries when we have so conspicuously failed to establish communion with so many of our neighbors. The critical question: do we really believe Jesus' eye–of–the–needle metaphor about the rich? If so, are we willing to accept its implications for Friends' institutions?

Kingdon Swayne, 1985

246   Love is a reciprocal relationship between independent personalities, each with rights and spheres of interest. So it is with groups—a proper loving relationship between groups must be based on their rights to co-exist and influence matters in their own spheres of interest. I do not see such group existence and group power as inconsistent with a loving relationship, but rather as the proper basis for such a relationship.

Our task then is not to oppose group differences or legitimate group power, i.e. power which does not place one group in a position of dominance or privilege with respect to another, but to welcome such diversity and reciprocity as the basis of creative dialogue in a spirit of love....

In order to be true to this goal, and to our own values as Quakers and Christians, we need to act in love, truth and responsibility, but also with frankness and radical strength of purpose.

A. Barrie Pittock, 1969

247   Looking at the historical expressions of gospel order raises provocative questions for the community of faith, particularly in regard to the nature of corporate commitment and the role of structure in faithful living. If, indeed, a living relationship with Christ is the basis of gospel order, what does it mean today to be a committed people in covenantal relationship with Christ? What does it mean to practice the mutual accountability that keeps this relation-

ship alive? Do our lives with each other in our meetings and homes reflect fidelity, love, and trust? Can we reclaim the socio-economic and political dimension of gospel order? Can we participate corporately in God's new order in a way that will allow our love to speak to a world dying from environmental destruction, violence, hatred, and entrenched systems of economic exploitation and injustice?

If the historical experience of Friends is applicable today, then corporate life needs pattern and structure to support faithful living. In turn, structures need care to prevent them from withering or becoming oppressive. Communities of commitment need to see what forms the patterns of faithfulness and the ministry of caring oversight will take today.

Sandra Cronk, 1991

248   The duty of the Society of Friends is to be the voice of the oppressed but [also] to be conscious that we ourselves are part of that oppression. Uncomfortable we stand with one foot in the kingdom of this world and with the other in the Eternal Kingdom. Seldom can we keep the inward and outward working of love in balance, let alone the consciousness of living both in time and in eternity, in timelessness. Let us not be beguiled into thinking that political action is all that is asked of us, nor that our personal relationship with God excuses us from actively confronting the evil in this world. The political and social struggles must be waged, but a person is more and needs more than politics, else we are in danger of gaining the whole world but losing our souls.

Eva I. Pinthus, 1987

249   Racism is one of the great evils of our times—as evil as war itself. It is at the root of strife in our city ghettos and of the guerilla warfare that has plagued Latin America and other parts of the world. John Woolman saw clearly that "The seeds of war have nourishment in the daily lives of men...."

The destructive nature of racism was made visible to the world when Hitler, acting on the theory of the inferiority of Jews and Eastern Europeans, invented Nazism—a system of segregation, exploitation, subjugation, and brutal physical atrocities which shocked the world. War resulted. Quaker pacifists rightly objected to our governments' participation in the war. But was our objection as firmly spoken to the underlying causes of the war?—to the glaring examples of racism as practiced in Nazi Germany; and to the insidious practices of racism in Asia, Africa, Latin America, the West Indies, and the United States—practices in which we all have shared. It was these pervasive practices of racism everywhere that lent support to the Master Race theory of the Nazis and Fascists, and that led to the most destructive war in the long history of violence.

Barrington Dunbar, 1969

250   Friends have always been especially sensitive to and questioning about the ways in which human beings relate to each other, in a continuing re-examination of their own inner and outer relationships. This consistent component of Quakerism has resulted in the equally consistent and insistent habit Friends have of looking upon and treating all human beings as persons, regardless of age, color, economic status, religion, occupation, or gender.

Mary Calderone, 1989

251   We are much concerned about the whole content of human relationship, about the meaning of "Thou shalt love thy neighbour as thyself" in the full range and depth of its implications. Loving does not merely mean doing good works; it goes further than feeding the hungry and clothing the naked. It means warmth and intimacy, open–heartedness and overwhelming generosity of hand and spirit. It means a desire to know and a courageous willingness to be known. Loving implies commitment to the other person, involvement in that person's life, whatever it may cost in suffering, whether that suffering comes through being repudiated or through identification and sharing.

The life of society desperately needs this warmth of giving and receiving. Everywhere we see sociability without commitment or intimacy, and especially in our towns, intense isolation and loneliness. We see human energy that should be creative and loving deflected into activities that are coldly power–seeking; we see love inhibited, frustrated, or denied, turning into its opposite—into ruthlessness and aggression.

Quaker Home Service, London Yearly Meeting, 1961

252   Care of the children of the meeting should be the responsibility of every Friend. Let us share with our children a sense of adventure, of wonder, and of trust and let them know that, in facing the mysteries of life, they are surrounded by love. Both parents and meetings need to guard against letting other commitments deprive children of the time and attention they need. Friends are advised to seek for children the full development of God's gifts, which is true education.

Revised Faith and Practice, New England Yearly Meeting, 1985

253   I hope the Society may be a community to which may turn: acknowledged Christians seeking an alternative to their present church; the searching humanist who comes to feel that there may be some power outside ourselves but who reacts violently against set forms and rigorous theology; the rationalist who begins to see that it is possible for a power to exist beyond the possibility of reasoning proof, but not in conflict with reason; someone from another culture who can respond to our approach....

David Hodgkin, 1971

254   It is a matter of grave anxiety that torture and secret imprisonment are being used by many governments, anti-government groups, and others to extract information, to suppress criticism, and to intimidate opposition, so that throughout the world countless numbers of men and women and children are suffering inhuman treatment. We believe in the worth of every individual as a child of God, and that no circumstances whatsoever can justify practices intended to break bodies, minds and spirits.

Both tortured and torturer are victims of the evil from which no human being is immune. Friends, however, believe that the life and power of God are greater than evil, and in that life and power declare their opposition to all torture. The Society calls on all its members, as well as those of all religious and other organisations, to create a force of public opinion which will oblige those responsible to dismantle everywhere the administrative apparatus which permits or encourages torture, and to observe effectively those international agreements under which its use is strictly forbidden.

Friends World Committee for Consultation, 1976

255   Our monthly and quarterly meetings were set up for reproving and looking into superfluous or disorderly walking, and such to be admonished and instructed in the truth, and not private persons to take upon them to make orders, and say this must be done and the other must not be done.... we must look at no colours, nor make anything that is changeable colours as the hills are, nor sell them, nor wear them: but we must all be in one dress and one colour.

This is a silly poor gospel! It is more fit for us to be covered with God's eternal Spirit, and clothed with his eternal Light, which leads us and guides us into righteousness, and to live righteously and justly and holily in this present evil world. This is the clothing that God puts upon us, and likes, and will bless.

Margaret Fell, 1700

256   The spirituality that is real to us finds its inner strength in the mystical experience of connectedness with each other and with the whole of creation. This is the deep, still, and vibrant centre that transcends time. From that dynamic place it is possible to turn outwards and work in one's own available and chosen action spaces to help make manifest the harmony that is already known.

Jillian Wychel and David James, 1991

257   Our life is love, and peace, and tenderness; and bearing one with another, and forgiving one another, and not laying accusations one against another; but praying one for another, and helping one another up with a tender hand.

Isaac Penington, 1667

258   Surely, one of the most moving days in my worship group was the day after we'd had a particularly Western-style argument that hadn't gotten us any place. After the argument the leader asked, "How would Friends like to structure this tomorrow? " In a touchingly quiet voice, a Kenyan woman said, "I would like an evangelical ...." The next day, we sang several hymns together, picking out unfamiliar tunes tentatively, hearing each other's voices, as we tried to blend ourselves into something that sounded like music. Then we took turns reading the Book of James in our different voices, different accents, and different languages.

As we read those remarkable and moving words, a magical thing happened that I hadn't experienced for many years. It had something to do with people reading the Bible together, the way those timeless words can take us outside ourselves and center us on what really counts. Somewhere along in there, we also began to hear each other in different ways, as we laid aside our opinions and really listened.

Melissa Kay Elliott, 1991

259   Are we too fearful of those with ideas different from our own? In one Meeting, the issue of whether or not to offer sanctuary to a refugee is a sword that divides people. Or our relationships may be severed due to differences in the way we interpret the Spirit guiding us or how we refer to God, whether in masculine or inclusive imagery. Quaker men and women who see military service as an integral and necessary part of American life are often branded as "strangers" in their Quaker community. Whether we define the Society of Friends in an inclusive or exclusive way will, in large measure, determine whether we grow, spiritually as well as numerically.

Nancy Alexander, 1987

260   Our language is often more revealing of our inner understandings than we realize. In recent years many Friends and Friends meetings have shifted terminology from "Social Order" to "Social Concerns"; Social Order committees have become Social Concerns committees, and Friends speak more of particular concerns than of a vision of divine social order. The former terminology speaks to Friends understanding that there is a Gospel Order, a Divine harmony intended for creation, in which human affairs can and should share.... Friends have lost the power of the vision of a social order which encompasses all of human society and which from its divine inspiration draws the power to transform all of society. This vision, and the inner transformation which enables one to see it and live in it, has the power needed to address the root causes of all our society's problems. In contrast the social concern approach does not carry with it a comprehensive concern; one is soon confronted with the need for a society-wide change in values that the visionless social concern approach cannot address.

Lloyd Lee Wilson, 1993

261   If we take seriously the nurture of our children in the worshiping group, we must start by re-appraising the whole life of the group. What kind of communication exists between us all? Do we know one another as people sharing joys and sorrows?

Do we have enough confidence in each other to know that our problems as well as our convictions and uncertainties can be shared with understanding? How is the child and the stranger received amongst us? Do we see our young people as individuals we want to know and care for and do we provide opportunities when they can get to know and care for us? Are they encouraged to feel that they have much to give us, that we value them and are the poorer without the insights and questioning they provide? Are we across all the ages a community learning together? Do we consciously look for experiences which can be shared by the whole community? Children and young people need their own peer groups but are encouragingly appreciative of the whole group sharing when they feel an integral part of it and can share in situations which deepen relationships and form lasting friendships. Part of that sharing is learning to know of our past as Quakers, our Christian roots, but even more necessary is the sharing of what we as Quakers believe today and how this should be shaping our lives both individually and corporately.

Peggy McGeoghegan, 1976

262   The roots of war can be taken away from all our lives, as they were long ago in Francis of Assisi and John Woolman. Day by day let us seek out and remove every seed of hatred and greed, of resentment and of grudging, in our own selves and in the social structure about us. Christ's way of freedom replaces slavish obedience by fellowship. Instead of an external compulsion He gives an inward authority. Instead of self-seeking, we must put sacrifice; instead of domination, co-operation. Fear and suspicion must give place to trust and the spirit of understanding. Thus shall we more and more become friends to all... and our lives will be filled with the joy which true friendship never fails to bring. Surely this is the way in which Christ calls us to overcome the barriers of race and class and thus to make of all humanity a society of friends.

All Friends Conference, London, Devonshire House, 1920

263   Our gracious Creator cares and provides for all his creatures. His tender mercies are over all his works; and, so far as his love influences our minds, so far we become interested in his workmanship and feel a desire to take hold of every opportunity to lessen the distresses of the afflicted and increase the happiness of the creation. Here we have a prospect of one common interest from which our own is inseparable, that to turn all the treasures we possess into the channel of universal love becomes the business of our lives.

John Woolman, 1763

264   In Friends' meetings also, from the fact that everyone is free to speak, one hears harmonies and correspondences between very various utterances such as are scarcely to be met elsewhere. It is sometimes as part-singing compared with unison. The free admission of the ministry of women, of course, greatly enriches this harmony. I have often wondered whether some of the motherly counsels I have listened to in our meeting would not reach some hearts that might be closed to the masculine preacher.

Caroline E. Stephen, 1890

265   I …was early convinced in my mind that true religion consisted in an inward life, wherein the heart doth love and reverence God the Creator and learn to exercise true justice and goodness, not only toward all men but also toward the brute creatures; that as the mind was moved on an inward principle to love God as an invisible, incomprehensible being, on the same principle it was moved to love him in all his manifestations in the visible world; that as by his breath the flame of life was kindled in all animal and sensitive creatures, to say we love God as unseen and at the same time exercise cruelty toward the least creature moving by his life, or by life derived from him, was a contradiction in itself.

John Woolman, c. 1765

266   Africa is full of discussions on democracy. We are telling our politicians that we do not want them to rule forever.… All of us say yes, we don't want this to happen. But look at our churches; look at our churches! The Kenyan situation: nobody wants to stop being chairman of some committee; nobody wants to give up being general secretary of one thing or another. We have become so preoccupied with power politics that we have lost the message of Quakerism as a community of believers who recognize we do not have bishops, we do not have popes, because we believe in the equal priesthood. If we who have been exposed to the Light cannot deal with each other peacefully, democratically, how do we expect those who have never been exposed to the Light to do it?

Miriam Were, 1992

267   Living out the immanent and transcendent aspects of spirituality as a Friend has never been a private matter. Quaker structures depend on the shared inward experiences of members as the basis for worship, the ordering of business, and social and humanitarian action. The Quaker way takes on faith the seemingly irrational proposition that the inspirations of individuals can lead a community to unity and spiritual power, not to chaos and dismemberment.

Ursula Jane O'Shea, 1993

268   As Quaker women become aware of the sexism in the society in which we live, and which they have for so long taken for granted as natural and normal, they are turning to their history to find out where they started and what

has gone wrong, and they are joining together and preparing themselves to take their rightful place as sisters in the new movement (feminism), contributing their own unique gifts of spiritual sensitivity to a movement that needs spiritual dimensions. They have caught the vision of the formation of a new society, once men and women alike escape the stereotyped roles of [gender]—a society where man need not prove his manhood by war and by acquisition, where he is free to be tender as women are free to be strong. They will be ready, perhaps soon, to join hands and walk cheerfully over the land, answering that of God in everyone.

Margaret Hope Bacon, 1974

269   We have been reminded vividly that women live under cultural, political, and economic oppression. All humanity is lessened by it; we are unwilling to tolerate its perpetuation, and must continue to work for justice and peace in the world....

We hope that we will act as leaven in our local meetings, churches, and yearly meetings, so that Quaker women everywhere will be encouraged by our new understanding. As we grow in solidarity with one another, enriched by how we express our faith, we will all be enabled to surmount the cultural, economic, and political barriers that prevent us from discerning and following the ways in which God leads us. We honour the lives of our Quaker foremothers as patterns which help us recognise our own leadings. Their commitment, dedication, and courage remain as worthy standards. May our lives be used as theirs were to give leadership to women everywhere to be vehicles of the love of God. We share a deep love for all creation, and cry with the pain of its desecration. We must realise we are a part of the natural world and examine our lives in order to change those attitudes which lead to domination and exploitation.

Epistle, First International Theological Conference of Quaker Women,
Woodbrooke, England, 1990

Integrity

270   One thing I understand now is that one's intellect alone won't pull one through, and that the greatest service it can perform is to open a window for that thing we call the divine spirit. If one trusts to it alone, it's like trusting to an artificial system of ventilation—correct in theory but musty in practice. How I wish it were as easy to throw everything open to the spirit of God as it is to fresh air.

Hilda Clark, 1908

271   Whichever sphere of activity we are involved in, we have to be responsive to the Spirit's leadings and try to put into practice our deepest beliefs, for our faith is a 24-hour-a-day, 7-day-a-week faith, which is not excluded from our workplace, wherever that may be. Everything in the end can be distilled to relationships—our relationships with each other and the earth. Our work must benefit our relationships rather than damage them, and we must ensure that neither the earth nor other people are exploited. Caring, not exploitation, is the key.

Jane Stokes, 1992

272   Friends are advised to consider our possessions as God's gifts, entrusted to us for responsible use. Let us free our time and our abilities to be able to follow the leadings of the Spirit. Let us cherish the beauty and variety of the world. Friends are urged to speak boldly against the destruction of the world's resources and the difficulties that destruction prepares for the future generations. Let us guard against waste and resist our extravagant consumption, which contributes to inequities and impoverishment of life in our own and other societies. Let us show a loving consideration for all God's creatures. Let kindness know no limits....

We are aware that there is no separation between caring for the land and caring for our fellow human beings, and the exploitation of the earth and the exploitation of human beings are part of the same sickness: a lack of connections among one another. Racism, sexism, pollution, drug abuse, causing the extinction of species, and war are all results of that disconnectedness.

Faith and Practice, New England Yearly Meeting, 1985

273   From time to time ... adherence to factual truth can give rise to profound dilemmas for Quaker Peace & Service workers if they are in possession of information which could be used to endanger people's lives or give rise to the abuse of fundamental human rights.... Some of us are clear that in certain difficult circumstances we may still uphold our testimony to truthfulness while at the same time declining to disclose confidences which we have properly accepted. Such withholding of the whole truth is not an option to be undertaken lightly as a convenient way out of a dilemma. We all accept that ultimately it is up to an individual's own conscience, held in the Light, to decide how to respond.

Quaker Peace and Service, London Yearly Meeting, 1992

274   A God we cannot be honest with is no God. If we bow the head and say, Thy will be done, when our heart is aflame with protest, we only increase our own pain. Better to rail, rail on God at the passing into night of this small sweet innocence than to assume unreal acceptance. And then, with small steps, treading the way of sorrows, we may gradually, or perhaps with blinding suddenness, look up from the dark road and see—see that He has been treading the Way with us, holding us when we faltered, giving us the strength to go hesitatingly forward.

Sheila Bovell, 1988

275   Where people love money and their hearts are ensnared with imaginary greatness, the disease frequently spreads from one to another, and children indulged in those wants which proceed from the this spirit, have often wants of the same kind in a much larger degree when they grow up to be men and women, and their parents are often entangled in contriving means to supply them with estates to live answerable to those expensive customs, which very early in life have taken hold of their minds.

In contriving to raise estates on these motives, how often are the minds of parents bewildered, perplexed, and drawn into ways and means to get money, which increase the difficulties of poor people who maintain their families by the labor of their hands?

A man may intend to lay up wealth for his children, but may not intend to oppress; yet in this fixed intention to increase his estate, the working of his designs may cause the bread of the needy to fail; and at the same time their hardships remain unnoticed by him.

John Woolman, 1772

276   Remember then--O my soul!-- the quietude of those in whom Christ governs, and in all thy proceedings feel after it.

Doth he condescend to bless thee with his presence? To move and influence to action? To dwell in thee and walk in thee? Remember then thy station as being sacred to God, accept of the strength freely offered thee, and take heed that no weakness in conforming to expensive, unwise, and hard–hearted customs, gendering to discord and strife, be given way to.

Does he claim my body as his temple and graciously grant that I may be sacred to him? Oh! that I may prize this favour and that my whole life may be conformable to this character!

Remember, O my soul, that the Prince of Peace is thy Lord; that he communicated his wisdom to his family, that they, living in perfect simplicity, may give no just cause of offence to any creature, but that they may walk as he walked.

John Woolman, 1764

277   I have never outgrown a sort of naive surprise and delight which I felt when I found out that there is one single thing that one can have without limit and not deprive anyone else—the love of God, His Presence.

Mildred Binns Young, 1961

278   All sorts of things "work" for us...as St. Paul declared. Not only does love "work", and faith and grace, but tribulation "works", and affliction, and the seemingly hostile forces which block and buffet and hamper us. Everything that drives us deeper, that draws us closer to the great resources of life, that puts vigor into our frame and character into our souls, is in the last resort a blessing to us, even though it seems on superficial examination to be the work of an "enemy"; and we shall be wise if we learn to love the "enemies" that give us the chance to overcome and to attain our true destiny. Perhaps the dualism of the universe is not quite as sharp as the old Persians thought. Perhaps too the love of God reaches further under than we sometimes suppose. Perhaps in fact all things "work together for good," and even the enemy forces are helping to achieve the ultimate good that shall be revealed "when God hath made the pile complete."

Rufus Jones, 1961

279   The catch is, we can't love God without loving our neighbor: whoever is next to us at this moment in time. We have to love, really love, with that same love we feel pouring into and loving us.

Some are easy to love. With some we feel at home. We run to them in joy. But we learn as we go that love is for each other one we encounter: those who are easy to love and those who are difficult. The love we feel loving us is as much for those who wound and betray us, and for those we perceive as "enemies", as it is for ourselves. This love is for the lost and the broken; the cantankerous, ugly, and lonely; yes, and even the brutal, the murderous, and cruel. If we are to love God we must love them as well, not for their cruelties, but for the hidden Seed that would live and grow in them. We, who are loved with a love that will not let us go, are to let that same love flow through us into the world.

Carol Reilley Urner, 1994

280   We have to be reminded that spirituality is not a separate compartment of life but life itself and...what is ordinary is the major part of our lives.... Ordinariness can be radical: it gets to the root of knowing God in everyday life.

Kathryn Damiano, 1996

281   I said to one of the Cuban Friends, "It must be hard to be a Christian in Cuba." He smiled, "Not as hard as it is in the United States," he said. Of course, I asked why he said that, and he went on, "You are tempted by three idols that do not tempt us. One is affluence, which we do not have. Another is power, which we also do not have. The third is technology, which again we do not have. Furthermore, when you join a church or a meeting, you gain in social acceptance and respectability. When we join, we lose those things, so we must be very clear about what we believe and what the commitment is that we are prepared to make."

Gordon M. Browne, Jr., 1989

282   There are few human activities in which perfection is possible; for in most things the human limitations of knowledge, time, energy, skill, and motive impede us; only in the arts do they work for us, so that we can truly say of certain works of music, poetry, painting, sculpture, and architecture that we can neither wish nor imagine them otherwise. When we find this degree of perfection and are able to respond to it, they become in sober truth a revelation of the divine in the sense that Jesus was: human yet complete.

John Ormerod Greenwood, 1978

283   God's revelations are more likely to be perceived and used to better advantage if the body has been trained for health, the hand for work, the mind for thought, and if the attention has been directed toward spiritual truth.

... When called to serve in public office, Friends should consider the public good rather than personal preference and convenience.

Philadelphia Yearly Meeting (Race Street), 1927

284   The love of money is apt to increase almost imperceptibly. That which was at first laboured after under pressure of necessary duty, may, without great watchfulness, steal upon the affections and gradually withdraw the heart from God. The danger depends not upon how much a man has, but upon how much his heart is set upon what he has, and upon accumulating more.

London Yearly Meeting, 1858

285   Friends, whatever ye are addicted to, the tempter will come in that thing; and when he can trouble you, then he gets advantage over you, and then you are gone. Stand still in that which is pure, after ye see yourselves; and then mercy comes in. After thou seest thy thoughts, and the temptations, do not think, but submit, and then power comes. Stand still in that which shows and discovers; and there doth strength immediately come. And stand still in the Light, and submit to it, and the other hushed and gone; and then content comes.

George Fox, 1652

286   We seem to be at a turning point in human history. We can choose life or watch the planet become uninhabitable for our species. Somehow, I believe that we will pass through this dark night of our planetary soul to a new period of harmony with the God that is to be found within each of us, and that S/He will inspire renewed confidence in people everywhere, empowering us all to cooperate to use our skills, our wisdom, our creativity, our love, our faith—even our doubts and fears—to make peace with the planet. Strengthened by this fragile faith, empowered by the Spirit within, I dare to hope.

Pat Saunders, 1987

287   As to our own planet which God has given us for a dwelling place, we must be mindful that it is given in stewardship. The power over nature that scientific knowledge has put into our hands, if used in lust or greed, fear or hatred, can bring us to utter destruction. Now as never before we have the choice of life and death. If we choose life we may now feed the hungry, clothe the naked, and heal the sick on a world scale, thus creating new conditions for spiritual advancement so often till now prevented by want. Many of our resources—of oil, of coal, and of uranium—are limited. If by condoning waste and luxury we over-spend the allowance God has given us, our children's children will be cheated of their inheritance....

Norfolk, Cambs., & Hunts Quarterly Meeting, London Yearly Meeting, 1957

288   ...that if any be called to serve the commonwealth in any public service, which is for the public wealth and good, that with cheerfulness it be undertaken, and in faithfulness discharged unto God.

Meeting of Elders, Balby, Yorkshire, England, 1656

289   To the present distracted and broken nation: We are not for names, nor men, nor titles of Government, nor are we for this party nor against the other . . . but we are for justice and mercy and truth and peace and true freedom, that these may be exalted in our nation, and that goodness, righteousness, meekness, temperance, peace, and unity with God and with one another, that these things may abound.

Edward Burrough, 1659

290   A good end cannot sanctify evil means; nor must we ever do evil, that good may come of it.... It is as great presumption to send our passions upon God's errands as it is to palliate them with God's name.... We are too ready to retaliate, rather than forgive, or gain by love and information. And yet we could hurt no man that we believe loves us. Let us then try what Love will do: for if men did once see we love them, we should soon find they would not harm us. Force may subdue, but Love gains: and he that forgives first, wins the laurel.

William Penn, 1693

291   Many yearly meetings hold very strong testimonies against any use of tobacco or alcohol. Within Britain Yearly Meeting some Friends advocate total abstinence from alcohol, others counsel moderation. Those who smoke tobacco, drink alcohol, or abuse other substances risk damage to their own health, and may hurt or endanger other people. Such use can deaden a person's sensitivity and response to others and to God. Consider whether you should avoid these products altogether, discourage their use in others, especially young people, and refrain from any share in their manufacture or sale. Maintain your own integrity and do not let social pressures influence your decisions.

Britain Yearly Meeting, 1994

292   We no longer need to dominate or take pride of place in respect
to any other creature. We can abandon the urge to rule at the office, at church, or
at home. We can treat everything God has made with gentleness and generosity,
rather than with grasping greed. In joyful dependence, we can grow to be as fully
human as possible, as thoroughly in the image of God as we are intended to be.
In reflecting the creativity and love of God, we can delight to sing and invent, to
work and to love. We can write poetry and tell stories, show mercy to one another and make one another laugh. Having given up the burden of usurping the
Creator's throne, we are now free to become who we are and to let our creature-
ly lives themselves, yielded gladly to God's will, shout praise to their Maker.
                                                   Howard R. Macy, 1988

293   Commonalities exist between addictive behaviours with these
substances and other compulsive actions such as in the areas of eating disorders,
gambling, overwork, and physical abuse. The causes go deep and may not be fully
understood; but the resulting pain, fear, desperation, and denial, damaging the
abuser and all around that person, need to be supportively recognized. A meeting
community should be ready to listen non-judgmentally, offer information about
sources of help, refuse to enable people to continue in harmful patterns, and continue to offer an environment free from addictive practices.
                       Faith and Practice, Baltimore Yearly Meeting, 1988

294   We feel that we should at this time declare once again our
unwavering opposition to capital punishment. The sanctity of human life is one
of the fundamentals of a Christian society and can in no circumstances be set
aside. Our concern, therefore, is for all victims of violence, not only the murder-
er but also those who suffer by his act.
    The sanctioning by the State of the taking of human life has a debasing effect
on the community, and tends to produce the very brutality which it seeks to
prevent. We realise that many are sincerely afraid of the consequences if the death
penalty is abolished, but we are convinced that their fears are unjustified.
                                             London Yearly Meeting, 1956

295   In the light of the resumption of executions in Pennsylvania
after a hiatus of thirty-three years, Philadelphia Yearly Meeting of the Religious
Society of Friends reaffirms its opposition to capital punishment, which has been
a deeply felt testimony of Friends since the establishment of our Religious Society
in the seventeenth century.
    We believe that the deliberate taking of human life by the state, under any
circumstances, is an absolute and irrevocable denial that there is that of God in
everyone.
    We urge all persons to press actively for the abolition of the death penalty
and to do so as a part of a broader effort to ensure equal justice for all.
              Philadelphia Yearly Meeting, Representative Meeting, 1995

296   We are faced at every hand with enticements to risk money in anticipation of disproportionate gain through gambling. Some governments employ gambling as a means of raising revenue, even presenting it as a civic virtue. The Religious Society of Friends continues to bear testimony against betting, gambling, lotteries, speculation, or any other endeavor to receive material gain without equivalent exchange, believing that we owe an honest return for what we receive.

Faith and Practice, Baltimore Yearly Meeting, 1988

297   Life is one. There is an invisible spiritual aspect and a visible material aspect of the same life. This life includes the whole world and all there is in it. Each aspect has its peculiar function: but the spiritual and the material are inextricably one. Each is to be known in and through the other. The material is infused with the spiritual. The spiritual is intrinsic to the material. In this scientific age we have tended to think that we could understand the world through the material aspect alone, but this one-sided approach to the real world may well prove disastrous. Many are alienated from the attempt to know the spiritual because to them it seems to be relegated to a world other than, separate from, the one in which we appear to live. Mysticism, the word used to describe the apprehension of the spiritual, is regarded by ordinary men and women as occult, abnormal, and unavailable even if they wanted it. But mysticism is the key to the whole. It is the recognition that there is a point of convergence of the material and spiritual qualities of man and the world.

Dan Wilson, 1951

STRUCTURES IN OUR YEARLY MEETING

It is earnestly recommended that, as Friends tend to the affairs of our Society, we bear in mind always that we are about God's work. We should endeavor humbly and reverently to conduct ourselves and our meetings in the wisdom and peaceable spirit of Jesus—with dignity, forbearance, honesty, and, above all, love.

-Source unknown

WHERE AND HOW DECISIONS ARE MADE

In the beginning, the Religious Society of Friends mistrusted church hierarchies, believing that the path to the Divine is inward for each individual and worshiping group. Friends have kept the power of decision in religious matters as close as possible to the primary worship group and the individual. The monthly meeting (see pp. 177-190), accordingly, has a freedom of action and responsibility in matters of membership not given to either the yearly meeting (see pp. 193-200) or to a regional gathering such as a quarterly or half-yearly meeting (see pp. 190-193). On the other hand, there are some matters on which a degree of uniformity among neighboring monthly meetings is essential to the good order of the Society. There are also a number of functions that are more efficiently accomplished centrally.

By virtue of membership in a monthly meeting, Friends also become members of a regional gathering and the yearly meeting. All members have the privilege and the responsibility to participate in decision-making within each body. Monthly meetings often designate certain members to attend sessions of their regional meetings, annual or called sessions of the yearly meeting, and Interim Meeting (see pp. 194-197), although all members are welcome and encouraged to attend.

Within its own area of responsibility, each body is autonomous. Friends do not attend regional meetings and yearly meeting as instructed delegates of their monthly meetings but join others in worship and decisions that respond to the moving of the Spirit in that time and place. Monthly meetings may adopt and forward minutes expressing unity on issues coming before a regional meeting, Interim Meeting, or yearly meeting, but such minutes do not limit the freedom of the body assembled to adopt alternate courses.

Monthly meetings, regional gatherings, and the yearly meeting share the common task of encouraging and sustaining members in their obedience to the Truth revealed in work and worship. Members' lives are made both harder and easier: harder, by the challenge to a higher level of commitment to a religious calling; easier, by the presence of a supportive structure within which that calling can be answered.

When presented with an urgent concern or proposal, whether by an individual under strong leading or by a group with a powerful sense of mission, bodies such as regional gatherings, yearly meeting, or Interim Meeting may be tempted to act precipitately. It is helpful in reaching a rightly ordered sense of the meeting to have in place a procedure for broad prior consideration in monthly meetings of such concerns or proposals.

REPORTING, OVERSIGHT, AND GUIDANCE

Monthly meetings, quarterly meetings, Interim Meeting, and the yearly meeting prepare and disseminate written annual reports. Many of these bodies also report informally to members through newsletters at more frequent intervals. There is also a strong tradition of oral reporting to monthly meetings of the deliberation of other bodies.

Monthly meetings send to quarterly meetings two separate forms of annual report: an overall "state of the Meeting" and a report of the committee on worship and ministry. Quarterly meetings report annually to yearly meeting on the same two subjects, drawing on the reports of monthly meetings.

Quarterly meetings should make provision for careful review of both annual reports of monthly meetings to identify situations in which it may be appropriate to offer oversight or guidance. The yearly meeting has a similar responsibility as it reviews annual reports from quarterly meetings.

The yearly meeting asks each year for two administrative reports:
• Membership statistics, provided by monthly meetings to both the quarterly and yearly meeting, for use in apportioning fair shares of yearly and quarterly meeting expenses, and for other purposes.
• Names of officers of quarterly and monthly meetings. The monthly meeting report goes to both the quarterly and yearly meetings.

The yearly meeting also notifies quarterly meeting clerks of publication deadlines for inclusion of their annual reports in the Yearbook.

This pattern of reporting, oversight, and guidance offers, but does not mandate, outside assistance to monthly and quarterly meetings. It is deliberately designed to affirm their autonomy. The only body in the structure that is specifically accountable to a parent is Interim Meeting, which reports on its actions annually to the yearly meeting in session.

Monthly Meetings

The monthly meeting is the fundamental spiritual community in the Religious Society of Friends. It is so called because its members meet monthly to conduct its business. It conducts meetings for worship weekly or more often, and is a caring community as responsive as it can be to the spiritual, social, educational, and material needs of its members. It may own and manage property, engage in significant social action, and operate schools or other institutions. It has sole authority to enroll or release members and to oversee marriages. It may undertake any action or assume any function consistent with the practices and principles of the Religious Society of Friends and not specifically the responsibility of some other body.

Governance, Officers, and Committees

Decisions are made by those gathered at regular monthly meetings for worship for business, or at special sessions called on reasonable notice by the clerk or by the committee of overseers. Such gatherings are meetings for fellowship and information sharing, as well as for worship and decision-making. Decision-making among Friends is discussed on pp. 21-26.

The entire range of a monthly meeting's activities—the conduct of worship, the care of members, religious education, the management of property, decisions on membership, issues of social action, oversight of institutions – should be given regular attention at monthly business meetings. While carrying out the day-to-day functions is often delegated to committees or designated officers, the monthly meeting remains the responsible body for all activities undertaken by its decision or on its behalf.

Each monthly meeting appoints a clerk (see p.187), a treasurer, and a recorder (see p.186), and usually a recording clerk. An assistant clerk may also be appointed, if needed. All other delegated functions are normally entrusted to committees rather than individuals.

Members are expected to serve on committees of the monthly meeting unless distance or disability is a significant hindrance. Acceptance of appointment is a commitment to be diligent, loving, and responsive in carrying out the committee's functions.

Committees serve the monthly meeting not only by carrying on routine delegated functions, but also by doing important background work in preparation for decisions at the monthly meeting for business. They examine designated matters in depth, identify the issues, gather the most useful information, and make seasoned recommendations for decision by the Meeting. When this work is done well, the monthly meeting in session is able to focus quickly on the matter at hand.

Monthly meetings should be clear about both what they expect of their officers and committees and what the limits are of their authority in performing those tasks. They should require full and timely reports. Such clarity and communication within an atmosphere of trust will liberate Meetings, officers, and committees to fulfill their respective tasks without wasteful duplication and frustration. Nevertheless, when good order requires, responsibilities and powers of decision delegated to an officer or a committee may be recalled and exercised by the Meeting.

The committees most commonly appointed by Meetings are mentioned under the function they perform for the monthly meeting.

The Individual and the Meeting

While the Religious Society of Friends accepts a variety of vocabularies for the expression of faith and encompasses a broad range of views on the way faith can be carried into action, there is a core of beliefs and standards of conduct which Friends hold in common. Monthly meetings, with the guidance of this Faith and Practice and supplementary sources have the on-going task of interpreting those beliefs and standards to prospective members, and may be called on to interpret them from time to time to experienced members as well. The individual should not hesitate to ask the Meeting for such interpretation.

A member under the weight of a spiritual or personal concern, or who feels a call to life-changing social action, may seek the assistance of the Meeting in testing this leading. The member may ask for individual counsel, or for a committee of clearness (see p. 29) chosen by the member or by the Meeting. Persons called to service on such a committee have a special concern to listen carefully, respond out of their own experience, and seek to promote individual and corporate faithfulness to spiritual leadings. Where no issue for Meeting decision arises, a committee of clearness will often have no need to report back to the monthly meeting.

Nurture of the Meeting Community

Members express their care for one another in many ways. They support one another's spiritual journeys. They participate in the intimate joys and sorrows of birth, marriage, death, and other rites of passage. Members facing important decisions receive counseling, as in the case of those contemplating marriage or those who are facing decisions about the military. At times of distress, the Meeting responds with the appropriate support, and, if needed, makes referrals to professional care-givers. A Meeting assumes responsibility for helping members resolve their differences. It responds to the special needs of the young and the elderly, and of new members, prospective members, and members at a distance.

All members share the duty and privilege of caring for one another. But except in small Meetings that act in all matters as a "committee of the whole," Friends have found it useful to identify specific duties and responsibilities and assign them to committees. A common practice is to assign pastoral care to a committee of overseers, care for the meeting for worship and members' spiritual development to a committee of worship and ministry, and oversight of programs for religious education to a religious education committee. The work of these committees is closely linked. Small Meetings often have a combined committee on ministry and oversight.

If separate committees are maintained, it is recommended that they meet together occasionally to assess the Meeting's programs of nurture, identify tasks undone or done poorly, and recognize those done well.

Monthly meetings should evaluate from time to time their effectiveness in nurturing members. If improvement is needed and continuing earnest attempts do not bring it, members may conclude that the Meeting either lacks sufficient numbers to do all that is necessary, or that its numbers have become so great that a sense of loving community is endangered. In either event, thought should be given to fundamental change, whether by merging with a neighboring Meeting or by dividing into two Meetings.

Meetings should view the division of the following duties described as illustrative, not prescriptive.

Committee on Worship and Ministry

(See also the section on Worship and the Meeting for Worship, pp. 17-21; queries on worship and ministry, p. 182-183)

The Committee on Worship and Ministry should be open to participation of members of all ages who are concerned for the spiritual life of the Meeting. It should include Friends in close fellowship with frequent speakers in meeting, ready when needed to help them keep sensitive to divine promptings. It should also include some Friends who are looked to as helpful counselors, to whom persons go for understanding and loving guidance. The vocations of ministry and of counseling are interwoven, and Meetings should encourage Friends to respond to a call to either service.

Giving Counsel   Those who are asked to give counsel should remember that often the best service is to be a good listener. When advice is given it should be offered in love and grounded in the Light.

Teaching by Example   Members of the committee teach by example as much as by precept and should therefore be chosen with consideration for the way in which Friends' testimonies are reflected in their lives. As they feel the call to be true to the essential testimonies of Friends, they help others to grow in loyalty to these testimonies. They encourage members and attenders to be ready and obedient should the leading come to enter into vocal ministry or prayer. They help members and attenders understand that all who attend the meeting for worship share responsibility for drawing the meeting together in expectant waiting and prayer.

Needs of the Young   The committee may need to take special pains to accommodate the needs of the young. Their interest in remaining Friends in later years may well be strengthened by the memory that as children they felt well prepared for meeting for worship and welcome there. Meetings fortunate enough to experience the murmurings of the very young, or the bustle of a group of children entering late or leaving early, should call themselves blessed.

Vocal Ministry and the Ministry of Stillness   Committee members should nurture the meeting for worship by giving appropriate attention to the quality of the vocal ministry and of the ministry of stillness that springs from centered silence. All Friends should be encouraged to give adequate time to study, meditation, prayer, and other ways of preparing themselves for worship. Sympathetic encouragement should be given to those who show promising spiritual gifts or who are timid or young in the ministry. Loving guidance may be needed by those whose ministry does not appear to come from deep centeredness in the Spirit. Some Friends may need to be counseled to avoid advance plans to speak on a specific topic in meeting for worship, thus closing themselves to the leading of the Spirit. Friends sometimes need to be counseled against self-centered activities that isolate them from the worship group. Both listeners and speakers may occasionally need guidance to assure that diversity of religious expression is enriching, not divisive.

Inappropriate Conduct   The committee should help the Meeting both to rise above occasional inappropriate conduct and to deal firmly with repeated behavior disruptive of corporate worship or business. The committee, not an individual, should make the decision to speak for the Meeting with a person whose vocal ministry is not acceptable. Committee members may praise or caution as individuals, but it should be clear that in doing so they are not speaking for the committee.

Interfaith Councils   The Committee on Worship and Ministry is often assigned the task of representing the Meeting on interfaith councils or ministeriums, and encouraging active involvement by the Meeting in ecumenical activities.

Recording of Ministers   Philadelphia Yearly Meeting no longer follows as a general practice the granting of formal recognition as "recorded ministers" to those with special gifts in the ministry. During the early years of this century the formal recording of ministers and elders was largely discontinued, first in London and then in Philadelphia, as a practice that had lost its usefulness. Nevertheless, some Meetings have continued its observance as a nurturing support to those individuals with unusual gifts in the ministry. Although Friends' practice of a free ministry is based upon the experience that the gifts of the Holy Spirit may be bestowed upon anyone at any time, a monthly meeting may, upon the advice of its Committee on Worship and Ministry, record as ministers those members who are recognized as having a clear leading to vocal ministry and prayer or counseling of individuals.

This recognition is not one of status or privilege and should be reviewed periodically. It is an affirmation based upon loving trust. The

Meeting's trust is that individuals so recorded will, in all humility, diligently nurture and exercise the gift of ministry in order that the Meeting as a whole may be nourished. The individual's trust is that the Meeting will on its part encourage and sustain them, and not only liberate them to undertake the disciplines of prayer and study and retreat that help clarify the springs of ministry but also lovingly and faithfully counsel them. Such nurture and encouragement and discipline are of special significance for younger members who, out of diffidence or unawareness, may discount their gifts and let them wither.

The gifts of the Spirit are diverse, and Friends' ministry includes pastoral care in settings such as hospitals and prisons. Friends' work in these areas may be especially benefited by the recording as ministers of those so gifted.

Reporting by Monthly Meeting Worship and Ministry Committees

The Committee on Worship and Ministry reports periodically to the monthly meeting for business. Also, in consultation with the monthly meeting, this committee submits a written report to the meeting on Worship and Ministry of PYM and to the quarterly meeting Committee on Worship and Ministry where such a group is active. In preparing these reports concerning the spiritual life of their meetings, monthly meeting committees on worship and ministry may be guided by the following queries that have been developed by the PYM Meeting on Worship and Ministry.

Concerning meeting for worship

•   In what ways does our meeting encourage members and attenders to prepare hearts and minds for meeting for worship?

•   How are we nurturing the sense that our meetings for worship are held in expectant waiting--joyfully patient to feel God's Spirit?

•   How are we helping Friends to find God's presence both in the silence and in the spoken ministry?

•   How are children and newcomers introduced and welcomed into meetings for worship?

•   What opportunities does our meeting provide for additional group worship to suppplement the main meeting for worship?

•   What problems do we perceive with our meetings for worship? How might we work to alleviate the problems we have identified?

Concerning ministry
• What evidence is there in our meetings for worship of vocal ministry that springs from obedience to the Living Spirit? How does our meeting nurture and support such ministry?
• If our meeting experiences inappropriate ministry, how do we address it?
• Have any of our members or attenders been called to a particular ministry within or beyond the meeting? If so , how has our meeting helped with discernment, encouragement, and support?
• Have any of our members or attenders suffered while trying to live their ministry? If so , what has our meeting done to help?

Concerning Spiritual Community
• How does our meeting nurture the spiritual lives of individual members and attenders, both adults and children?
• What evidence is there of God's presence in our meeting community?
• What are visitors to our meeting looking for in worship and in the spiritual life of the meeting? What causes visitors to stay or leave?
• What evidence is there in our meeting of lives transformed by the Spirit of God?

Committee of Overseers

A *Committee of Overseers* is appointed to assume leadership in maintaining a caring community, helping all members to find their right roles as nurturers of others. Its tasks may be shared with other committees.

Pastoral care and counseling are the special responsibility of the members of this committee. They should take a personal interest in the spiritual and physical welfare of each member of the Meeting. Membership on this committee calls for dedication, tact, and discretion. It should be entered into prayerfully, with an alert willingness to be of service. Overseers should meet together regularly and carry on their work in a spirit of consecration and love.

While the Meeting places special responsibilities and duties on this committee, others should also be conscious of their duty and privilege of caring for the members of the Meeting. In some cases pastoral care can be carried out to better advantage by Friends who are not on the Committee of Overseers. Also, especially in small meetings, the resources of the yearly meeting can be used where the action could not appropriately be performed by any Meeting member.

Responsibilities of overseers for the Meeting as a caring community include:
Care of the Meeting family Overseers should become acquainted with Meeting members, should visit them in their homes, if possible, and should maintain contact with all members and attenders in a spirit of affectionate interest.

Care of young people The members of this committee should be aware of and foster influences that develop the religious life of the children and young people of the Meeting, whether members or non-members, and should assist in giving them an understanding of the principles and practices of Friends. Overseers should seek to strengthen the work of the Committee on Religious Education or other committees seeking similar ends. Young people desire and need to have a creative part in the life of the Meeting; Friends should recognize the contributions that young people can make.

New members Overseers should pay special attention to new members, making them feel welcome, introducing them to other Friends, and offering them means of deepening their knowledge of Friends' beliefs. This special attention should continue for some months or years, if necessary.

Marriage Overseers see to it that the Meeting responds in good order to requests to be married under its care (See details under Marriage Procedure, pp. 47-54). Overseers should also take the lead in bringing into the fellowship of the Meeting the nonmember fiancé(e)s or spouses of members.

Divorce When a couple within the Meeting has decided to divorce, the overseers should first explore the possibility of reconciliation. If the effort fails, overseers should encourage an equitable, non-adversarial separation, and seek to maintain the Meeting's connections with both individuals.

Differences If differences arise among members of the monthly meeting, members of the Committee of Overseers should take steps to provide a framework for reconciliation, perhaps seeking help from other Meeting members, from the quarterly meeting, Interim Meeting, or conflict resolution services within the yearly meeting. If all such endeavors fail to bring disputing members together to work out a resolution, and a third party would be helpful in resolving the dispute, overseers should endeavor to persuade the parties to find a mediator rather than go to court.

Members in material need   Overseers, or a committee especially appointed for the purpose, should provide for those members in need of financial assistance. Meetings are advised to exercise tactful and watchful care in ascertaining and meeting those needs. Such care may involve aid in finding employment, in establishing eligibility for public income maintenance programs, in defraying the living expenses of individuals or of families, and in providing for the education of young people. Friends are urged to be open-hearted and liberal in providing funds for these purposes but are cautioned not to expose unnecessarily the names and conditions of the fellow members assisted.

Visiting in case of illness or other trouble   Visiting the sick and extending sympathy and assistance to families in time of serious illness, bereavement, or other trouble are important services.

Funeral and memorial meetings   Overseers assure that a memorial meeting or funeral is held upon the death of a member, and may offer to do so upon the death of a nonmember. (See Death & Bereavement and Memorial Meetings, pp. 58-59.)

Yearly meeting and other resources   Overseers should know when and where to seek professional help in care and counseling, whether from services of the yearly meeting or from community agencies.

Responsibilities of overseers for the Meeting as a body of members include:
Inquirers   The overseers should give information to persons interested in learning about the Religious Society of Friends. Attenders at meeting for worship should be given loving attention and invited to consider applying for membership when they become convinced of the principles of Friends. (See Membership, pp. 34-39.)

Application and transfer of membership: The Committee of Overseers should receive all letters of application for membership and all requests for transfer of membership to or from other Meetings within the Religious Society of Friends. Both new applications and transfers should receive careful consideration before being brought to the monthly meeting. (See details under Membership, pp. 39-40)

Membership list   This committee should keep an accurate list, with addresses and telephone numbers, of all members of the monthly meeting. This list should be compared annually with the recorder's list, before the Checklist for Monthly Meetings (p. 190) is answered. Endeavor should be made to keep in touch with all members. Letters should be written to those who are nonresident to give them news of the Meeting and its activities and to let them know that the Meeting is interested in their welfare. When appropriate, such members should be urged to consider the advantages of transferring membership to a Meeting closer to their residence. A list of non-members who attend with some regularity should also be kept.

Delinquencies or lack of interest   Members who neglect the obligations of membership should be cautioned by overseers in a loving spirit and with the hope of restoring their interest in the Meeting. If this proves unavailing, overseers should follow the guidance in the section on membership (pp. 41-43).

Religious Education
Religious education is a lifelong endeavor. It begins in the family, as parents take responsibility for the religious education of their children. Monthly meetings have a special responsibility to bring children under their care into full participation in the life of the Meeting and into an understanding of the beliefs and practices of Friends.

Meetings are expected to offer religious education programs for young and adult members and attenders, drawing on the many resources made available by the Religious Education Committee of yearly meeting, Friends General Conference, and others. A thriving First Day School has proven to be important to the life of many Meetings. Religious education programs can also include study groups, conferences, retreats, service projects, and libraries.

Outreach
By extending a welcome to people in the community and interpreting our faith to them, we practice a traditional form of Quaker ministry. In larger meetings, an Outreach Committee can assist the overseers in the care of seekers, attenders, and new members, helping to include them in the life of the Meeting and encouraging them to join in membership.

Peace and Social Justice
Meeting members may feel a responsibility to address a variety of issues in their community, state, nation, or world. Common ways of giving life to

these leadings include:

• Planning and carrying out service projects as corporate activities of the Meeting.

• Maintaining a committee to address peace and social justice issues. This committee may recommend particular action to individuals and to the Meeting itself as a corporate body.

• Encouraging members to participate in the work for social change of larger Quaker groups or other bodies, or to independently pursue leadings to social actions consistent with Friends' testimonies. Members who appear to be moved by a genuine prompting of the Spirit may be supported in leadings that not all share.

• Supporting a member or members in seeking assent to a particular expression of social concern by a quarterly meeting or yearly meeting (see pp. 65-67).

• Contributing services or money to help free a member to pursue a social concern as a 'released Friend'.

Property and Finance

Monthly meetings may hold and maintain real property; hold and maintain trust funds; solicit, maintain, and disburse operating funds for their own purposes; and raise funds for a quarterly meeting, yearly meeting, and other such bodies as they may decide to support. These tasks and responsibilities are entrusted to a treasurer, trustees, and, if needed, committees charged with such functions as property maintenance, graveyard management, fundraising, and investment management. The books of those holding funds are audited at least annually, usually by a committee of Meeting members. For guidance in property matters, including an expression of Quaker attitudes toward the exercise of economic power, see pp. 80-81.

Records

A recorder keeps records of births, adoptions, deaths, marriages, divorces, and changes in membership (see pp. 35-43). The recorder, or another person or committee specially designated, periodically publishes a directory of members and persons associated with the Meeting.

Care should be taken that minutes of monthly meetings for worship and business, when approved, are recorded on acid-free paper, appropriately bound, held in safekeeping, and, when no longer required for current reference, deposited in one of the Friends' historical libraries at Swarthmore and Haverford Colleges. Records of other meeting bodies may be treated similarly, if desired.

Guidance of Meeting Affairs

The Clerk as Manager

The clerk conducts business sessions (see pp. 24-28) and, with the assistance of a secretary or assistant clerk, sees to the management in good order of the affairs of the Meeting. The clerk carries out the instructions of the Meeting on all matters pertaining to the accomplishment of its business. In addition, the clerk is often in the best position to identify weaknesses or failings in the committee structure and to initiate corrective action. The annual reporting process (see pp. 188-190) is supervised by the clerk and provides an occasion for assessment and correction as needed.

The Nominating Committee

Monthly meeting officers and committee members are given substantial autonomy within their areas of responsibility, so their wise selection is essential to the Meeting's welfare. The Nominating Committee bears the important responsibility of discerning the gifts of members, recommending the right people for these and other services to the Meeting, and seeing to their replacement at appropriate intervals by others equally well qualified. To provide for a broad sharing of the nominating functions, Meetings are encouraged to specify short terms for Nominating Committee members, and to choose an ad hoc "naming" committee to nominate people to the Nominating Committee. At a minimum, a Nominating Committee can offer:

•   A procedure for the identification, recruitment, training, and rotation of clerks. The office of assistant clerk or recording clerk is often used as a training ground for clerks.

•   A roster of officer positions and standing committees of the Meeting, with job descriptions and numbers of members in each committee.

•   Where warranted, a plan for the staggering of terms and the regular rotation of members serving in various offices and committees.

•   A reporting procedure which permits the Meeting to weigh nominations thoughtfully before final action.

Volunteers and paid staff

Friends have been reluctant to deviate from the tradition of volunteerism that has marked the Society from its beginnings. Volunteers, as they work together for the Meeting, often find their religious lives mutually strengthened, their sense of community deepened, and their commitment as members affirmed. These dividends of volunteerism diminish when volunteers find themselves overcommitted. Some Meetings have found themselves strengthened spiritually when they have employed staff to perform a few essential functions, such as child care, general secretarial work, and maintenance of buildings and grounds.

Annual or Biennial Checklist for Monthly Meetings

Friends have found that the regular consideration of these inquiries is helpful for maintaining good order as the Meeting community fulfills its responsibilities.

STATE OF THE MEETING
• Is the Meeting in a reasonable state of health, its problems manageable with its own resources? If not, has it considered calling on the quarterly or yearly meeting for assistance?

COMMITTEES
• Do committees have clear responsibilities assigned by the Meeting? Are they functioning in ways that meet the needs of the Meeting, and do they report regularly to the Meeting?

ECONOMIC RESOURCES
• Are endowments and working capital invested in a socially responsible way? Does the Meeting employ the services of the Friends Fiduciary Corporation? Is the income of restricted endowments put to the uses specified or the concerns indicated by the donor?
• Is title to real property:
    1) held by the Meeting as a permanent corporate body, as recommended by the yearly meeting?
    2) held by the Friends Fiduciary Corporation? If so, is the Meeting aware of the potential inconveniences?
    3) held by trustees? If so, are the trustees all living and competent to serve?

- Are fire and liability insurance in good order?
- Is real property managed with care for nature's integrity? Are burial grounds simple in style and carefully maintained, with accurate records in the hands of a responsible committee?
- Are policies and practices for hiring and dismissal of employees consonant with Friends' belief? Do employees receive caring oversight and equitable compensation?
- Are patterns of spending and consumption socially and environmentally responsible?

FINANCE

- Does the monthly meeting have a long-term financial plan? Does it establish clear policies, through an annual budgetary process, for the raising, custody and spending of money?
- Are routine operating budgets financed by the living?
- Are the accounts of custodians of Meeting funds regularly audited, and reports made to the monthly meeting? Does the Meeting require bodies under its care to undergo regular audits and to send the auditors' reports to the Meeting?
- Have the Meeting's treasurer and Finance Committee observed all state and federal regulations governing the handling of their finances? Where there is doubt, has the yearly meeting or legal counsel been consulted?
- Is the burden for financial support spread equitably within the Meeting?
- Does the Meeting have a process for extending financial aid to members suffering as a result of a witness to Friends testimonies, or experiencing hard circumstances?
- What activities or programs strengthen the Meeting's ability to devote financial resources to good works?

RECORDS

- Are official membership records in the hands of a competent recorder? Are they reviewed at least annually by overseers?
- Are informal records of members and attenders kept in a computer data base or data bases, from which can be drawn useful information for building the Meeting community, such as newsletter mailing labels, lists of children by age group, and telephone numbers?

- If the Meeting is incorporated, are its records maintained and its corporate procedures conducted in accordance with good practice and legal requirements?
- Are minutes of the monthly meeting and of significant committees accurately and neatly kept on acid-free paper and retired from time to time to a designated depository?

Quarterly (Regional) Meetings

Regional gatherings of Friends were first advocated by George Fox in 1666 when he also established monthly meetings, realizing that the Society of Friends had thus far been held together mainly by the leadership of a few traveling ministers. Groups of neighboring monthly meetings within Philadelphia Yearly Meeting have likewise felt strengthened by joining to form quarterly or half-yearly meetings. These bodies traditionally have met two to four times a year as occasions for Friends to encourage and strengthen one another through worship, and to deal with matters of regional concern. Today the importance of some of these gatherings has diminished, and their benefits are felt to be better supplied by the yearly meeting. Others have found new roles that have given them new vigor. Members of each regional meeting decide how often they will gather for worship, business, and mutual support.

Such a regional meeting is composed of all the members of its constituent monthly meetings. It may be established upon the initiative of the yearly meeting; or when the yearly meeting approves a request from one or more monthly meetings; or when a regional meeting wishes to divide. In all cases the yearly meeting should appoint a committee to be present and assist in the organization. With the consent of their constituent monthly meetings, two or more regional meetings may merge. (See p. 203) Sessions of a quarterly meeting, thoughtfully planned, can provide religious fellowship, spiritual enrichment for Friends, and a forum for cooperation and exchange of information and ideas among the members of the constituent monthly meetings. Those gathered may develop plans to deal regionally with broader issues and special concerns and may also test concerns that a monthly meeting wishes to bring before the yearly meeting. Those named as monthly meeting representatives should be faithful in reporting to the members of their monthly meeting the proceedings of such gatherings.

Some quarterly meetings within Philadelphia Yearly Meeting have substantial institutions under their care, are custodians of property, employ paid staff, and have active programs in matters of ministry and worship, peace and social concerns, and youth. These activities are usually overseen by committees whose members are nominated by constituent monthly meetings.

Quarterly meetings maintain a structure of administrative officers and committees. These include at a minimum a clerk, a recording clerk, and, when financial matters are addressed, a treasurer. There may be committees to assist the clerks, to plan gatherings, to conduct routine business between sessions, to prepare the annual budget, and to provide sensitive oversight of staff.

• A nominating committee nominates the officers as well as the quarterly meeting's appointees to the yearly meeting Nominating Committee (see p. 199). It oversees the process by which the quarterly meeting committee members are nominated by monthly meetings; or, where appropriate, it makes the nominations. A quarterly meeting should give periodic attention to the structure of its on-going bodies to assure that they are appropriately representative and suited to its needs. (For the roles of the Clerk and Recording Clerk, see pp. 24-28).

• The treasurer receives, holds, invests, and disburses the quarterly meeting's funds in accordance with that meeting's instructions. The treasurer receives the covenants from its constituent monthly meetings to provide for the quarterly meeting's expenses and to be used toward developing the income budget of Philadelphia Yearly Meeting. Auditors, appointed annually, should audit the treasurer's books, submit a written report to the quarterly meeting, and guide the treasurer as needed in good accounting practices.

• A committee on worship and ministry can enrich the lives of the members of the quarterly meeting. It may also respond sensitively when a monthly meeting is in need of special nurture.

• A committee focussing on peace and social concerns can enable members of different monthly meetings to coordinate more effectively their public witness or service.

• A committee concerned principally with activities may provide programs such as retreats, service projects, and workshops for adults and youth. In addition to its own resources and help from the yearly meeting, with monthly meeting consent this committee may employ staff to assist in giving vitality to its regular meetings and to the ongoing social and religious life and activities—especially of the younger members of its constituent monthly meetings.

• A quarterly meeting which has a school, health facility, or other institution under its care should appoint to the governing body members with dependable commitment and proven qualifications. The quarterly meeting should entrust operating responsibility to those appointed and seek through legal means to limit the Meeting's liability for their actions. It has the obligation to offer encouragement and spiritual nurture to the governing body and to intervene if the viability of the institution is in question. It should maintain a regular reporting process from the institution to the quarterly meeting that will promote diligence in management, good stewardship, and regular attention to maintaining the Quaker character of the institution in all aspects of its policies and operation.

• A property committee or trustees can assume responsibility for property such as meetinghouses or burial grounds under the care of the quarterly meeting.

OVERSIGHT AND ASSISTANCE

Quarterly meetings may guide individual monthly meetings through transitional stages and on request provide assistance for specific need. When a monthly meeting faces difficult problems, needs encouragement, or wishes guidance in making decisions concerning membership, it may ask for the quarterly meeting's assistance; or the quarterly meeting may take the initiative in offering assistance. Interim Meeting may also be of assistance in such circumstances.

To assure such support, the quarterly meeting should establish its schedule of regular annual reports from each of its constituent monthly meetings as a means of constructive self-assessment. When a quarterly meeting for whatever reason cannot fulfill its functions of oversight or assistance, or is unable to receive and forward Meeting reports and funds, the condition should be reported to Interim Meeting for its advice and assistance.

Philadelphia Yearly Meeting

Philadelphia Yearly Meeting was founded in 1681 to provide assistance and oversight for the monthly meetings then established or in prospect in the middle Atlantic colonies. In its early years it was called the "General Yearly

Meeting for Friends of Pennsylvania, East and West Jersey and of the Adjacent Provinces." Its geographical boundaries today are more limited but no more precise. They are the unplanned result of a series of affiliation decisions by monthly meetings in the border areas. From 1827, when the yearly meeting split, to 1955, when the branches reunited, two yearly meetings functioned in the same general geographic area and each called itself Philadelphia Yearly Meeting.

Annual Sessions

All members of its constitutent monthly meetings are members of the Philadelphia Yearly Meeting of the Religious Society of Friends and should feel under the weight of duty to attend the annual sessions and participate in its deliberations and decisions. In meeting for worship for business and other forums, members come together in annual or special sessions for assessment of the life of the Society, the conduct of business, spiritual refreshment and commitment, and the renewal of the bonds of friendship.

Monthly meetings appoint two or more representatives, to assure both a large pool of wisdom and insight at each session and full and careful reports of these sessions to their home Meetings. Members of other yearly meetings and other interested persons are welcome to attend; but decisions should be made, under divine guidance, by the members present. Continuity of attendance is of great value.

The annual sessions may change in format or emphasis from year to year. They are occasions for sharing information and concerns from individual members, constituent meetings, yearly meeting committees, and other Friends' groups, or organizations in sympathy with Friends. Some messages are in the form of epistles from other yearly meetings, to which it is customary to reply with an epistle approved near the close of the sessions.

Information, insight, and concern are received in a worshipful spirit and often evoke deeply felt responses. The yearly meeting may be led to unite in an expression of concern or in a decision for specific action. Since such expressions or actions speak for the entire membership, responsible bodies should carefully review in advance any concerns or proposals for action which are to come before the annual or special session.

Annual sessions can also play a role in the chain of assessment and oversight through the reception of and response to the annual reports of the quarterly meetings and Interim Meeting.

An annual session may have before it many actions to consider or few, but each year one of the weightiest is the budget. Budgetary proposals are given wide circulation well in advance of the annual session, with ample opportunity for comment. The discussion of the budget is most useful when it explores the spiritual and testimonial implications of budgetary decisions and elicits and weighs ideas that will influence future budgets.

The yearly meeting in annual session appoints clerks for terms of one year. In addition to a presiding clerk, these may include alternate clerks and recording clerk(s). It also appoints a treasurer and assistant treasurer for terms of three years, as well as the holders of such other offices as it may create. It establishes, funds, oversees and lays down standing and ad hoc committees and working groups; and it appoints or provides for the appointment of their members.

The yearly meeting in annual session is supported by a committee to plan a proposed agenda and schedule, and by committees to make arrangements that will contribute to the care of those in attendance. During the sessions the clerk and alternate clerk are supported by a committee to assist the clerk chosen by the clerk.

The Yearly Meeting Between Sessions: Interim Meeting

History of Interim Meeting

In the year 1756 the Meeting for Sufferings was established in Philadelphia to represent Philadelphia Yearly Meeting between sessions and to carry out its work. It consisted originally of twelve Friends appointed at large by the yearly meeting and four Friends from each quarterly meeting. It was in every sense a Select Meeting. In the course of time the name was changed to Representative Meeting, and in the 1970s it was decided that attendance at the sessions would be open. In 1996 the name was changed to Interim Meeting.

Any significant change in the makeup and function of Interim Meeting is the sole responsibility of the yearly meeting in session.

Interim Meeting membership

The number, selection, and terms of service of members of Interim Meeting are from time to time reviewed and determined by the yearly meeting upon recommendation from Interim Meeting.

Participation in the sessions of Interim Meeting

Friends gather in worship at Interim Meeting just as they do at their quarterly or yearly meeting, not as instructed delegates but as individuals guided by the Spirit at that time and place. Interim Meeting is representative of the yearly meeting in annual session; it is not a gathering of representatives of constituent bodies. In any representative body members will, nevertheless, experience the tensions that are implicit among the dictates of individual conscience, the desires of the bodies that appointed them, and the best interests of the whole.

The designation of individuals as members encourages both continuity of attendance and seasoned judgment. Continuity of attendance is imperative for satisfactory communication between the Interim Meeting and monthly or quarterly meetings and their members. Information and understanding must constantly flow into and out of Interim Meeting so that policies and decisions may be made with widespread help and be widely understood and implemented when made.

Interim Meeting has adopted these queries to guide its members:

• As part of Interim Meeting in a worshiping community, am I faithful to the responsibility of seeking God's will in carrying out the business of our yearly meeting? Do our practices provide us with spiritual refreshment? In what ways do I contribute to this?

• Am I faithful in sharing the decisions reached by Interim Meeting with my monthly meeting, including all information appropriate to the understanding of those decisions? Do I share other reports and information about events?

• Do I participate in a way that helps the clerk accomplish the agenda of the meeting?

Am I careful not to speak too easily or too often, careful to discern whether my speaking is rightly ordered?

Am I careful to listen to the Spirit as it is reflected in the contributions of others as well as within myself?

If I am not in agreement with the discussion, do I strive to present alternatives in a way that both helps others understand my concerns and maintains the spirit of worship?

Do I assist the clerk by remaining focused on the agenda item under discussion? Do I hold the clerk in the Light, especially when there are tensions in the decision-making process?

Functions and responsibilities of Interim Meeting

Interim Meeting acts for the yearly meeting when the yearly meeting is not in session and ensures that the work and witness of yearly meeting are carried forward in the spirit of yearly meeting in session. It reports annually to that body.

The yearly meeting has delegated the following duties to Interim Meeting:

• Accepting responsibility for those concerns specifically referred by yearly meeting in session.

• Providing general oversight and coordination of the work of the committees of the yearly meeting and of other groups of Friends acting under leading with yearly meeting approval.

• Representing the yearly meeting and appearing in its behalf whenever the cause of truth, public welfare, or the interest and reputation of the Society of Friends may require.

• Providing for widespread consultation and discussion on matters of major import to the Society of Friends.

• Providing for the printing and distribution of literature that will extend the knowledge of Friends' faith and practice, and reviewing both communications and publications specifically issued in the name of the yearly meeting.

• Providing advice and assistance to monthly or quarterly meetings, upon their request, in the administration of property and trust funds, or in dealing with difficult situations.

• Providing advice and assistance for any persons suffering because of adherence to Friends' testimonies.

• Receiving and endorsing minutes of Friends traveling in the ministry or under other circumstances related to Friends' concerns.

• Establishing contact with other Quaker bodies and other religious organizations on matters of common concern.

• Designating the duties and responsibilities of the treasurer and assistant treasurer of the yearly meeting.

• Appointing the general secretary and associate secretaries of the yearly meeting, designating their duties and responsibilities; and providing for each oversight, support, and regular evaluation of performance.

Interim Meeting appoints, customarily for one year, its clerk and such officers as it finds necessary, and designates their duties and responsibilities. The clerk shall not be concurrently the clerk of yearly meeting.

Experience has shown that eight sessions a year are usually necessary to perform the duties of Interim Meeting. Its clerk may call special sessions as needed.

When need arises, Interim Meeting may ask the clerk of yearly meeting to call special sessions of the yearly meeting. When vacancies occur among the officers of the yearly meeting, Interim Meeting makes interim appointments.

Interim Meeting may not make any changes in **Faith and Practice**, issue any statement of faith, or act upon any matters specifically reserved for the yearly meeting. It should advise the yearly meeting when a revision of the text of **Faith and Practice** is indicated.

Any significant change in the makeup and function of Interim Meeting is the sole responsibility of the yearly meeting in session.

The Yearly Meeting Between Sessions: Committees of the Yearly Meeting

Philadelphia Yearly Meeting (PYM) is empowered to appoint, fund, oversee, and require regular reports from its five standing committees and these, in turn, have authority to create, oversee, and lay down services and projects in program areas assigned to them by PYM. This authority is subject to budgeting and program direction from Interim Meeting or PYM in session. In addition, each standing committee oversees representatives to those external organizations and granting groups which PYM has assigned to that specific committee.

The principal functions of the standing committees are as follows:

1.   Education – review, guide and support the religious and academic education of young people and those who serve them within PYM. This committee thus oversees such activities as curriculum development for First Day Schools, non-violence and children's projects, and also support for Friends Schools and for Friends in public education.

2.   General Services – provide oversight for the various elements of administration that enable PYM to pursue its ministry. These elements include finance, personnel and office services, coordination of granting groups, conference management, and property management.

3.   Peace and Concerns – select, enable and monitor projects that implement Friends testimonies both locally and in the wider world, in order thereby to help bring about a more just and peaceful world. Such

projects arise from the leadings of individual Friends who find support within their monthly meetings or from a group of Friends, including established working groups.

4.	Support and Outreach – provide essential services that will strengthen monthly meetings as fundamental units within PYM. Such services include the PYM library, publications, support for monthly meetings in their outreach efforts, and support for regional coordinators.

5.	Worship and Care - support and encourage members and meetings in enhancing their temporal and spiritual lives. The committee has oversight of various groups and projects dealing with spiritual enrichment and pastoral care such as aging concerns spiritual formations and adult religious education.

Worship and ministry are essential to the life of the Religious Society of Friends. In recognition of this fact, the Meeting on Worship and Ministry of Philadelphia Yearly Meeting is specifically charged with the responsibility of nurturing the quality of worship, ministry, and spiritual life throughout the yearly meeting. Annual sessions of Philadelphia Yearly Meeting have traditionally opened with consideration of matters laid before it by the Meeting on Worship and Ministry.

Prior to the restructuring of Philadelphia Yearly Meeting in 1998, this group was known as the Committee on Worship and Ministry, and was itself a standing committee. Under the new structure, the Meeting on Worship and Ministry continues to perform these functions under the aegis of the Worship and Care Standing Committee.

Members for the five standing committees are proposed by the Nominating Committee and approved by Interim Meeting or PYM in session. Determination of how members of a working group are selected is the responsibility of its standing committee. The standing committee may request the assistance of PYM's Nominating Committee or delegate the responsibility to the working group itself when that seems to be suitable. However, members of groups that make monetary grants must be selected by the standing committee and their names reported to Interim Meeting.

NOMINATING COMMITTEE

The Nominating Committee presents to the annual sessions nominations for the following yearly meeting positions:

Clerks of the yearly meeting, for terms of one year. These include alternate clerk(s) and recording clerks in addition to the presiding clerk.

Treasurer for a term of three years, but not serving more than 4 terms; and an assistant treasurer as needed.

Such other officers as the yearly meeting may direct.

The Nominating Committee presents either to the annual sessions or to Interim Meeting nominations of the following:

Persons to serve on the five yearly meeting standing committees, on the Financial Stewardship Committee, and on other bodies as directed by the yearly meeting.

Persons to represent the yearly meeting at other gatherings and organizations that are consonant with Friends' practices and beliefs.

The Nominating Committee also prepares a list of nominees to the Friends Fiduciary Corporation from which it appoints its members according to its by-laws.

FINANCIAL STEWARDSHIP COMMITTEE

The Financial Stewardship Committee is charged with preparing the PYM budget. The process of budget development includes gathering funding requests from the standing committees as well as the perceptions of monthly and quarterly meetings regarding the relative value of the various yearly meeting projects and services. The committee is made up of a representative from each of the standing committees and five to nine at-large members appointed by PYM through its nominating committee.

Friends Fiduciary Corporation

This corporation is a tax-exempt, church-related, legally separate, Pennsylvania non-profit corporation whose sole mission is to provide services for Friends meetings, schools and other Friends organizations. Its main service, acting as either agent or trustee, is to provide discretionary investment of the funds placed in its care. Friends Fiduciary also holds "bare" legal title of real estate, where necessary, on behalf of some unincorporated Meetings, schools and burial grounds.

The corporation appoints the members of its board from a list of nominees presented by the Nominating Committee of Philadelphia Yearly Meeting.

Meetings: Growth and Changes in Formal Relationships

WORSHIP GROUPS

When a group of people have been drawn to Friends worship and testimonies but find no organized Meeting nearby with whom to worship, they may form a Friends' worship group. The worship group can be as formal or as informal as is desired and can assume as little or as much structure as it feels is rightly ordered. It may not, however, present itself as an official body of the Religious Society of Friends or act in its name.

A facilitator or correspondent may help by maintaining contact among the worshipers, arranging for the time and place for worship sessions, and issuing whatever publicity the group may wish. Such leadership is especially helpful when a group draws its members from scattered communities, experiences a lull in its activities, or decides to broaden its activities and relationships.

Some Friends' worship groups fulfill their purposes by remaining in a temporary state, meeting seasonally or only briefly. Those that have achieved some permanence may choose whether to remain informal or to seek a formal relationship with the Society of Friends.

The latter choice requires individuals to decide whether to apply for membership in the Society of Friends or, for those already members, to apply for a transfer of membership. For the group, the issue, decided in consultation with the regional meeting within which they reside and with neighboring monthly meetings as appropriate, is whether to apply to the regional meeting for status as a preparative meeting or as a monthly meeting.

Status as a preparative meeting serves as an intermediate step between that of a worship group and an established monthly meeting. It also serves the needs of a group wishing to have membership in the Religious Society of Friends but not ready to assume the full responsibilities of a monthly meeting.

A preparative meeting is a Meeting under the care of a monthly meeting, reporting regularly to it, yet holding its own meetings for worship and having its own officers and meetings for business. Insofar as it wishes, it may have its own committees and financial structure and its own programs and activities, including the holding of memorial meetings or funerals. It may own property and trust funds. A preparative meeting may not admit members or conduct marriages under its care or in other ways act as an established monthly meeting.

When a monthly meeting, with quarterly meeting approval, accepts the request of a worship group for status as a preparative meeting of that monthly meeting, it enrolls as its members those individuals in the group who apply and are accepted. Thereby the monthly meeting affirms its role as nurturer of these additional members and of this new Meeting and appoints a committee of oversight composed of Friends experienced in worship and business after the manner of Friends. The monthly meeting should promptly inform the yearly meeting of this change in status and of the names of the members involved.

Given that there may well be experienced Friends and different but valid customs in the new preparative meeting, an established Meeting has much to learn as well as to offer when called upon to assist a worship group. A tender and sensitive spirit must prevail in this process and consultations should be grounded in worship.

Changes in Established Meetings

MONTHLY MEETINGS

When members of a worship group or of a preparative meeting wish to form a monthly meeting, they should first consult with the appropriate monthly meeting and the regional meeting. If it is evident that the group is fully aware of the responsibilities of an established monthly meeting (see pp. 177-190), a formal minute should be prepared and forwarded to the monthly meeting. If the monthly meeting approves this minute, it is forwarded to the regional meeting. When the regional meeting gives approval, it appoints a committee of oversight to assist in matters of membership and responsibilites for finance and property. The regional meeting should also inform the yearly meeting of such a change in status along with the names of the members involved.

A large established monthly meeting, in order better to meet members' needs, may wish to divide; or a Meeting, feeling itself to be too small to fulfill its various obligations of property, finance, and spiritual nurture, may wish to become a preparative meeting of another Meeting or to merge with it. The Meetings involved should minute their intentions and seek the approval of the regional meeting. If the proposal is approved, the yearly meeting should receive prompt notice of the change and of the names of the members involved.

QUARTERLY (REGIONAL) MEETINGS

For reasons such as convenience of attendance, a monthly meeting may request transfer of affiliation from one quarterly (or regional) meeting to another. The parties involved should consult carefully and, if the change is approved by all concerned, the matter should be reported to the yearly meeting or Interim Meeting for its approval.

Similar consultation and discernment should occur when one or more monthly meetings wish to form a new regional meeting; or when a large regional meeting feels it right to divide; or when smaller regional meetings wish to join into one. In such cases a committee from the yearly meeting or Interim Meeting should be party to the discussions and assist as needed. Final approval rests with the yearly meeting or Interim Meeting.

WHENEVER MEETINGS MERGE

When any merger of Meetings occurs, all property both real and fiscal of the bodies involved becomes the property of the newly established body. Meetings are cautioned to prepare proper minutes to take care of all legal matters involved in the merger.

If the members of a Meeting believe it desirable either to lay it down or to unite with another Meeting, they should make their request to the regional meeting to which they regularly report. If approval is granted, this regional meeting should appoint a committee to assist in making the necessary arrangements. In the case of the closing of a monthly meeting, this committee should arrange for the transfer of individual memberships to another Meeting. Notification of such action should be forwarded promptly to the yearly meeting.

In the case of the laying down of a preparative, monthly, or regional meeting, all rights and responsibilities of property vested in it and all responsibility for records shall be transferred to the larger meeting of which it has been a part.

Revising Faith and Practice

A regular review of **Faith and Practice** should be undertaken to keep our statements on faith and practice in step with changes both in understanding our call to obedience to the Light and in our procedures for such matters as marriage and membership.

Revisions should not be undertaken lightly nor under pressure from groups eager to press their special concerns. Major revision should be initiated only by action of the yearly meeting in session, usually upon recommendation of Interim Meeting. Such revision places heavy demands upon those individuals so entrusted, and careful consideration should be given to their selection, to the expected extent and process of the revision, and to the staff and financial support required.

Minor changes, especially in matters of procedure, may originate at any level. Such experiments are to be encouraged, but should be laid before Interim Meeting prior to consideration by the yearly meeting in session.

Any proposed revisions should be widely circulated and discussed prior to formal acceptance and publication by the yearly meeting. To assure full opportunity for responsible consideration by the membership, all changes in **Faith and Practice** laid before the yearly meeting in annual session for preliminary reading may not be finally accepted until a year later.

Friends have assessed the state of this religious society through the use of queries since the time of George Fox. Rooted in the history of Friends, the queries reflect the Quaker way of life, reminding Friends of the ideals we seek to attain. From the Christian tradition, Friends have taken as a standard the life and teaching of Jesus, not only as recorded in the New Testament, but even more importantly as revealed inwardly, as we seek God's truth and its expression through our lives today. Friends approach queries as a guide to self-examination, using them not as an outward set of rules, but as a framework within which we assess our convictions and examine, clarify, and consider prayerfully the direction of our lives and the life of the community.

Over the years, the content of the General Queries has changed, as each generation finds its own voice. The earliest General Queries of London Yearly Meeting asked for specific facts and figures: which Friends imprisoned for their testimonies had died, which present prisoners there were, and what sufferings. Even in the more abstract question, "How does Truth prosper among us?" there was an expectation of a quantifiable answer—in this case, the number of new Friends. Today, queries that are looking for specific factual answers are not included in the general queries. Rather, they are considered supplementary to the queries (see the checklist, pp. 188-190) and their focus is the 'right ordering' of the monthly meeting organization.

The language of the General Queries today is language that encourages the probing-in-depth of an issue or a concern. While changes in specific focus and language are inevitable over time, the queries have been marked by consistency of convictions and concerns within Friends testimonies— simplicity, peace, integrity, stewardship, equality and community—as well as by strength derived from worship, ministry, and social conscience.

Meetings consider the General Queries in a variety of ways. Some Meetings value the preparation of written answers; some use them as an aid to inward reflection; some make them part of the meeting for worship, some of the meeting for business. Friends may consider each in turn, or may consider several together that meet a current need. There may be times when a Meeting will reword a query or contemplate a new one to meet its particular situation. Friends will benefit from review of the full cycle of queries over a year or two. It has been common practice to use the responses to the queries addressed to Meetings as a basis for reports to the quarterly meeting. Whatever the approach, Friends' faithful attendance to the queries in openness to the Spirit enriches the life of the Meeting.

The following General Queries are arranged with a set for the Meeting and a set printed in italics for the individual. In addition, within the section of *Care for One Another* there is a set for the family to consider. While some Meetings read aloud and consider both the corporate and individual sets, others consider only the corporate sets, leaving the individual sets for personal reflection and response.

GENERAL QUERIES

1. Meeting for Worship
Are our meetings for worship held in stilled, expectant waiting upon God?

As we worship is there a living silence in which we are drawn together by the power of God in our midst?

Is the spirit of our worship together one that nurtures all worshipers?

How does our Meeting respond when the vocal ministry seems inappropriate, or when the meeting for worship is consistently not gathered?

Do I faithfully attend meeting with heart and mind prepared for worship, clear of any predetermination to speak or not to speak, and expecting that worship will be a source of strength and guidance?

Does worship deepen my relationship with God, increase my faithfulness, and refresh and renew my daily life, both inwardly and in my relationship with others?

Have I experienced in worship that direct leading to listen or to speak, and have I been faithful to my own experience?

2. Meeting for Business
Is our meeting for business held in the spirit of a meeting for worship in which we seek divine guidance?

Are we careful to keep in the spirit of worship each of the concerns that emerge, whether of nurture, of Spirit, of social concerns, of property, or of finance?

Are Meeting decisions directed by prayerful consideration of all aspects of an issue and are difficult problems considered carefully with patient search for truth, unhurried by the pressures of time?

How do we respond if we notice the meeting has lost an understanding of the presence of God?

Do we recognize that we speak through our inaction as well as our action?

Do I regularly attend meeting for business and in a spirit of love and unity? If unable to attend, how do I attend to my responsibility?

Do I consider prayerfully the many concerns that are lifted up on any issue, acknowledging that the search for truth in unity involves what God requires, being open to personal transformation as the community arrives at the sense of the meeting?

3. Spiritual Nurture, Ministry, and Religious Education

Does our Meeting encourage the ministry of both word and deed? How does our Meeting recognize, develop, and nurture the gifts of our members and attenders of all ages?

Does our Meeting prepare all its members and children for worship and for a way of life consistent with the principles of the Religious Society of Friends? How do we teach about Quaker practices in business and worship and their importance to the functioning of our Meeting community?

In what ways do we support each other in order to seek God's will and act upon our understanding of truth? Is there opportunity in our Meeting to share the excitement of religious discovery and the possiblity of religious transformation?

Does our Meeting provide opportunities for all in the Meeting to learn about:

-the Inner Light, the living Christ within, the Bible, the writings of Friends, our Christian heritage, other religious traditions and their respective roles in the history and formation of Friends' principles?

-the common testimonies Friends declare?

-the variety of expression Quaker faith takes today?

Do I maintain as part of my personal and family life those daily practices that focus on continued spiritual growth, with disciplined worship, inward retirement, and communion with the divine spirit?

Do I frequently read the Bible and other religious literature, including the records of the lives and experiences of Friends? Do I take the time to explore these resources with others, and likewise encourage my children?

Do I share my own faith and spiritual journey, and encourage such sharing within my family?

4. Care for the Meeting Community

Care for one another

Are love and unity maintained among us? When conflicts exist, are they faced with patience, forbearance, and openness to healing? Are avenues for exploring differences kept open? To what extent does our Meeting ignore differences in order to avoid possible conflicts?

Is the Meeting a safe, loving place? When we become aware of someone's need, do we offer assistance? Are the meetinghouse and the Meeting property physically accessible to all?

Do all adults and children in our Meeting receive our loving care and encouragement to share in the life of our Meeting, and to live as Friends? Do we truly welcome newcomers and include them in our Meeting community?

When a member's conduct or manner of living gives cause for concern, how does the Meeting respond?

How does our Meeting keep in touch with all its members?

Am I ready to offer assistance as part of my religious community serving its members? Am I equally willing to accept graciously the help of others?

Do I recognize and face disagreements and other situations that put me in conflict with others? Do I manifest a spirit ready to give or receive forgiveness?

Do I treat adults and children alike with respect and without conde-scension? Is my manner with visitors and attenders to my Meeting one of welcome?

Care in my home
(This set of personal queries may be helpful for the family to consider within the family setting. Families may also wish to explore other General Queries as part of regular family worship.)

Is my home a place where all members of the family receive affection and understanding, and where visitors are welcome? Do I choose recreation and a manner of living that enriches the body, mind, and spirit; and shows a high regard for family, community, and creation?

Is our family prepared to discuss such sensitive topics as death, faith, money, even sex and drugs, in a manner that allows openness and honesty, and also direction?

How do I help to arrange life at home so that there is an opportunity for all to learn and absorb by example what it means to live a life of Spirit-led commitment?

5. Education
What is our Meeting's role in the life and support of Friends' education? If supporting or maintaining a Friends school, have we developed an appropriate relationship of Meeting and school? What is our role in the spiritual life of the school and its maintenance of Friends' principles?

What does our Meeting do to support education in the wider community?

What help do we provide for the children and adults in our Meeting to pursue the education they seek, whether academic, technical, or voca-tional? Do we make provision for children in our Meeting to attend a Friends school?

How do I show my concern for the improvement of public education in my community and in the world?

Am I aware of what Friends schools are doing and of their plans for the future? How do I show encouragement and support?

6. Equality

How does our Meeting help to create and maintain a society whose institutions recognize and do away with the inequities rooted in patterns of prejudice and economic convenience?

Is our Meeting open to all regardless of race, ability, sexual orientation, or class?

What steps are we taking as a Meeting to assure that our Meeting and the committees and institutions under our care reflect our respect for all and are free from practices rooted in prejudice?

Do I examine myself for aspects of prejudice that may be buried, including beliefs that seem to justify biases based on race, gender, sexual orientation, disability, class, and feelings of inferiority or superiority?

What am I doing to help overcome the contemporary effects of past and present oppression?

Am I teaching my children, and do I show through my way of living, that love of God includes affirming the equality of people, treating others with dignity and respect, and seeking to recognize and address that of God within every person?

7. Social Responsibility and Witness

How does our Meeting work:

-to overcome social, legal, economic, and political injustices, locally and in the wider world?

-for the funding of community services that does not rely on gaming income?

Does our Meeting serve the community through action on concerns for civic improvement? What actions are we taking to assure everyone equal access to education, health care, legal services, housing, and employment as well as equal opportunities in business and in the professions?

When a member has lifted up a concern, how does our Meeting respond?

Does our Meeting encourage those seeking clearness for their convictions of conscience to hold up such convictions with prayerful openness to the Light?

Am I mindful of how my lifestyle and my investments can contribute to the improvement of the human condition, or to the exploitation of others?

Am I open to seeking clearness on matters of conscience and to assisting others in doing so? How do I respond and support one who acts out of a clear leading when I am under the weight of another?

What am I doing to work for the betterment of my community to assure the maintenance of effective public services which do not rely on funding from gaming?

Do I fulfill my civic responsibilities when they do not conflict with divine leadings?

8. Peace

How does our Meeting act to advance peace, to oppose violence, and to support the constructive use of authority in our community, our nation, and the world?

What are we doing as a Meeting:

— to free our nation from militarization, so evident in our society and in its economy?

— to understand the causes of war and violence and to work for the development of the attitudes and institutions of peace?

— to recognize and correct the causes of violence within our communities, and to work toward overcoming separations and restoring wholeness?

— to increase the understanding and use of nonviolent approaches for the resolution of conflicts?

Do I live in the power of that Life and Spirit that takes away the occasion of all wars?

How do I maintain Friends' testimony that military training and all participation in war and its preparation are inconsistent with the teaching and the spirit of Christ?

Do I work for the establishment of alternative ways of settling disputes? Am I aware that to build a world community requires that we all face our differences honestly, openly, and in trust?

Do I treat conflict as an opportunity for growth, and address it with careful attention? Do I seek to recognize and respect the Divine in those with whom I have a basic disagreement? Do I look for ways to reaffirm in action and attitude my love for the one with whom I am in conflict?

9. Ministry of Outreach

Outreach

What are we doing as a Meeting to communicate our presence and our principles to the community around us? Does our Meeting's ministry of outreach lead Friends to share their spiritual experiences with others?

What are we doing to invite persons not in membership to attend our meetings for worship and to encourage their continued attendance? How does the Meeting welcome visitors? Are we sensitive to the needs and hesitations of each visitor?

Are we tender to the needs of isolated Friends and Meetings, and to nearby Meetings seeking support?

How do I ground myself in the understandings of my faith? Am I clear about my beliefs? How do I prepare myself to share my faith and beliefs with others?

Does my manner of life as a Friend attract others to our religious society?

Do I seize opportunities to tell others about the Religious Society of Friends and invite them to worship with us?

Is my manner with visitors and attenders to our Meeting one of welcome?

Collaboration

In what ways does our Meeting respond to opportunities to join with other faiths in worship, in social action, and in spiritual dialogue?

How does our Meeting encourage its members to seek opportunities to meet and work with Friends world wide?

What opportunities have I taken to know people from different religious and cultural backgrounds, to worship with them, and to work with them on common concerns?

What opportunities have I taken to know, to work, and to worship with Friends outside of my own Meeting?

10. Stewardship of the Environment

Is the Meeting concerned that human interaction with nature be responsible, guided by a reverence for life and a sense of the splendor of God's continuing creation?

Are the decisions of the Meeting and its committees relating to the uses of property, goods, services, and energy made with sensitivity toward the environmental impact of those choices?

How does our Meeting learn about environmental concerns and then act in the community on its concerns?

How am I helping to develop a social, economic, and political system which will nurture an environment which sustains and enriches life for all?

Am I aware of the place of water, air, and soil in my life? Do I consider with care the necessity of purchasing substances hazardous to the environment? Do I act as a faithful steward of the environment in the use and disposal of such hazardous substances?

Do I choose with care the use of technology and devices that truly simplify and add quality to my life without adding an undue burden to essential resources?

11. Stewardship of Resources

Does our Meeting serve social and economic justice in its uses of property and money?

How does our Meeting engage its members in the support of the Meeting's work, its ministry, and the upkeep of its property?

How does our Meeting engage its members in the support of the quarterly and yearly meetings and other Quaker organizations?

To what extent does our Meeting rely on current members for financial support, and what role does endowment income serve? Does the Meeting consider carefully the appropriate role of invested funds?

Am I clear that I am the steward, not the owner, of property in my care?

Do I simplify my needs, making choices that balance self-sufficiency (to avoid unnecessary dependence on others) and fair sharing of resources? Do I make choices as a consumer that support the equitable distribution of income?

Do my employment and other activities allow for use of time and energy in spiritual growth and in service to the Religious Society of Friends?

Do I contribute generously within my means to the funding of the work of Friends in my Meeting, in the yearly meeting, and in the wider world of Friends?

12. Integrity and Simplicity

What does our Meeting understand to be the meaning and implication of our testimonies on simplicity and integrity?

How do our Meeting's actions demonstrate this understanding?

As a Meeting, what are we doing to encourage members to embody integrity and simplicity in their everyday lives?

How do I strive to maintain the integrity of my inner and outer lives— in my spiritual journey, my work, and my family responsibilities? How do I manage my commitments so that overcommitment, worry, and stress do not diminish my integrity?

Am I temperate in all things? Am I open to counsel and advice on overindulgence and addictive behavior, such as gambling? Do I take seriously the hazards associated with addictive and mood-altering substances?

Am I careful to speak truth as I know it and am I open to truth spoken to me? Am I mindful that judicial oaths imply a double standard of truth?

Do I refrain from membership in organizations whose purposes and methods compromise our testimonies?

Note: Some of the terms that follow are in common usage, but Friends have given them a particular meaning. Others are essentially limited to Quaker usage.

Advices: Extracts from minutes and epistles of early Friends intended to supply guidance, caution and counsel to monthly meetings and their members on various aspects of daily life. The collection of such extracts prepared for the previous edition of Faith and Practice is included at the beginning of the Section of Extracts. The word Advices is also sometimes used to encompass the whole of a Friends book of discipline (*See also* Preface).

Affirmation: A legal declaration provided for Friends and others who conscientiously refuse to take (or swear) judicial oaths.

Allowed or Indulged Meeting: A worship group of Friends under the care of an organized body of Friends, usually at quarterly or monthly meeting level, but less formally organized than a preparative meeting. This term has been applied to Friends from various monthly meetings who gather at a common vacation site during the summer, or to the occasional use of an historic Friends meetinghouse.

Birthright Friend: In early practice, an individual whose parents were both members of a Friends Meeting was automatically registered at birth as a member of that Meeting. Such automatic registration has generally been replaced by a system which requires a definite decision on the part of the parent or parents regarding the membership status of a newborn child.

Book of Discipline: A book describing a yearly meeting's history, structures, and procedures, including advices, queries, and often quotations, or extracts, from the experience of Friends. Faith and Practice is a Book of Discipline. The word discipline comes from the root word *disciple.*

Breaking Meeting: The act of bringing a meeting for worship to a close by shaking hands. Usually, an individual has been designated to initiate this process.

Called Session: A meeting of the monthly, quarterly, or yearly meeting specially called by its clerk to address some concern or item of business. In a called meeting for business, decisions are recorded as in a regular meeting for business.

Centering/Centering Down: The initial stage of worship when Friends clear their minds and settle down to achieve a spiritual focus.

Clearness: Confidence that an action is consistent with the divine will.

Clerk: The person responsible for the administration of a Friends body and sensitive to the guidance of the Spirit in the conduct of the business of that body. This includes preparation, leadership, and follow up of meetings for business.

Concern: A quickening sense of the need to do something about a situation or issue in response to what is felt to be a direct intimation of God's will.

Conscientious Objection: A principled refusal to participate in certain social or political practices; commonly applied to the refusal to undertake military service or pay war taxes.

Conservative Friends: Three unaffiliated yearly meetings – Iowa, North Carolina and Ohio – call themselves Conservative. Historically, they share John Wilbur's objections to the pastoral system; at the same time they are more explicitly Christ-centered than most meetings in Friends General Conference.

Continuing Revelation: A central Quaker belief that the revelation of God's will is an ongoing process.

Convinced Friend: A person who, after deciding that the Religious Society of Friends provides the most promising home for spiritual enlightenment and growth, becomes a member of a monthly meeting. Traditionally distinguished from a birthright Friend.

Elder: The verb *to elder* is used for the exercise of spiritual leadership either to support and encourage members or attenders in their ministry or to question or discourage an individual whose behavior is deemed inappropriate. The noun *elder* is occasionally used to designate individuals recognized as having significant spiritual gifts and expected to exercise special oversight of the spiritual life of the meeting and its members. In the past such individuals were specifically recorded by a monthly meeting, and their names were then reported to the quarterly meeting, and yearly meeting; this practice was discontinued in Philadelphia Yearly Meeting by 1962.

Epistle: A public letter of greeting and ministry. Such letters are sent from a Friends meeting or organization to other Friends groups, to supply information, spiritual insight, and encouragement.

Evangelical Friends International, North American Region (EFI NAR): Six yearly meetings in the United States constitute this group. Through their deep concern for mission, they have parented groups of Friends in Latin America, Africa, and India; many have now become independent yearly meetings. Their worship is programmed and their theology is evangelical, with a strong scriptural base. Like other Friends, they hold testimonies of peace, simplicity, and equality.

Experiential Religion: A religion in which personal spiritual experience is the foundation for belief and practice. The word experimental was used by early Friends with this meaning.

Facing Benches: In older Friends meetinghouses, rising tiers of benches facing the meeting, traditionally occupied by recognized ministers and elders. Metaphorically, the group of leaders occupying those benches.

First Day School: Friends' designation for the Sunday religious education program provided by a monthly meeting for children and adults.

Friends General Conference (FGC): An association of yearly meetings and other bodies of Friends in North America. Its purpose is to nurture their members by developing and providing resources and opportunities for spiritual growth. Those meetings belonging to FGC tend to be liberal in theology and to have an unprogrammed form of worship.

Friends United Meeting (FUM): A confederation of yearly meetings whose pattern of worship is largely programmed and led by pastors. While FUM Friends make a corporate faith commitment to the ministry of Jesus Christ, their social testimonies are similar to FGC. FUM has member Meetings in Cuba, Jamaica, and East Africa, as well as North America. Some of its Meetings also belong to FGC.

Gathered Meeting: A meeting for worship or for business in which those present feel deeply united in the divine presence.

Good Order: Those procedures for the conduct of Friends business and witness that encourage a meeting to carry out its corporate activities under divine leading. The term rightly ordered is also used in this sense.

Gospel Order: A term used by George Fox and others to describe the new covenant order of the church under the headship of Christ. It concerns how we live faithfully in relationship with God and with each other. This term is coming into renewed use among Friends.

Hold in the Light: To desire that divine guidance and healing will be present to an individual who is in distress or faces a difficult situation; also, to give prayerful consideration to an idea.

Inner Light/Inward Light/The Light Within: Terms which represent for Friends the direct, unmediated experience of the Divine. Some other equivalent terms often found in Quaker writings are: the Spirit, the Spirit of Truth, the Divine Principle, the Seed, the Guide, the Christ Within, the Inward Teacher, that of God in every person.

Integrity: One of the basic practical principles or testimonies of Friends. It involves both a wholeness and harmony of the various aspects of one's life, and truthfulness in whatever one says and does. Friends commonly link this principle with the testimony of simplicity.

Interim Meeting: In Philadelphia Yearly Meeting, a broadly representative body meeting to conduct the business of the yearly meeting between its annual sessions. (Formerly called Representative Meeting.)

Laying Down: A decision to discontinue a committee when its work is complete; occasionally, a decision to discontinue a Meeting or other Friends organization when it is no longer viable.

Laying Over: To postpone the discussion of an issue or the presentation of a report from one meeting for business to another.

Leading: A sense of being called by God to undertake a specific course of action. A leading often arises from a concern.

Lift Up: To emphasize or make explicit a particular point or concern.

Meeting for Worship: A gathering of individuals in quiet waiting upon the enlightening and empowering presence of the Divine; the central focus of the corporate life of the Religious Society of Friends.

Meeting for Worship for Business: A meeting for worship during which the corporate business of the meeting is conducted – often referred to as meeting for business.

Mind the Light: An admonition to attend to the Light Within for guidance in one's life. It means both active obedience to divine leadings and careful nurturing of one's openness to the Light.

Ministry: Sharing or acting upon one's gifts, whether in service to individuals, to the meeting, or to the larger community. [*See also* Vocal ministry]

Minute: The record of a corporate decision reached during a meeting for worship for business. More broadly, the account of a single transaction in the written record of a meeting for business or other body.

Minute of Exercise: An expression of a clerk's insights and concerns at the close of a meeting for business. Historically, a closing summary of vocal ministry and spiritual concerns expressed during yearly meeting sessions.

Monthly Meeting: 1] A congregation of Friends who meet regularly for worship and to conduct corporate business. 2] A monthly gathering of such a body for worship and business.

Opening: A term often used by early Friends to designate a spiritual opportunity or leading.

Overseers: Those members who are appointed by the Meeting to give pastoral care and nurture to all members and attenders.

Pacifist: A person who renounces war and any use of violence and seeks to resolve conflicts peacefully.

Passing Meeting: Acceptance by a monthly meeting of a written request, usually for membership or for marriage under its care.

Pastoral Meeting: See Programmed Meeting.

Peace Testimony: The corporate commitment of Friends to pacifism and nonviolence.

Plain Dress/Plain Speech: The witness of early Friends to the testimonies of equality and integrity by dressing and speaking simply. These served into the 20th century as outward symbols and reminders of our distinctive beliefs.

Preparative Meeting: An organized group of members of an established monthly meeting which ordinarily gathers for worship at another place.

Proceed As Way Opens: To undertake a service or course of action without prior clarity about all the details but with confidence that divine guidance will make these apparent and assure an appropriate outcome.

Programmed Meeting: A Friends meeting under the leadership of a pastor, with an arranged order of worship that usually includes a period of silent worship. [*See also* Unprogrammed Meeting].

Quaker: Originally, a derogatory term applied to Friends because their excitement of spirit when led to speak in a meeting for worship was sometimes expressed in a shaking or quaking motion. Now this term is simply an alternative designation for a member of the Religious Society of Friends.

Quarterly Meeting: A regional gathering of members of constituent monthly meetings, traditionally on four occasions each year. Some quarterly meetings also oversee the operations of institutions.

Queries: A set of questions, based on Friends' practices and testimoniees, which are considered by Meetings and individuals as a way of both guiding and examining individual and corporate lives and actions. As such, they are a means of self examination. Queries to be considered regularly are included in Faith and Practice; others may be formulated by a committee or Meeting that seeks to clarify for itself an issue it needs to address.

Recorder: The person appointed by a Meeting to maintain statistics of the members and attenders of that Meeting.

Recording Clerk: The person appointed to take minutes at regular and called meetings for business of a Meeting or other Friends body.

Released Friend: A Friend whose leading to carry out a particular course of action has met with approval from a Meeting which then promises to provide such support as would enable the Friend to follow that leading.

Sense of the Meeting: An expression of the unity of a meeting for worship for business on some issue or concern; the general recognition, articulated by the clerk or some other person, that a given decision is in accordance with the divine will.

Simplicity: One of the traditional Quaker testimonies that is closely associated with integrity, equality, and stewardship. Essentially, to limit the material circumstances of one's life in a way that allows/enables one to follow divine leadings.

Sojourning Friend: A member of a monthly meeting who may temporarily reside at some distance from that Meeting, but close to another monthly meeting, and upon formal request is accepted by the latter as an active member without financial obligations.

Speaking to My/One's Condition: The conviction that a message, whether directly from God or through the words or actions of another, meets one's own deepest needs and purposes.

Standing Aside: An action taken by an individual who has genuine reservations about a particular decision, but who also recognizes that the decision is clearly supported by the weight of the Meeting. The action of standing aside allows the Meeting to reach unity.

Stewardship: For Friends, stewardship is an element of integrity. Good stewardship directs Friends' investment of time and money in sustainable and renewable resources and in work that supports Quaker values and beliefs.

Stop/Stop in the Mind: A clear uneasiness in the face of a proposed decision or action, and an unwillingness to follow it.

Testimony: A guiding principle of conduct that bears witness to the presence of God in the world and in our lives. Though there is no official list of such testimonies, Friends have traditionally identified peace and nonviolence, equality, simplicity, stewardship, community, and integrity as their practical principles.

Threshing Session: A gathering of Friends to consider in depth a controversial issue but in a way that is free from the necessity of reaching a decision.

Truth: The revealed will of God, as experienced in communion with the Inner Light or Inward Christ. Early Quakers called themselves the Religious Society of Friends of the Truth.

Under the Care Of: Describes an activity, program, or event for which a Meeting takes responsibility and to which it gives oversight: thus, a marriage, a preparative meeting, and a school might all be said to be under the care of a monthly meeting.

Under the Weight Of: Giving high priority to an issue arising from a deep feeling of concern. Said of an individual or Meeting that is struggling to reach an appropriate decision about such an item of business.

Unity: The spiritual oneness and harmony whose realization is a primary objective of a meeting for worship or a meeting for business.

Unprogrammed Meeting: A Friends meeting whose worship is based on quiet waiting for the presence of God revealed through spirit-led vocal ministry and the gathered communion; sometimes called open worship. [cf., Programmed Meeting]

Vocal Ministry: The sharing of a message or prayer during a meeting for worship.

Weighty Friend: An informal term for a Friend who is respected for spiritual depth, wisdom, and long service to the Religious Society of Friends.

Worship Group: A group of worshipers who meet regularly, but who may or may not have established a formal affiliation with an established meeting.

Worship Sharing: A modern group practice in which participants share personal and spiritual experiences, thoughts, and feelings, often in response to a prearranged theme or questions, and in a manner that acknowledges the presence of God.

Yearly Meeting: Those Friends from a geographically extended area who gather in annual session to worship and conduct business together. This term is also used to denote the total membership of the constituent monthly meetings of a designated yearly meeting.

SOURCES OF EXTRACTS
FROM THE WRITINGS OF FRIENDS

Please note that the following information reflects the sources that the committee used; additional information is sometimes also provided in square brackets.

The years provided on the extract itself refers to the original writing or publishing as we understand it. The year used in this listing refers to the publication of the source material, whether an original publication date or subsequent reprint. The number appearing at the end of the entry of the quote is its location in the extract section.

Abbott, Margery Post; *An Experiment in Faith: Quaker Women Transcending Differences,* Pendle Hill Pamphlet 323, 1995, p. 14: #70.

Alexander, Nancy; *Practicing Compassion for the Stranger in the World,* Pendle Hill Pamphlet 271, 1987, p. 9: #259

All Friends' Conference; Devonshire House, London, 1920: #262

Anonymous; 1995: #233

Bacon, Margaret Hope; **The Quaker Struggle for the Rights of Women,** American Friends Service Committee, 1974, pp. 20-21: #268
——. **Mothers of Feminism,** San Francisco, Harper, 1986, p. 232: #243

Barclay, Robert; **An Apology for the True Christian Divinity:** *Proposition 2, Section 1;* Friends Book Store, Philadelphia, 1908, pp. 27-28. [Current edition: edited by D. Freiday, Philadelphia, 1967, p. 17]: #13
——;Ibid.; *Introduction,* p. 72 [1967 edition, p. 46]: #96
——;Ibid.; *Prop. 10 Sect. 2,* p. 263. [1967 edition, p. 178]: #14
——;Ibid.; *Prop. 11 Sect. 7,* p. 340 [1967 edition, p. 254]: #49
——;Ibid.; *Prop. 11 Sect. 6,* p. 336. [1967 edition, pp. 248-249]: #51
——;Ibid.; *Prop. 11 Sect. 17,* p. 364-365 [1967 edition, p. 280]: #50

Bathurst, Elizabeth; *The Sayings of Women...in several places of the Scriptures,* 1683, pp.13, 23: #95

Bellers, John; *Watch unto Prayer,* 1703, p. 7: #55

Berks and Oxon Quarterly Meeting Ministry and Extension Committee; (London Yearly Meeting), 1958: #48

Bishop, Molly; *Reading the Bible: A feminist viewpoint, **Friendly Woman,** 1994,* vol. 11, no. 5, p. 19: #69

Blom, Dorothea; *A living present in the Bible,* chapter 10 in **Seek, Find, Share,** *Study Volume Number Two,* 4th World Conference of Friends, 1967, p. 34: #110

Bond, Elizabeth Powell; **Works by the Way,** Philadelphia, Friends Book Association, 1895, pp. 147-149: #79

Boobyer, George; *Friends and the Bible,* 1988, pp. 3-4 [**Quaker Faith and Practice,** Britain Yearly Meeting, 1995, segment 27.30]: #105

Boulding, Elise; *Born Remembering,* Pendle Hill Pamphlet 200, 1975, pp. 15-16: #161
———;Ibid.; p. 7: #109
———;*The Quaker Journey,* Address to Friends General Conference, 1954: #3

Boulding, Kenneth; *Friends and Social Change,* Friends General Conference, 1988: #210

Bovell, Sheila; *I Wish It Would Always Be Wednesday, The Friend* (London), 1988, vol. 46, p. 1013: #274

Bownas, Samuel; **Life and Travels,** reprint, Wm Taber, ed., Pendle Hill/Tract Association, 1989, p. 4: #150

Braithwaite, William Charles; **Memoir and Papers,** ed. by two of his sisters, Anna B. Thomas and Elizabeth B. Emmott, New York: Longmans, Green, 1931, p. 118: #33

Brinton, Howard; *Ethical Mysticism in the Society of Friends,* Pendle Hill Pamphlet 156, 1967, p. 5: #21
———;*Quaker Education in Theory and Practice,* Pendle Hill Pamphlet 9, 1940, pp. 11-12: #24
———;*Friends for 300 Years,* Pendle Hill, 1964; p. 59: #61

Brown, Alfred Barrett; *Wayside Sacraments,* London, Friends' Book Centre, 1932, pp. 9-10: #18

Brown, Thomas Shipley; *When Friends Attend to Business,* Philadelphia Yearly Meeting, 1963: #128

Browne, Gordon M., Jr; *Today Was Tomorrow Yesterday,* address to Ohio Valley Yearly Meeting, Wider Quaker Fellowship, 1989, p. 13: #281

Burnell, S. Jocelyn; *The Kingdom in our Midst,* Introduction to London Yearly Meeting Session, 1976: #27
———;*Broken for Life,* Swarthmore Lecture, 1989, p. 47: #189
———;Ibid.; pp. 51-52: #125

Burrough, Edward; **The Memorable Works,** London, E. Hookes, 1672, p. 604: #289
———;**Testimony in Letters, etc., of Early Friends,** A. R. Barclay, ed., 1841, vol. VII, p. 305: #126

Cadbury, Henry; Shrewsbury Lecture, June 17, 1961: #121

———;*After Thirty Years: 1917-1947: AFSC,* Margaret Hope Bacon, ed. [quoted in **Let This Life Speak,** M. H. Bacon, University of Pennsylvania Press, 1987, pp. 144-145]: #211
———;*A Quaker Approach to the Bible,* Ward Lecture, 1953, pp. 14-15: #106

Calderone, Mary; *Friends and Womankind,* Friends General Conference, 1989, p. 9: #250

Capper, Mary; **Day By Day**- *a compilation from the writings of ancient and modern Friends,* William Henry Chase, ed., Auburn, NY, Dennis Bros. & Co., 1869, p. 132: #153

Cary, Steven; *The Quaker Proposition, Friends Journal,* Nov. 1979, p. 4: #204

Catchpool, Corder; quoted by William R. Hughes, in **Indomitable Friend: the life of--; 1883-1952,** London, Allen & Unwin, 1956, pp. 218-219: #172

Cedergren, Elsa; quoted by Ingeborg Borgström in *In Search of Integrity,* Friends World Committee for Consultation, 1983, p. 18: #178

Chetsingh, Ranjit; *The ground on which you stand is holy ground; Friends World News,* Spring 1975, p. 2: #209

Clark, Hilda; **War and Its Aftermath: Letters,** E. M. Pye, ed., London, Clare, 1956, p. 7: #270

Cobin, Martin; *From Convincement to Conversion,* Pendle Hill Pamphlet 134, 1964, p. 12: #136

Coffin, Rhoda;--: **Her Reminiscences, Addresses, Papers and Ancestry,** Mary

Coffin Johnson, ed., New York, Grafton Press, 1910, p. 69: #112

Crisp, Stephen; *The Kingdom of God Within*, Sermon, Grace Church St., London, 9 VII 1691 [Philadelphia, Thompson, 1863]: #145

Cronk, Sandra; *Peace Be With You*, Tract Association, c. 1983, p. 16: #30
——;Ibid.; p. 2: #222
——;*Dark Night Journey*, Pendle Hill, 1991, p. 91: #68
——;Ibid.; p. 8: #139
——;*Gospel Order*, Pendle Hill Pamphlet 297, 1991, p. 44: #247

Dale, Jonathan; *Rediscovering Our Social Testimony, Friends Journal*, September 1996, p. 17 [reprint from *Friends Quarterly*, April 1996, vol. 30 #2,]: #195

Damiano, Kathryn; presentation at School of the Spirit retreat, 1996: #280

Dewsbury, William; *Epistle from York Tower, 10th day, 12th Month, 1660: The Faithful Testimony of --*, London, 1689, p. 185: #148.

Dodson, Shirley; *Theology for Each of Us, Friends Journal*, September 1, 1980: #29

Doncaster, Hugh; *The Quaker Message: A Personal Affirmation*, Pendle Hill Pamphlet 181, 1972, p. 9 [Quoted from *God in Every Man*]: # 22
——;God in Every Man, Swarthmore Lecture, London, George Allen & Urwin, 1963, pp. 38-39: #25

DuBois, Rachel Davis; quoted by Leonard Kenworthy in **Nine Contemporary Quaker Women Speak,** Kennett Square, Pa., Quaker Publications, 1989, p. 27: #173

Dunbar, Barrington; from **Break the new Ground: Seven Essays by Contemporary Quakers,** Charles W. Cooper, editor, Friends World Committee for Consultation, Birmingham, England, 1969, p. 87: #249

Dunstan, Edgar G; **A Little Book on Prayer,** London, Friends Book Centre, 1946, pp. 19-21: #75

Durland, William; *The Apocalyptic Witness,* Pendle Hill Pamphlet 279, 1988, pp. 29-30: #118

Duvenek, Josephine; **Life on Two Levels: An Autobiography,** Los Altos, CA, W. Kaufmann, 1978, p. 166: #177

Elders at Balby; *The Elders and Brethren send unto the Brethren in the North,* **Letters, etc., of Early Friends,** A. R. Barclay, ed., London, Harvey and Darton, 1841, p. 280: #288

Elliott, Melissa Kay; **Faith in Action: Fifth World Conference of Friends,** Friends World Committee for Consultation, 1992, pp. 171-172: #258

Elliott, Rosemary M.; *Friends in a living community,* Chapter 29 in **Seek, Find, Share,** Study Volume Number Two, Fourth World Conference of Friends, 1967, Friends World Committee for Consultation, 1967, p. 97: #135

Farrow, Jo; *On Keeping a Journal,* **Gifts and discoveries,** Unit 1, background paper 2, 1986, pp. 1-2 [Reference cited in **Quaker Faith and Practice,** Britain Yearly Meeting, 1995, p. 618]: #187

Faulkner, Jenifer; *Out of the Depths, The Friend* (London), 1982, vol. 140, pp. 805-806: #163

Fell, Margaret; *Epistle against uniform Quaker Costume,* quoted by Jessamyn West in **Quaker Reader,** Pendle Hill, 1992, pp. 226-227: #255

Ferguson, Val; **Faith in Action: Fifth World Conference of Friends,** Friends World Committee for Consultation, 1992, p. 183: #34

First International Theological Conference of Quaker Women; *Epistle,* 1990: #269

Fitch, Joan; The Present Tense: Talking to our time. Discussion paper, 1980, pp. 22, 23: #86
——;*Handicap and bereavement*, 1988, pp. 4-5 [**Quaker Faith and Practice**, Britain Yearly Meeting, 1995, segment 21.59]: *#124*

Flexner, Helen Thomas; **A Quaker Childhood**, 1940, New Haven, Yale University Press, p. 78: *#176*

Fogelklou, Emilia; **Reality and Radiance**, trans. by Howard Lutz, Richmond, IN, Friends United Press, 1985, p. 63: *#190*

Foster, Richard; **Celebration of Discipline**, San Francisco, Harper, 1978, p. 148: *#140*

Foulds, Elfrida Vipont; **A Faith to Live By**, Friends General Conference, 1962, p. 1: *#28*
——;*The Candle of the Lord*, Pendle Hill Pamphlet 248, 1983, p. 13: *#83*
——;*The heart of the Quaker Faith*, **Quaker Life**, June 1981, p. 13: *#205*

Fox, Caroline; **Memories of old Friends**, H. N. Pym, ed., 1882, vol. 1, 3rd ed., p. xxii: *#155*

Fox, George; **A collection of Epistles**, London: T. Sowle, edited 1698, *Epistle 227*, p. 199,: *#4*
——;Ibid.; *Epistle 10*, p. 11: *#285*
——;Ibid.; *To Friends in New Jersey and Pennsylvania, Epistle 376*, *#241*
——;*Epistle 151*, quoted by Cecil W. Sharman in **No More But My Love: Letters of George Fox**, London, Quaker Home Service, 1980, p. 59: *#2*
——;**Journal**, Nickalls, ed., London Yearly Meeting, 1975, p. 33: *#6*
——;Ibid.; p. 11: *#111*
——;Ibid.; p. 19: *#39*
——;Ibid.; p. 65: *#215*
——;Ibid.; *Letter of. . to Lady Claypool*, p. 346: *#93*
——;Ibid.; p. 169 : *#234*
——;*The True Christians Distinguished*, 1689; quoted by Hugh McGregor Ross in **George Fox Speaks for Himself**,

York, Sessions Ltd., 1991, p. 41: *#94*
Franklin, Ursula; *Perspective on Friends Testimonies in Today's World*, Gardner Lecture, 1979, pp. 3-4: *#65*
Friends World Committee for Consultation; *Statement adopted at 13th Triennial*, Hamilton, Ontario, 1976[Quaker Faith and Practice, Britain Yearly Meeting, 1995, segment 23.31]: *#254*

Fry, Elizabeth Gurney; **Memoir of the life of --**, ed. by two daughters, 1847, vol. 1, pp. 35-36: *#154*
——; Ibid.; vol. 2, p. 509, [Also quoted by Jessamyn West in **The Quaker Reader**, Pendle Hill, 1992, p. 310]: *#156*

Fry, Joan Mary; *Thoughts of a British Friend*, **Friends World News**, No. 23, Spring 1947, p. 9: *#107*

Gates, Tom and Liz; *Stories fom Kenya*, Pendle Hill Pamphlet 319, 1995, pp. 6-7: *#207*

Gillman, Harvey; *Spiritual Hospitality*, address for Adult Religious Education Conference, Swarthmore Meeting, Nov. 20, 1993, unpublished: *#36*

Glover, Margaret; *Letter from --*, **The Friend** (London), 1989, vol. 147, p. 830: *#186*

Gorman, George; *Quaker Spirituality* from **Quakerism: a way of life.** Norwegian Quaker Press, 1982, pp. 87-88: *#60*

Greenwood, John Ormerod; **Signs of Life**, Swarthmore Lecture, London, Friends Home Service Committee, 1978, p. 64: *#282*

Grellet, Stephen; Attributed, Oxford Dictionary of Quotations, 3rd edition, 1979, p. 236: *#203*

Gurney, Joseph John; **Memoirs of --**, ed. by J.B. Braithwaite, Philadelphia: Lippincott, 1862, pp. 42-43, : *#100*

Gwyn, Douglas; **The Apocalypse of the Word,** Richmond, IN, Friends United Press, 1986, p. 93: *#114*

Haines, Deborah; *Living in Harmony with Heaven on Earth,* **Friends Search for Wholeness,** John Bond, ed., 1978, p. 139: *#213*

Harvey, T. Edmund; **The Spiritual Message of the Religious Society of Friends,** Friends World Conference, Commission Report, 1937, p. 18: *#57*
——;Ibid.; p. 18: *#76*

Heales, Brenda Clifft, and Chris Cook; **Images and Silence,** Swarthmore Lecture, London, Quaker Home Service, 1993, p. 16: *#146*

Hermann, Eva; *Gefangen und dochfrei; In Prison Yet Free,* Tract Assoc., c. 1947: *#175*

Hicks, Elias; *To William B. Irish,* **Letters of --,** 1st month 15th 1820, I. T. Hopper, New York, 1834, p. 57: *#101*

Hodgkin, David; *Quakerism: A Mature Religion for Today,* **Quaker Universalist Fellowship,** 1995, [Reprint of James Backhouse lecture, 1971, Australia Yearly Meeting], p. 17: *#253*

Hodgkin, George Lloyd; quoted in **George Lloyd Hodgkin [a memoir],** by L. Violet Holdsworth, 1921, p. 129 (also included in **Christian Faith and Practice,** 1960, selection 106): *#91*

Hole, Helen; *Prayer, The Cornerstone,* Pendle Hill Pamphlet 123, 1962, p. 16: *#85*

Holmgaard, Elisabeth; *Be Still and Know that I am God: Thoughts on prayer,* Birmingham, England, Woodbrooke, 1984, p. 17: *#84*

Howgill, Francis; *A Lamentaton for the Scattered Tribes;* reprinted in **The Dawning of the Gospel Day,** London, 1676, p. 46: *#9*

Hutchinson, Dorothy H; *The Spiritual*

Basis of Quaker Social Concerns, Friends General Conference, 1961, p. 2: *#202*

Imani, Ayesha (Clark-Halkin); *Blacks and Quakers: Have We Anything To Declare, Friends Journal,* June 1988, pp. 6-7: *#26*

Irie, Yukio; *My Religion: by a Japanese Friend, The Friend* (London), 1957, vol. 115, pp. 163-4: *#157*

Jones, Rufus; **The Spiritual Message of the Relgous Society of Friends,** Friends World Conference, Commission Report, 1937, p. 65:*#19*
——;**Swords into Ploughshares, An Account of the American Friends Service Committee 1917-1937,** New York, Macmillan, 1937, pp. vii-viii: *#212*
——;**A Call to What is Vital,** New York, Macmillan, 1948, p. 65: *#20*
——;*Quakerism and the Simple Life,* London, Headley, 1906, pp. 16-17: *#227*
——;*Spiritual Energies in Daily Life,* Philadelphia Yearly Meeting, 1962 reprint. [Essay first appeared in *The Friend* (London), July 1919, p. 1]: *#278*

Karger, Ilse; **Living Adventurously,** York, England, Sessions, 1995, pp. 188-189: *#171*

Kelly, Thomas; *Reality of the Spiritual World,* Pendle Hill Pamphlet 21, 1942, p. 33: *#78*
——;Ibid.; p. 45: *#158*
——;*The Gathered Meeting,* Tract Assoc. of Friends, 1945: *#59*
——**A Testament of Devotion,** New York, Harper, 1941, p. 111: *#201*
——;Ibid.; p. 110: *#239*
——;Ibid.; p. 71: *#15*

Lacey, Paul; **Leading and being Led,** Pendle Hill Pamphlet 264, 1985, p. 3: *#198*

Lampcn, Diana; **Faith in Action: Fifth World Conference of Friends,** Friends World Committee for Consultation 1992, pp. 71-72: *#164*
——;*Facing Death,* London, Quaker Home Service, 1979, p. 27: *#193*
——;Ibid.; p. 35: *#92*

Landstrom, Elsie; *Friends, Let Us Pray,* Pendle Hill Pamphlet 174, 1970, p. 14: #80.

Littleboy, William; *The Appeal of Quakerism to the Non-mystic,* 1964 edition, p. 5: #185
——;*The meaning and practice of prayer,* London, Friends Home Sevice Committee, 1937, pp. 7-9: #122

Lonsdale, Kathleen; I believe..., Eddington Memorial Lecture, Cambridge University Press, 1964, pp. 54-55: #159
——;*A Scientist tries to answer some of her own questions about religion,* London, Friends Home Sevice Committee, 1962: #180

Loring, Patricia, *Spiritual Discernment,* Pendle Hill Pamphlet 305, 1992, p. 24: #127
——; Ibid.; p. 29: #137

Lugalya, Mable; **Faith in Action: Fifth World Conference of Friends,** Friends World Committee for Consultation, 1992, p. 26: #44

Macphail, Gordon; *The Pastoral Care of Gay Friends, The Friend* (London), 1988, vol. 146, p. 1371: #165

Macy, Howard R.; **Rhythms of the Inner Life,** Fleming Revell & Co, NY, 1988, pp. 153-154: #292

Marsden, Lorna; **The Prepared Heart; an anthology of the writings of LMM,** London, Quaker Home Service, 1988, p. 98: #196

McGeoghegan, Peggy; *Can you tell me? Quaker monthly,* 1976, vol. 55, p. 223: #261

McNeill, Margaret; unpublished, 1990: #191

Michaels, Walter C.; *Commander Michaels, USNR, Pacific Fleet, to his daughter Leslyn, September 9, 1945:* #219

Morris, Jennifer; **Quakers in the eighties:**

What it's like to be a Friend, Anne Hosking and Alison Sharman, eds., London, Quaker Home Service, 1980, p. 15: #162

Mott, Lucretia; **--: Her Complete Speeches and Sermons,** ed. by Dana Green, New York, E. Mellen Press, 1980, pp. 236-237: #42

Murer, Esther; *Notes from the Extreme Middle, Newsletter, Central Phila. Monthly Meeting,* Dec. 1986: #41
——;*On 'Standing in the way',* ibid., Aug. 1986: #133
——;*Quench not the Spirit,* ibid., Jan. 1988: #149

Murphy, Carol; *Milestone 70,* Pendle Hill Pamphlet 287, 1989, pp. 32-33: #38
——;unpublished, c. 1993: #179
——;*Nurturing Contemplation,* Pendle Hill Pamphlet 251, 1983, pp. 25, 26, : #143

Mustin, Janet; *Dedication at Firbank Re-Opening,* Pendle Hill, Oct. 1992, #169

Nayler, James; **Works,** 1716, p. 696: #16

Newell, Kara Cole; *Things Important to Friends Today, Evangelical Friend,* Feb. 1982: #67
——;Ibid. #228

Norfolk, Cambs. & Hunts Quarterly Mtg.; London Yearly Meeting, 1957: #287

Nühn, Ferner; Fourth World Conference of Friends, 1967, p. 29: #40
——;*A Quaker Approach to Christ,* **Quaker Understanding of Christ and of Authority,** T Canby Jones, ed., Faith and Life Movement, Friends World Committee for Consultation, Section of Americas, 1974, pp. 15-16: #103

O'Shea, Ursula Jane; *Living the way, Quaker Spirituality and Community,* The twenty-eighth James Backhouse lecture, 1993, Australia Yearly Meeting, pp. 12-13: #267

Palmer, Charles Warner (1879- 1963);

unpublished prayer: #89

Palmer, Parker J.; *A Place Called Community,* Pendle Hill Pamphlet 212, 1977, p. 27: #63

Parker, Alexander; **Letters, etc., of Early Friends,** A. R. Barclay, ed., 1841, London, Darton & Harvey, Vol. 7, pp. 365-366: #45

Parker-Rhodes, Damaris; **The Way Out is the Way In,** 1985, London, Quaker Home Service , p. 16: #168

Peck, George; *What is Quakerism?* Pendle Hill Pamphlet 277, 1988: #88

Penington, Isaac; **The Works of --,** Philadelphia, 1863
——;*To a parent,* vol. 1, p. 506: #12
——;*To Friends in Amersham, from Aylesbury Gaol,* vol. 1, p. 532: #257
——;*The Consideration of a Position Concerning the Book of Common Prayer,* vol. 2, p. 111: #87
——;*To Thomas Walmsley,* vol. 2, p. 517: #120
——;*Vol.* 2, p. 544: #98
——;*Vol.* 2, p. 545: #99
——;*To the Women Friends That Meet at Armscot in Worcestershire,* vol. 3, p. 520: #208
——;*Inward Journey of --,* Robert J. Leach, Pendle Hill Pamphet 29, 1944, p. 29: #54
——;*A month with --,* Beatrice Saxon Snell, compiler; London, Friends Home Service, 1966, Day 16: #98
——;Ibid.; Day 17: #12
——;Ibid.; Day 30: #257

Penington, Mary Proude Springett; **Experiences in the Life of --,** Norman Penney, ed., Philadelphia, Biddle Press, 1911, [1992 reprint, Friends Historical Soc., London] pp. 30-32: #151
——;Ibid.; pp. 38-40: # 152
——;Ibid.; pp. 20-21: #73

Penn, William; **Collection of the Works**

of --, by Joesph Besse, London, 1726, vol. 2, p. 899: #238
——**Select Works of --,** New York, Kraus Reprint Co., 1971, *A Brief Account of the Rise and Progress of the People Called Quakers,* p. 757: #10
——;*A Tender Visitation,* p. 438: #52
——;*No Cross: No Crown;* p. 29: #8
——;**Reflections and Maxims, Part I,** Philadelaphia, H. Longstreth, 1901
——;*Maxim* 50, p. 28: #231
——;*Maxim* 519, p. 120: #11
——;*Maxims* 537, 540, 543-546: p. 123-125: #290

Pickett, Clarence E.; **--: A Memoir,** Walter Kahoe, ed., 1966, p. 52: #160

Pinthus, Eva I.; *Faith and Politics, Hand in Hand?,* **The Friend** (London), 1987, vol. 145, p. 483: #248

Pittock, A. Barrie; **Toward a Multiracial Society,** The 1969 James Backhouse Lecture, Australia Yearly Meeting, p. 33: #246

Punshon, John; **Encounter with Silence,** Richmond, IN, Friends United Press, 1987, pp. 94-95: #58
——;**Faith in Action: Fifth World Conference of Friends,** Friends World Committee for Consultation 1992, pp. 186-7: #167
——;**Encounter with silence,** op. cit., p. 44-45: #197

Quaker Home Service. London Yearly Meeting, 1961: #251

Quaker Peace and Service; *Integrity and Truthfulness in Quaker Work,* background document for Quaker Peace and Service workers, unpublished, 1992 [**Quaker Faith and Practice,** Britain Yearly Meeting, 1995, segment 20.45]: #273

Richards, Phyllis; *What Do Ye Do To Excess, The Friend* (London), 1948, vol. 107, p. 306: #117

Sansom, Clive; *Heart and Mind Prepared,*

The Friend (London), 7 September
1962, published as pamphlet by Friends
Home Service Committee, 1967 (1995
reprint), p. 3: #147

Santos, Heredio; *A Bridge of Love (Un
Puente D'Amor)*, address to New
England Yearly Meeting, 1991: #35

Saunders, Joolz; Unpublished, 1994: #170

Saunders, Pat; **Dare We Hope? Quaker
approaches to development;** Quaker
Peace and Service Committee on
Sharing Word Resources, 1987, p. 97:
#286

Sawyer, Deb; *Creating a Nonviolent
Society, Friends Journal,* March 15, 1987,
p. 14: #220

Schenck, Patience; *Courage and Spiritual
Leadings, Friends Journal,* March 1988,
p. 11: #166

Schurman, Virginia; *A Quaker Theology of
the Stewardship of the Creation,* paper
delivered at Quaker Theological
Discussion Group, George Fox College,
Newberg, OR., June 1990: #43

Scott, Janet; **What Canst Thou Say;**
Swarthmore Lecture, London, Quaker
Home Service, 1980, pp. 41-42: #242

Scott, Job; **Journal,** 1797, pp. 13-15: #116

Seeger, Daniel A.; *I have called you
Friends: A reflection of understandings of
Jesus among Friends,* address to
Hanover Meeting (NH), Nov. 18, 1994:
#37

Sharman, Alison; *Women in Search of
Truth, The Friend* (London), 1986, vol.
144, p. 1392: #32

Smith, Bradford; *Dear Gift of Life,* Pendle
Hill Pamphlet 142, 1965, p. 7: #181

Smith, Hannah Whitall; quoted by
Leonard S. Kenworthy in **Quaker
Quotations of Faith & Practice,** c. 1983,
p. 177: #183

Snell, Beatrice Saxon; *Letter from --;*

The Friend (London), 1961, vol. 119, pp.
60-61: #23
See also Isaac Penington

Steere, Dorothy; unpublished, 1995: #194

Steere, Douglas; **Bethlehem Revisited,**
Pendle Hill Pamphlet 144, 1965, pp., 8-9:
#113
——;*On Speaking Out of the Silence,*
Pendle Hill Pamphlet 182, p. 17: #138
——;*Introduction,* **Quaker Spirituality,**
Paulist Press, N. Y., 1984, p. 16: #31
——;*Dimensions of Prayer,* 1962, p. 97; #81
——;**Where words come from,**
Swarthmore Lecture, London, George
Allen & Unwin, 1955, p.58-59: #62

Stephen, Caroline E.; **Quaker
Strongholds,** London, 1890, pp. 55, 56,
[1923 edition, London, Society of
Friends Bookshop, p. 46]: #264
——;Ibid.; pp. 11-13, [1923 edition, pp. 3-
4]: #53

Stokes, Jane; unpublished, 1992: #271

Swayne, Kingdon; *Stewardship of Wealth,*
Pendle Hill Pamphlet 259, 1985, p. 22:
#245

Taber, Frances Irene; **Friends Face the
World,** Leonard Kenworthy, editor,
Quaker Publications, 1987, p. 59: #225

Taber, William; *Toward a Broader Quaker
Message, Friends Journal,* Feb 1, 1984, p.
6: #119
——;*The Prophetic Stream,* Pendle Hill
Pamphlet 256, 1984, pp. 8-9: #104

Tierney, Agnes L.; *Effective Prayer,* reprinted by Philadelphia Yearly Meeting, 1972,
p. 3: #77

Tolles, Frederick, *Quakerism and Politics,*
Ward lecture, 1956, p. 20: #206

Toomer, N. Jean; *An Interpretation of
Friends Worship,* Friends General
Conference, 1947, pp. 14-15: #132
——;Ibid.; p. 10: #141
——;Ibid.; p. 7: #64

Torrie, Margaret; **Begin Again: A Book for Women Alone,** London, Dent, 1970, p. 146: *#182*

Tritton, Frederick J.; *Friends and Spiritual Healing, The Friend* (London), 1958, vol. 116, pp. 5-6: *#82*

Urner, Carol Reilley; *The Kingdom and the Way,* Pendle Hill Pamphlet 317, 1994, p. 15: *#279*
——;Ibid.; p. 36: *#123*

Vail, James G.; *Science and the Business of Living,* Pendle Hill Pamphlet 70, 1953, pp. 12-15, : *#216*

Vallentine, Jo; **Faith in Action: Fifth World Conference of Friends,** Friends World Committee for Consultation, 1992, p. 213: *#219*
——;Ibid.; p. 215: *#232*

Vining, Elizabeth Gray; *Beauty from Ashes, Strength from Sorrow,* Philadelphia Yearly Meeting, c. 1979: *#188*
——;Being seventy: the Measure of a Year, New York, Viking Press, 1978, pp. 4-5: *#108*
——;Ibid.; pp. 131-132: *#90*

Watson, Elizabeth; **Guests of my life,** Burnsville, NC, Celo Press, 1979, p. 137: *#184*

Were, Miriam; **Faith in Action: Fifth World Conference of Friends,** Friends World Committee for Consultation, 1992, p. 205: *#266*

Wilbur, Henry W.; **A Study in Doctrine and Discipline,** Friends Book Association, 1908, pp. 45-46: *#200*

Wilbur, John; **Republication of the Letters of John Wilbur to George Crosfield,** Providence, 1895, pp. 60-61: *#102*

Wilson, Dan; *Promise of Deliverance,* Pendle Hill Pamphlet 60, 1951, pp. 16-17: *#297*

Wilson, Lloyd Lee; **Essays on the Quaker Vision of Gospel Order,** Burnsville, NC, Celo Valley Books, 1993, p. 23: *#260*

Wilson, Roger; **Authority, Leadership and Concern,** Swarthmore Lecture, London, George Allen & Unwin, 1949 p. 12: *#199*

Woolman, John; **Journal and Essays of --,** *Considerations on the true harmony of mankind,* A.M. Gummere, ed., New York, McMillan Co.,1922, p. 470: *#275*
——;--, the Journal and Major Essays, Phillips P. Moulton, ed., New York, Oxford Univ. Press, 1971, p. 184: *#72*
——;Ibid.; p. 160: *#74*
——;Ibid.; p. 157: *#97*
——;Ibid.; p. 95: *#129*
——;Ibid.; p. 31: *#142*
——;Ibid.; p. 255: *#230*
——;Ibid.; p. 28: *#265*
——;Ibid.; p. 143: *#276*
——;Ibid.; p. 35: *#235*
——;Ibid.; *A Plea for the Poor,* p. 241: *#263*
——;Works, *Considerations on Keeping Negroes;* 1774, p. 325: *#17*

Wychel, Jillian and David James; *Loving the Distances Between,* The Twenty-Seventh James Backhouse Lecture, Australia Yearly Meeting, 1991, p. 43: *#256*

Yamanouchi, Tayeko; *Ways of Worship, Friends World News* No. 113, p. 13 (also reprinted by Philadelphia Yearly Meeting as pamphlet, 1979-80): *#66*

Yates, Elizabeth; **A Book of Hours,** Noroton, Connecticut, Vineyard Books, 1976, pp. 60-61: *#174*

Yearly Meeting, Aoteraoa/New Zealand; *Minute on Peace,* 1987: *#224*

Yearly Meeting, Baltimore; **Faith and Practice of -- of the Religious Society of Friends,** 1988, pp. 17-18: *#293*
——;Ibid.; p. 18: *#296*

Yearly Meeting, Britain; **Quaker Faith and Practice,** 1995, segment 20.40: *#291*

——;Ibid.; segment 3. 28: *#134*
——;Ibid.; segment 10.05: *#131*

Yearly Meeting, London; *An essay by a group of Friends, Towards a Quaker view of sex,* London, Friends/Home Service Committee, 1963: *#192*
——;*Epistle,* 1858 Yearly Meeting Proceedings, pp. 25-26 (also included in **Christian Faith and Practice,** 1960, selection 423): *#284*
——;*Industry and the Social Order Conference,* Preparatory Document 5, 1958 (also included in **Christian Faith and Practice,** 1960, selection 533): *#229*
——;1888 Yearly Meeting Proceedings, p. 60 (also included in **Christian Faith and Practice,** 1960, selection 310): *#71*
——;*Statement on the Death Penalty, Minute* 39, 1956 Yearly Meeting Proceedings, p. 241 (also included in **Christian Faith and Practice,** 1960, selection 577): *#294*
——;Revision Committee; 1911(also included in **Christian Faith and Practice,** 1960, selections 261, 282): *#46*

——;Revision Committee; 1925 and modified in 1994 (also included in **Quaker Faith and Practice,** 1995, section 2.11): *#56*

Yearly Meeting, New England; **Faith and Practice of New England Yearly Meeting of Friends,** 1985, p. 205: *#1*
——;Ibid.; pp. 208-209: *#272*
——;Ibid.; p. 114 : # *130*
——;Ibid.; p. 208: *#252*

Yearly Meeting, North Carolina, Conservative; **Faith and Practice,** 1983, p. 7: *#240*

Yearly Meeting, Philadelphia; *Minute,* 4/4/1970: *#221*
——;Ibid, *Minute,* 1723 [Appeared in Race St. (Hicksite) Disciplines through 1888, in the Arch St. (Orthodox) Disciplines through 1912]: *#144*
——;**Book of Discipline,** 1806, p. 114: *#223*
——;*Minute,* Representative Meeting, 1995: *#295*

——;*Minute 26,* **Statement on Race,** 1969: *#5*
——;Ibid.; *#244*
——;Race St.; **Book of Discipline,** 1894, pp. 38-39: *#226*
——;Ibid.; 1927 [1950 printing, some changes], p. 29: *#214*
——;Ibid.; pp. 46, 58: *#283*
——;Ibid.; p. 31: *#236*
——;Ibid.; p. 29: *#47*
——;*Report,* Friends Peace Committee, 1940: *#217*

Young, Mildred Binns; *Insured by Hope,* Pendle Hill Pamphlet 90, 1956, pp. 4-5: *#237*
——;*The Candle, The Lantern, The Daylight,* Pendle Hill Pamphlet 116, 1961, p. 23: *#277*

Yungblut, John; *Quakerism of the Future: Mystical, Prophetic and Evangelical,* Pendle Hill Pamphlet 194, 1974, p. 24: *#115*

BIOGRAPHICAL NOTES OF AUTHORS

"May the light prevail over the darkness, may those who are here speak for all the children of the Light, to the needs of other times as well as their own."

--**Christian Faith and Practice** in the Experience of the Society of Friends (London Yearly Meeting 1960), Introduction to Chapter 1, p. 2.

The notes below are for the convenience of readers who, after reading one of the quotations that are in this book, would like to know a little about its author. Every effort has been made to present accurate information in brief form, but we realize there may be errors. Please send corrections in writing to the attention of the Publications Service Group, Philadelphia Yearly Meeting, 1515 Cherry Street, Philadelphia, PA 19102-1479.

Note that entries are in alphabetical order with years of the person's life when known and then followed by the numbering of the extract(s) by the author which are given as follows: *[#000]*. Abbreviations include:

AFSC = American Friends Service Committee,
FCNL = Friends Committee on National Legislation
FGC = Friends General Conference
FWCC = Friends World Committee for Consultation
PYM = Philadelphia Yearly Meeting

MARGERY POST ABBOTT *[#70]* gathered a group of women Friends from her own unprogrammed meeting and an Evangelical Friends Church -- both in Portland (OR) -- to discuss Quaker literature. The anthology she edited, **A Certain Kind of Perfection**, is one of the fruits of this experience. She is a graduate of Swarthmore College.

NANCY C. ALEXANDER *[#259]* has a special interest in "how religion, psychology and politics converge to change hearts and societies." She has worked in conflict resolution as applied to energy and environmental policies and served as a lobbyist for FCNL.

MARGARET HOPE BACON *[#268]* is a Quaker author and historian who wrote **Mothers of Feminism** and biographies of Henry Cadbury and Lucretia Mott. Much of her research and writing were done while she was holding down a full-time job in the public relations department of AFSC.

ROBERT BARCLAY (1648-1690) *[#13]* with the advantage of a good education -- part Presbyterian and part Catholic -- at the Scottish College in Paris, was able to write the famous **Apology** which first organized Quaker beliefs in a theological format. Barclay felt that, in his own time, God had "chosen a few despicable and unlearned instruments, as He did fishermen of old, to publish His pure and naked Truth, and to free it of these mists and fogs wherewith the clergy had fogged it."

ELIZABETH BATHURST (1655-1685) *[#95]* traveled widely in the ministry in England in the seven years between becoming a Quaker and her death. Her theological work *Truth's Vindication* had almost disappeared until it was republished in **Hidden in Plain Sight: Quaker Women's Writings 1650-1700** (Pendle Hill, 1996).

JOHN BELLERS (1654-1725) *[#55]* was a reformer who proposed -- alas, with little success -- workingmen's colleges, rehabilitation of prisoners rather than capital punishment, peaceful settlement of international disputes, and the investment of private capital in community betterment. His motives were religious, but he tried to convince others that such policies would lead to greater prosperity for England.

MOLLY BISHOP *[#69]* of Duncan Mills (CA) is a teacher of reading to children who need extra help. She characterizes herself as "a feminist and a Bible reader."

DOROTHEA BLOM (1911-1991) *[#110]* published nine books on design and color before the contemplative temperament and the artist in her converged, yielding a new career emphasizing art as a link between the spiritual life and the outer world. She has taught adults in Quaker and other settings, including six years at Pendle Hill.

ELIZABETH POWELL BOND (1847-1926) *[#79]* was called matron when she came to work at Swarthmore College in the late 1880s. She eventually became the institution's first dean. Apparently a believer in the goodness of young people and the possessor of an even temperament and a serene religious faith, she became a beloved figure on campus.

GEORGE BOOBYER (1902-1999) *[#105]* was a Quaker Biblical scholar and head of the Divinity School at Newcastle University in Great Britain until 1967. He served on the committee responsible for the **New English Bible** translation.

ELISE BOULDING (1920---) *[#3]* has been a sociologist, feminist, envisioner of a peaceful world, and a wise mother of five. She is admired by Friends as a workshop leader and writer. In retirement, she lives in Massachusetts. Her latest project was the founding of Friends Peace Teams.

KENNETH E. BOULDING (1910-1993) *[#210]* was born into a working-class family in Liverpool, England. He obtained a scholarship to Oxford and became a world class economist who taught at the University of Michigan and the University of Colorado. A quick-witted "idea man" of abundant originality, he wrote widely on a variety of topics, especially conflict resolution. Friends knew Kenneth as a sincere Christian and a Quaker poet who wrote poems only in the sonnet form (see especially his poems on James Naylor's last words).

SHEILA BOYELL *[#274]*, a British Friend, wrote a poignant essay in 1988 on a thorny theological problem: if God is love, why do tragic things happen to blameless people? It was occasioned by the crib death of a three-week-old infant.

SAMUEL BOWNAS (1676-1753) *[#150]*, a blacksmith's apprentice, became one of the most powerful Quaker ministers. Though he had little schooling, he became thoroughly versed in the scriptures, and was able "by the force of their testimony to confute gainsayers" and deliver his message to multitudes on both sides of the Atlantic.

WILLIAM CHARLES BRAITHWAITE (1862-1922) *[#33]* was a British Quaker historian and New Testament scholar. He was the author of **The Beginnings of Quakerism** and **The Second Period of Quakerism.**

HOWARD BRINTON (1884-1973) *[#21]* and his wife Anna Cox taught at Earlham and Mills Colleges. In 1938 they went to Pendle Hill, where Howard became director of studies and Anna director for administration. Together they helped define the mission of Pendle Hill as a religious community and retreat center for the study of Quaker mysticism. They began the Pendle Hill pamphlet series and edited 100 of them. Howard wrote the classic **Friends for 300 Years.**

A. BARRET BROWN (1887-1947) *[#18]* was principal of Ruskin College at Oxford University. British Friends valued his writing and spoken ministry in spiritual matters.

THOMAS S. BROWN (1912---) *[#128]* has been a Quaker educator who taught Classics, English and religion at Westtown School for 22 years. Decisive and fair-minded, Tom is a master of the Quakerly art of clerking a meeting for business. He has been clerk of everything in sight, including PYM and the general board of Pendle Hill.

GORDON M. BROWNE (1923---) *[#281]* is a writer and teacher of English. He has served as executive secretary of the FWCC, Section of the Americas, and as clerk of New England Yearly Meeting. In the 1950s and 1960s he was instrumental in reviving Quakerism on Cape Cod. He now lives in Hanover (NH).

C. JOCELYN BURNELL *[#27, 125 and 189]* received her Ph.D. in radio astronomy at Cambridge University where she was involved in the discovery of pulsars. She is chairman of the department of physics in the Open University (Great Britain) and has served as vice-president of the Royal Astronomical Society. She is an active member of the Religious Society of Friends and a former clerk of Britain Yearly Meeting.

EDWARD BURROUGH (1633-1663) *[#126 and 289]* was a young farmer and separatist preacher of Underbarrow near Kendal when convinced by Fox in 1652. Burrough was accounted the greatest Quaker preacher in London. In 1655 he went with fellow-worker Howgill to establish Quakerism in Ireland. IIe is the best-known early tract writer on Quaker doctrine and politics. Burrough died in Newgate prison. His death was a setback for the young Quaker movement.

HENRY J. CADBURY (1883-1974) *[#106, 121 and 211]* was among the foremost Biblical scholars of his day. He was the only Quaker in the group of translators who produced the **Revised Standard Version** of the **Bible.** Henry Cadbury taught at Haverford College and the Harvard Divinity School. Friends loved him for his dry wit and his immense knowledge of Quaker history. We remember that he accepted the Nobel Peace Prize for the AFSC wearing a tuxedo borrowed from its clothing workroom.

MARY CALDERONE (1904-1998) *[#250]* has been one of the great interpreters of human sexuality. She collected the results of research on sex and shared them in a warm, understanding way. Mary was the first medical director of the Planned Parenthood Federation of America and then a founder of SIECUS (Sex Information and Educational Council of the U.S.). She served this organization as executive director and president for 18 years. She was a member of Manhasset Monthly Meeting on Long Island (NY).

MARY CAPPER (1755-1845) *[#153]* was a "convinced Friend" at a time when there were probably not many of these in Britain. She remained faithful all her long life to the decision she made as a young girl to cast her lot with Quakers.

STEVE CARY (1915---) *[#204]* was a conscientious objector in World War II. He has since devoted his life to Quaker work, especially with the AFSC and Haverford College. He worked at AFSC from 1946-1969 in various positions, ending as associate general secretary, which meant supervising all programs in the United States. In 1969 he became director of development at Haverford College, later serving as acting president for a year and a half. From 1979-1991, he was clerk of the AFSC board.

CORDER CATCHPOOL (1883-1952) *[#172]*, a British Friend, was imprisoned as a draft resister during World War I. From then on he devoted himself to peace and reconciliation between peoples, especially in Germany. Always a lover of mountains, he died in his 70th year while climbing Mount Rosa in the Alps.

ELSA CEDERGREN (1893- ?) *[#178]* was born a member of the Swedish royal family (Count Bernadotte was her brother). Elsa became sensitized to poverty and injustice and exposed to pacifism through her work and travels for the international YWCA. After joining Friends in 1943 she became caught up in the international work and gatherings of Friends and from 1959-61 was chairman of the Friends World Committee.

RANJIT CHETSINGH *[#209]* was secretary/convenor of the General Conference of Friends in India. For sixteen years he was a vice-chairman of the Friends World Committee and was its general secretary in 1954-56. He gave a lifetime of service to adult literacy work in India.

HILDA CLARK (1881-1955) *[#270]* was a British medical doctor. During World War I she was an organizer of the Friends War Victims Relief Committee and worked to set up a maternity hospital in France. From 1919-22 she was head of the Friends Relief Mission in Austria and helped to rescue a whole generation of children there from starvation. She had the gift that "lit up sparks in others, and released in them powers they didn't know they possessed."

MARTIN COBIN (1920--) *[#136]* was a professor of Drama who taught at the University of Illinois and the University of Colorado. He served as clerk of the Friends Meeting in Champaign-Urbana. Of Jewish background, he outlined his personal theology in the Pendle Hill pamphlet **From Convincement to Conversion.** He defined conversion this way: "when you come in contact with God, not as a freak accident, but as an experience you can keep repeating."

RHODA COFFIN (1826-1909) *[#112]* was a Friends minister of the Orthodox branch from Richmond (IN). She was particularly interested in prison reform and the care of the insane.

STEPHEN CRISP (1628-1692) *[#145]*, though only a prosperous bays* maker from Colchester in England, was among the best educated of the early Friends. After his convincement, he began a series of visits to Holland and Germany — his mother and his second wife were Dutch. Active in London Quaker affairs, he wrote 21 books and tracts. His journal and 5 books of sermons were published posthumously.

*bays (mod. baize) was a type of fabric introduced into England in the 16th century by refugees from Holland and France.

SANDRA CRONK (1942---) *[#30, 68, 139, 222, and 247]* has been a spiritual nurturer, teacher and historian of religions. For ten years, she taught Quaker faith and thought, spiritual life studies, and religious community at Pendle Hill. In 1990 she became a founding member of the School of the Spirit, a ministry of contemplative prayer and religious study.

JONATHAN DALE *[#195]*, a social activist, author and birthright Friend, was active in peacework during the Cold War. Latterly, he has felt called to give up his comfortable university life to live very simply in the deprived area of Ordsal (England) and try to put his Quaker social witness into practice.

KATHRYN DAMIANO *[#280]*, as a spiritual director and retreat leader, founded the School of the Spirit (a ministry of contemplative prayer and religious study) with Sandra Cronk. She has also been on the staff at Pendle Hill.

WILLIAM DEWSBURY (1621-1688) *[#148]* was a weaver from Allthorpe in Yorkshire. He had served in the Puritan Army but left it and had reached his own inner experience of Light when he and his wife were won as colleagues by Fox in a moonlight walk in 1651. He preached throughout the Midlands and suffered long imprisonments, including 19 years at Warwick. Wisest of letter writers in counseling, he helped heal the Fox-Naylor split. He was apocalyptic in tracts and thundering sermons.

SHIRLEY DODSON *[#29]* graduated from of the Earlham School of Religion and wrote and edited adult curriculum materials for PYM. She now serves as director of conferences and retreats at Pendle Hill.

HUGH DONCASTER (1914-1994) *[#22]* was trained as a natural scientist, but began his career as a social worker among unemployed miners in Wales. Between 1942-64 he taught Quaker history at Woodbrooke, the English Quaker study center for adults. He traveled widely among Friends in England, South Africa and Australia.

RACHEL DAVIS DuBOIS (1892-1993) *[#173]* was a pioneer in inter-group relations. She developed the Living-room Dialogues method, which may have been the beginning of our present worship-sharing. Originally, she used it with inter-racial groups as an aid to mutual understanding. She later spread the method to the Society of Friends through her Quaker Dialogues which involved sessions on meeting for worship, meeting for business and outreach. With the help of Friends General Conference, Quaker Dialogues were introduced to over 400 groups in the United States, Canada, Mexico and eight European countries.

BARRINGTON DUNBAR (1901-1978) *[#249]* was born in British Guyana and educated in the United States. He devoted his life to social work, as the director of settlement houses, camps for refugees, etc. He joined 57th Street Meeting in Chicago and later was active with 15th Street Meeting in New York City. Committed to both black liberation and Quakerism, he explained the Black Power movement to whites as a need to express rage as a step toward self-esteem. Dunbar said that it is easy for Quakers to believe in non-violence because we are insulated from the life that poor people know; noting that we create "beautiful islands which help individuals to develop but often aren't enough concerned with the ugly world outside."

EDGAR DUNSTAN (1890-1963) *[#75]* was for many years a professional journalist. He worked with the Friends Home Service (London) from 1929-52. During those years he was in correspondence with enquirers about Friends' beliefs in many parts of the world. In his Swarthmore Lecture of 1956 (these are traditionally given at London, now Britain, Yearly Meeting and later reprinted) he stated firmly that Quakerism is a Christian religion by tradition and should remain so.

WILLIAM DURLAND (1931---) *[#118]* is a socially-concerned Friend with a strong interest in international communities. He and his wife Genie are Intermountain Yearly Meeting representatives to the Friends Peace Team Project. At one time, they were on the staff at Pendle Hill. They now are members of Lamb's Community Worship Group in Trinidad (CO).

JOESPHINE DUVENEK (1891-1978) *[#177]* was born to wealth but she devoted her life to education and activist public service. She was founder and director of the Peninsula School of Creative Education in California and a supporter of Cesar Chavez's Agricultural Workers Union. Religiously, she was a mystic who needed to serve others, not retreat from the world.

MELISSA KAY ELLIOTT *[#258]* is director of publications of the AFSC and a member of Germantown (PA) Monthly Meeting. She formerly served as associate editor of *Friends Journal.*

ROSEMARY ELLIOTT *[#135]* is the wife of a citrus farmer and a member of Eastern Cape Regional Meeting, South Africa Yearly Meeting. She is a participant in many community activities with persons of other religious and racial backgrounds, especially through the Quaker Service Fund, Sunday River Branch.

JO FARROW *[#187]* is from Arundel in England. For a time, she was a Methodist deaconess. Though a latecomer to the Society of Friends, she became general secretary of Quaker Home Service. **The World in my Heart** is her spiritual autobiography. She is a feminist and a member of the Quaker Women's Group.

JENIFER FAULKNER *[#163]* is a British Friend.

MARGARET FELL (1614-1702) *[#255]* was the wife of Judge Thomas Fell of Swarthmoor Hall, near Ulverston in Lancashire. After meeting with George Fox in 1652 she made her house (with her husband's permission) the center for the Quaker "Publishers of Truth" and became the nursing mother of the new movement. In 1669, eleven years after Judge Fell's death, Margaret Fell married George Fox, though their incessant labours, travels and imprisonments prevented them from living much together at Swarthmoor Hall.

VAL FERGUSON *[#34]* was for a long time a staff member at the London office of FWCC, including being general secretary from 1986-91. He has also been interim head at Woodbrooke.

JOAN FITCH (1908-2001) *[#86 and 124]* was active in the Friends Fellowship of Healing. She was a member of Harting Grove Meeting in Cambridge, England. From her writings one learns of a person who overcame tragedy in her personal life and that she had a gift for pastoral care.

HELEN THOMAS FLEXNER (1871-1956) *[#176]* was a graduate of Bryn Mawr College, where she taught English and was vice-president of the national Collegiate Equal Suffrage League. She is known for her one published book **A Quaker Childhood** and her ties to others: her husband, pathologist Simon Flexner; her sister, the president of Bryn Mawr; her aunt, evangelist Hannah Whitall Smith; and her friend, Bertrand Russell.

EMILIA FOGELKLOU (1878-1972) *[#190]* was the first woman in Sweden to earn a doctorate in theology. She became a Quaker and devoted her long life to teaching, writing and the support of peace and women's concerns.

RICHARD FOSTER *[#140]* is the author of several books, including the best-selling **Celebration of Discipline.** He has been part of the pastoral team at Newberg Friends Church in Oregon, and taught theology at Friends University in Wichita (KS) and spiritual formation at Azuza Pacific University. He is the founder of RENOVARE, "an effort working for the renewal of the church in all her multifaceted expressions."

ELFRIDA VIPONT FOULDS (1902-1992) *[#28, 83 and 205]* was a noted British Quaker. Countless Quakers have visited the 1652 country in Northwestern England in her company—either on Quaker pilgrimages she conducted or with her guide book in hand. Many others learned our history through her book **The Story of Quakerism** (1954, revised 1977) and her writings for young people.

CAROLINE FOX (1819-1871) *[#155]* with her charm and intelligence won the friendship of the Coleridges, Carlyles and Mills. Her journal is an important source of information about them. She called her form of religion Quaker-Catholicism. Today we might say Quaker Universalism.

GEORGE FOX (1624-1691) *[#2, 4, 6, 39, 93 and 94]* was a charismatic preacher, strong in prayer and healing, who gathered the first Seekers, survived persecution and, with his wife, Margaret Fell, laid the administrative foundation of the Religious Society of Friends.

URSULA FRANKLIN (1921---) *[#65]* is a retired university professor, activist for peace and justice, a feminist and member of Voice of Women. Born in Munich, Germany, she is a materials scientist, specializing in the physics of ancient archeological materials. She gathered and analyzed data on the strontium-90 accumulation in the teeth of Canadian children that was the result of fallout from nuclear weapons tests.

ELIZABETH GURNEY FRY (1780-1845) *[#154, 156]* was the daughter of a banker and member of a prominent Quaker family. Her conscience was first reached by the American evangelist, William Savery. In 1813 she began visiting women and children in Newgate Prison, London. By 1817 she had established a school and founded a prisoners aid society. Marriage to fellow Quaker Joseph Fry resulted in a family of 10 children, but she continued to travel widely, preaching and visiting in Britain and elsewhere in Europe. After her husband's bankruptcy in 1823 her public activities were curtailed, but she continued her prison visiting and interest in employment schemes for London's poor.

JOAN MARY FRY (1862-1955) *[#107]* was active in Friends' work in Germany during World War I and she worried that the large financial and commercial dealings necessary for relief work might be "too heavy a burden for the inner strength of the Society." As chairman of the Friends Allotment Committee, she helped 135,000 people to cultivate garden plots during the Great Depression.

TOM AND LIZ GATES *[#207]* went with their two young sons to live and work at Friends Hospital at Lugulu in Kenya from 1991-1994. Tom, a family physician, and Liz, a public school teacher, concluded that "Africa is not a joyless place, despite all the hardships and suffering. Most Africans continue to be sustained by traditional loyalties to family, community and God in a way that is hard for us from the individualistic West to fully comprehend ... in our time there we have, in that wonderful old Quaker phrase, been made tender." The Gates now live near Lancaster (PA).

HARVEY GILMAN *[#36]* for many years did outreach work for Friends Home Service Britain. He is known for his writings on spiritual hospitality and the necessity for welcoming strangers and minorities to our Meetings.

MARGARET GLOVER *[#186]* lives in London, England where she is an artist and peace activist. She attended the Rio summit and is studying for a Ph.D. on Peace Art.

GEORGE GORMAN (1916- ?) *[#60]* was the highly successful head of Quaker Home Service for London Yearly Meeting. He produced a striking set of outreach posters and invented the seekers' weekend.

JOHN ORMEROD GREENWOOD (1907-1989) *[#282]* joined the Society of Friends while a student at Cambridge University. His main interests were in the theatre. He was executive secretary of the Group Theatre of London, which presented the plays of Eliot, Auden, Isherwood, etc. Later he was a radio producer at the BBC and for 18 years he taught at the Royal Academy of Dramatic Art. His Swarthmore Lecture at the 1978 London Yearly Meeting dealt with religion and the arts.

STEPHEN GRELLET (1773-1855) *[#203]* was born of a noble Roman Catholic family in Limoges, France. He fought in a counter-revolutionary army, was taken prisoner and then emigrated to Long Island in the United States. There he had a St. Paul-like conversion experience. He became a Quaker and carried his messages through all grades of society and all parts of the United States and Europe. It was he who inspired Elizabeth Fry to visit Newgate Prison.

JOSEPH JOHN GURNEY (1788-1847) *[#100]*, the son of a baker, affirmed his Quaker heritage but "shared the concerns of Anglican evangelicals for theology, slavery, prisons and the poor." He approved of the doctrine of the atonement and urged Friends to set up Sunday schools and study the **Bible.** In 1837 Gurney toured the United States where 3,000 heard him preach in Ohio and Indiana. He also went to North Carolina, New England, New York and Canada. Gurney's writings and travels gave strength to Quaker evangelicals during the Hicksite controversy.

DOUGLAS GWYN (1948---) *[#114]* has been a Friends pastor, a teacher, and a scholar in residence at Pendle Hill. He is now on the staff of Woodbrooke in England. Much of his writing has been devoted to exploring the spirit of early Quakerism.

DEBORAH HAINES (1947---) *[#213]* coordinated the Centennial observances of FGC in 2000. She was a prime mover at New Swarthmoor, a "Quaker Commune" of the 1970s which was located in a farmhouse near Clinton (NY) that was owned by her parents. Deborah is a professionally-trained historian and a member of Swarthmore Meeting (PA).

T. EDMUND HARVEY (1875-1955) *[#57 and 76]* was born in Leeds, England. "He sat in Parliament about 18 years, which covered both the great wars. There his constant advocacy of magnaminity, justice and peace won him the high regard of men of all opinions. He worked in defense of conscientious objectors to military service, and in relief work for the victims of war....In our meetings his ministry was deeply valued, being simple and personal as well as profound."

BRENDA CLIFT HEALES and CHRIS COOK *[#146]* are now living in Worcester, England and often work at Woodbrooke in Birmingham. Their concern with ministry through the experience of art led them to set up the Appleseed Quaker Ministry; they travelled widely through Britain in a motor home on this concern.

EVA HERMANN *[#175]* and her physicist husband Carl (1898-1961) were on the German Quaker list of Vertrauens Leute (Trusted Friends) who could be counted on to help Jews. Before the war, Eva had helped a number of Jews to emigrate and had hidden a Jewish family in her flat for several weeks, although her own father was a Nazi. In 1943 the Hermanns were arrested and charged with listening to the BBC. They were to stay in prison for two years.

ELIAS HICKS (1748-1830) *[#101]* was a prosperous farmer and recorded minister from Long Island (NY). He visited meetings throughout America but never went abroad. His preaching was eloquent. "To Hicks, the emerging evangelical emphasis upon the authority of Scripture, the Trinity and the atonement seemed to be putting intellectual notions above surrendering self-will to the inward Christ." He encouraged his followers to resist what he viewed as attempts to change the beliefs of Friends and to erect a hierarchy of elders; but he took no role in the maneuverings in PYM which led to the separation of 1827.

DAVID HODGKIN (1914-1977) *[#253]* met his wife Bridget when they both were serving at the Quaker Centre in Vienna in 1939. In 1953 they moved to Australia, where David was on the administrative staff of the Australian National University in Canberra. From 1957 to 1965 he was clerk of Australia Yearly Meeting. In retirement, he was its executive secretary. He said, "Our faith is never in conflict with our reason. This keeps Quakerism a modern and mature religion."

GEORGE LLOYD HODGKIN (1880-1918) *[#91]* was described as possessing "a radiant and dedicated spirit." In 1918, leaving a young family behind, Hodgkin set out on his second war-time journey to Armenia on behalf of the lord mayor of London's Armenian Relief Fund. He was taken ill at Baghdad and died there.

HELEN HOLE (1906-1983) *[#85]* was involved in Quaker education throughout her life as a student, teacher, wife of a teacher, administrator and board member. She served as dean of Earlham College and was a member of the Pendle Hill Board.

ELIZABETH HOLMGAARD *[#84]* is a Danish educator who has worked at Woodbrooke and lived in Africa. She is the author of pamphlets on prayer and is an enthusiastic weaver who was part of the Quaker Tapestry Project. She lives in Selly Oak, England.

FRANCIS HOWGILL (1618-1669) *[#9]* was a preacher and pamphleteer from the north of England. As one of the "Valiant 60" he carried Quakerism to London and helped organize its spread elsewhere. Falsely accused of political sedition, he was jailed in 1663 and died in prison five years later.

DOROTHY HUTCHINSON (1905-1984) *[#202]* was "a shy person inwardly compelled into a career of obedience." She joined the Society of Friends in 1948. During the war, she had founded Peace Now, an effort to shift American policy from unconditional surrender to negotiation. A decade later, she journeyed from home to home around the world with a message of friendship from her Meeting (Abington, PA). In May 1958 she fasted in the lobby of the

Atomic Energy Commission to protest nuclear testing. In the 1960s, as president of the U.S. Section, Women's International League for Peace and Freedom, she visited Poland and the USSR.

AYESHA (CLARK -HALKIN) IMANI *[#26]* is valued for her workshops which have helped many Quakers and others uncover racism in themselves. She now lives in Germantown (PA).

YUKIO IRIE (1908--) *[#157]* was a Japanese Friend who was a professor of English at Tokyo University. He studied at Woodbrooke (England) in 1956-57.

RUFUS JONES (1863-1948) *[#19, 20, 212, 227 and 278]* was a writer, scholar, orator and skilled administrator. Believing that both quietists and evangelicals of his time distorted the original message of Quakerism, he worked to turn Friends toward a mystical and prophetic Christianity. As a major figure among Protestant religious leaders, he exerted more influence on other denominations than any previous American Quaker. He was a professor at Haverford College for 40 years, edited the **American Friend** for 20 years, and was the first chairman of the board of the AFSC, serving from 1917 to 1928.

ILSE KARGER (1902--) *[#171]* was born in Berlin into a family of "free thinkers." She became a Quaker and worked as a nursery school teacher and a nurse for sick children in the United States and Australia.

THOMAS R. KELLY (1893-1941) *[#15]* was raised in Ohio. He earned a Ph.D. at Hartford Theological Seminary and became a professor of religion and philosophy. He taught at several Quaker colleges: Wilmington, Earlham and Haverford. Failure to obtain a second doctorate at Harvard threw him into a depression from which he emerged spiritually stronger. In the last three years of his life he produced several devotional classics, including **A Testament of Devotion** and **The Reality of the Spiritual World.** They fruitfully combine evangelical language and a mystical Quaker emphasis.

PAUL LACEY *[#198]* first became acquainted with Quakers through weekend work camps. He teaches English literature at Earlham College, where he has been provost and served as acting president. He has written extensively about teaching and conducts a workshop for teachers new to Friends schools under the auspices of the Friends Council on Education.

DIANA LAMPEN *[#92, 164 and 193]* with her husband has worked in a school for delinquent boys and on peace-making projects in Northern Ireland. She now leads workshops on mediation and death and dying issues.

ELSIE LANDSTROM *[#80]* is a member of Wellesley (MA) Meeting and is now living at Kendal-at-Longwood (PA). She was one of the original editors of **Approach**, a literary magazine born at Pendle Hill in the 1950s. Later she worked as a writer and editor for AFSC and edited non-technical publications for M.I.T.

WILLIAM LITTLEBOY (1853-1936) *[#122 and 185]* was a highly respected clerk of London Yearly Meeting. He attended the Manchester Conference and wrote on mysticism and prayer.

KATHLEEN LONSDALE (1903-1971) *[#159 and 180]* was a crystallographer and a world-class scientist. She was the first woman elected to the Royal Society (British) in the physical sciences. She and her husband joined the Society of Friends in 1935. In 1943 she spent a month in Holloway prison as a conscientious objector. She published books and articles on issues of war and peace as well as her scientific papers.

PATRICIA LORING *[#127 and 137]* is released by Bethesda (MD) Friends Meeting for a ministry in the nurture of the spiritual life. She is a graduate of Hartford Theological Seminary and spent 5 terms at Pendle Hill. She creates and leads adult religious education courses and retreats. Her two-volume book **Listening Spirituality** is much valued.

MABLE LUGALYA *[#44]* is co-pastor with her husband, Alfred, of a large Quaker meeting in Nairobi, Kenya.

GORDON MACPHAIL (1956-1991) *[#165]* was a British Friend who gave up general practice as a physician to do full-time hospice work for people with AIDS. He urged the Society of Friends to come out from behind Quaker euphemisms and openly recognize committed homosexual relationships.

HOWARD MACY *[#292]* is professor of religion and biblical studies at George Fox College in Newberg (OR). He has served as a Friends pastor, led retreats, and worked with young people. His book **Rhythms of the Inner Life** helps us find clues to deeper spirituality through the *Psalms*.

LORNA MARSDEN *[#196]* was a founding member of the Open Letter Movement in Britain. She is the author of several books on Quaker spirituality and theology.

PEGGY McGEOGHEGAN *[#261]* worked in the children and young peoples section at Friends House (headquarters of Britain Yearly Meeting) in the 1970s. She is a librarian and the author of books and study materials on and for children, including **Quaker Meeting & Its Children**.

MARGARET McNEILL (1905-1994) *[#191]* was the extension secretary at Woodbrooke, the British Quaker study center in Birmingham. She retired to Ireland.

WALTER C. MICHAELS (1906-1975) *[#219]* was a professor of physics at Bryn Mawr College from 1932-72. He was a naval officer during World War II.

JENNIFER MORRIS *[#162]* was born into an English Quaker family in the 1940s. She trained in speech and drama and has taught in different settings. She is the mother of two daughters.

LUCRETIA MOTT (1793-1880) *[#42]* was a recorded Hicksite minister. She became a major figure nationally in two reform movements: anti-slavery and feminism —— working for these causes with non-Quakers. This and her increasingly liberal theology led some Friends to try to disown her or get her to resign from the Society of Friends, but she stayed within Quakerism and worked for change.

ESTHER MURER (1935---) *[#41]* writes for the newsletter of Central Philadelphia Monthly Meeting and edits *Types and Shadows*, a quarterly published by the Fellowship of Quakers in the Arts. She has prepared a computerized index to scriptural references in the writings of George Fox and other early Friends.

CAROL MURPHY (1916-1994) *[#38]* said of herself "my abilities ran in the groove of reading, thinking and observing rather than participating." Though she was solitary and introverted, her messages during worship were treasured in her home Meeting of Swarthmore (PA). She sensitively explored religious philosophy, psychology, comparative religion and methods of spiritual growth in her 17 Pendle Hill pamphlets -- the largest number written by a single author.

JANET MUSTIN *[#169]* is an artist who works in print making and with oils. She is a member of Lansdowne (PA) Meeting. Graduating from Swarthmore College in 1945, she obtained her art education at the Pennsylvania Academy of Fine Arts, the Art Institute of Chicago, and the Wallingford (PA) Art Center.

JAMES NAYLOR (1617-1660) *[#16]* is famous today for his last words; but he was once reckoned the best speaker in the Quaker movement and perhaps more its leader than Fox. Sadly, he seemed to lose his mental balance and, in 1656, he permitted enthusiastic followers to strew garments in his path as he rode into Bristol, England. He was tried for blasphemy and cruelly punished. Released from prison in 1659, Naylor died the following year after being robbed and beaten while travelling toward his home in the north.

KARA COLE NEWELL *[#67 and 228]* was raised among Evangelical Friends, but she has shared her administrative talents and speaking ability widely among different branches of Quakers. Kara has been general secretary of Friends United Meeting. Later she was executive director of the AFSC.

FERNER NUHN (1903-1989) *[#40]* taught at Claremont College in California. He published a book about Friends and the ecumenical movement and was active with the Friends World Committee for Consultation.

URSULA JANE O'SHEA *[#267]* is an Australian Friend who was formerly an Ursuline nun. She served on the staff at Woodbrooke (England) for three years.

CHARLES WARNER PALMER (1879-1963) *[#89]* was a beloved member of Middletown (PA) Meeting where he frequently said this prayer during meeting for worship.

PARKER J. PALMER *[#63]* is a writer and teacher with a particular interest in the spiritual life of educators. He has been dean of Pendle Hill and a staff member at the ecumenical St. Benedictene Retreat Center in Madison (WI). He is now a senior associate of the American Association for Higher Education and in demand as a speaker and retreat leader.

ALEXANDER PARKER (1628-1689) *[#45]*, a Quaker of the first generation, pled with Charles II to release imprisoned Friends. In Fox's later years, Parker was his travelling companion.

DAMARIS PARKER-RHODES *[#168]* was first an Anglican, then a communist, and then a convinced Quaker. She is active in peace and social issues and has great interest in oriental meditative traditions. Her book **The Way Out Is the Way** In expanded her previous Swarthmore Lecture in the light of her experience with cancer.

GEORGE PECK (1916---)*[#88]* was trained as a historian, with a doctorate from the University of Chicago, and he then worked in his family business for twenty years, mostly in advertising. In 1970 he returned to college teaching and was a founding member of Brunswick (ME) Meeting. He has been clerk of the general board at Pendle Hill. His pamphlet **Quakerism: a Primer** is widely used.

ISAAC PENINGTON (1617-1679) *[#12, 54, 87, 98, 99, 120, 208 and 257]* was the son of a leader in Cromwell's Parliament. He was 42 when he joined Friends. Scholarly and retiring by nature, his spiritual writings continue to inspire us. As a person of some wealth, he was both fined and imprisoned for his faith.

MARY PROUDE SPRINGETT PENINGTON (1644-1682) *[#73, 151 and 152]*, "after earnest search and some disillusionments she, with her husband, at length found her goal in worship with Friends." Though at first she was "still exercised against taking up the cross to the language, fashions, customs, titles, honour and esteem in the world" she found her voice and began to write her own prayers. Eventually she produced an autobiography, a manuscript that she hid in a wall. It was found forty years later and has been reprinted in modern times.

WILLIAM PENN (1644-1718) *[#8, 10, 11, 52, 231 and 290]* was an Admiral's son who cast his lot with Friends and became a promoter of religious freedom and the proprietor of the Holy Experiment in Pennsylvania. He was the author of many pamphlets, most notably **No Cross, No Crown and the Fruits of Solitude.**

CLARENCE PICKETT (1884-1965) *[#160]* was raised in Illinois as a Gurneyite Friend and educated at Hartford Theological Seminary. He served as a Friends pastor, and as secretary of the American Young Friends Movement. He headed the AFSC from 1929 to 1950. Pickett directed the agency's growth as its mission moved beyond relief toward aiding the economic development of the poor, promoting better race relations, etc. It was he who persuaded Eleanor Roosevelt to tour the coal regions of Appalachia during the Great Depression.

EVA J. PINTHUS *[#248]* was a German Friend who fled the Nazis and settled in England. By profession she was an occupational therapist.

A. BARRIE PITTOCK (1938---) *[#146]* is a physical scientist —— specializing in atmospheric ozone —— with a deep sense of social responsibility. As a member of Melbourne Monthly Meeting, he has been a lobbyist and worker for Aboriginal rights and immigration reform for Australia. He is on the board of the Quaker Service Council of Australia.

JOHN PUNSHON (1935---) *[#58, 167 and 197]* is a lawyer who once ran for Parliament. He became widely known as a tutor at Woodbrooke and, later, a professor at the Earlham School of Religion. He is a recorded minister of Indiana Yearly Meeting. Punshon's **Portrait in Grey** is a readable modern history of the Society of Friends.

PHYLLIS RICHARDS (1900-1976) *[#117]* did not formally become a Friend until she was 47, after she had worked with Jewish children in Vienna during World War II and raised a family of her own. Thereafter, valued for her skill in ministry and pastoral care, she was an elder in several Meetings in different parts of Britain.

CLIVE SANSOM (1910-1981) *[#147]* was an Australian Friend and a published poet.

HEREDIO SANTOS *[#35]* is a beloved Quaker pastor from Cuba. He visited New England Yearly Meeting in 1991, as part of the Puente des Amigos exchange program between Cuban and New England Friends.

JOOLZ SAUNDERS *[#170]* and her husband, David, live in Worcester, England. She is a social worker by profession.

PAT SAUNDERS *[#286]* is a Canadian Friend who worked on environmental and development issues for Quaker Peace & Service (Britain) and now runs a small bookshop in the north of England.

DEB SAWYER *[#220]* has attended Friends Meetings in Salt Lake City (UT) and Boulder (CO). In her **Friends Journal** article she said, "We can create a non-violent society but it will involve interrelated changes in the way we think, the way we raise our children, in our economic system, and the way we resolve conflicts."

PATIENCE SCHENCK *[#166]* was an administrator for the American College of Obstetricians and Gynocologists in Washington (DC) during the 1980s. She is a member of Annapolis (MD) Meeting. In a **Friends Journal** article she said "Being open to the spirit has an element of fear for all of us. We don't know what we'll be called to do. It might be hard for us."

VIRGINIA SCHURMAN *[#43]* serves on the board of the Tract Association of Friends and is active in the Spiritual Formation Program of Baltimore Yearly Meeting. A microbiologist, she wrote **George Fox and the Care of Creation**. She has travelled in the ministry with a Friend from Ohio Yearly Meeting Conservative.

JANET SCOTT *[#24]*, a British Friend and theologian, is a member of the Faith and Order Plenary Commission of the World Council of Churches. She is head of the religious studies department of Homerton College at Cambridge University where she teaches **New Testament** and religious education.

JOB SCOTT (1751-1793) *[#116]* has been called "the most creative theologian in 18th century America." He made three extended journeys, two in America and one to Europe —— where he died of smallpox in Ireland. "Scott was a quietist who saw all outward means —— including the Bible, reason, learning —— as irrelevant or a hindrance to salvation....He refused to use the term trinity and denigrated the atonement. Like Hicks, Scott made the Inward Light the entire substance of faith." He was not criticized during his lifetime, but statements in his **Journal** (published in 1797) upset evangelicals.

DANIEL A. SEEGER *[#37]* is an active Universalist Friend. He headed the regional office of AFSC in New York City and served as executive secretary of Pendle Hill. The law case he brought during the Korean War establishes the right of conscientious objection for those not officially members of any church but who are believers in a Supreme Being, which was his own position at the time.

ALISON SHARMAN *[#32]* is a British feminist and writer. She was editor of the *Friends Quarterly* and edited various pieces of literature put out by London Yearly Meeting.

BRADFORD SMITH (1909-1964) *[#181]* was a writer who taught English in this country and Japan. He published books on social history, biography and religious philosophy. During World War II, Smith worked for the Office of War Information in Japan. He retired early, only to find he had cancer, and then wrote the beloved Pendle Hill pamphlet *Dear Gift of Life:* "the message now comes home, strange and yet familiar: I, too, am mortal."

HANNAH WHITALL SMITH (1832-1911) *[#183]*, after her marriage to Robert Pearsall Smith, embarked with him on a career of religious evangelism in both America and Europe. She took part in the founding of the Women's Christian Temperance Union and Women's Suffrage movements. Her **Christian's Secret of a Happy Life** is still in print and sold widely. (President M. Carey Thomas of Bryn Mawr College was her neice; Bertrand Russell and Bernard Berenson were her sons-in-law.)

BEATRICE SAXON SNELL (1900-1982) *[#23]* was a British writer whose perceptive essays, frequently on the subject of worship, were originally published in the magazine *The Friend.*

DOROTHY STEERE (1907---) *[#194]* confessed that during the earliest days of their marriage, she sometimes felt inferior to her charismatic and better educated husband. At the same time, he felt inferior to her when it came to dealing with people. Eventually they became a partnership in which the whole was greater than its parts. She typed and edited his manuscripts, helped him teach work-campers at Pendle Hill and shared his ecumenical interests.

DOUGLAS STEERE (1901-1995) *[#31, 62, 81, 113 and 138]* was for many years a member of the department of religion at Haverford College. He was intensely mystical but also had a strong practical side. He was prominent in the rebirth of Radnor (PA) Monthly Meeting and led the work camp movement in Finland after World War II. Receptive to insights from other faiths, he studied Buddhism in Japan and kept in touch with Catholics during Vatican II. His book **Dimensions of Prayer** has become a Quaker classic.

CAROLINE E. STEPHEN (1834-1909) *[#407]* was a gifted newcomer to the Society of Friends. She was able to interpret the Quaker heritage in a dynamic way to young people and others who may have taken it for granted. Her **Quaker Strongholds,** published in 1890, influenced a whole generation.

KINGDON SWAYNE (1920---)*[#245]* was born into the Society of Friends. His first career was as a foreign service officer for the U. S. State Department. After 1967, he taught for many years at the Bucks County Community College. He has been elected to several local political offices and served Quakers in various capacities, including a term as clerk of PYM.

FRANCES IRENE TABER *[#225]* grew up among Conservative Quakers in Iowa and Ohio Yearly Meetings. She has lived and worked among Friends in New England, Indiana and Pennsylvania, between intervals at Barnesville (OH) where she had a variety of roles at Olney School, and where she now lives. While at Pendle Hill she became particularly interested in solitary silent retreats. After a two-year course at the Shalem Institute, she became a core teacher on spiritual nurturing for the School of the Spirit.

WILLIAM P. TABER *[#104]* has life-long roots among the Conservative (unprogrammed) Friends of eastern Ohio. He was a teacher and administrator at the boarding school in Barnesville (Olney School) for 20 years. He was made a recorded minister in 1966. He taught Quaker Studies and the Prophets at Pendle Hill. He and his wife Frances have retired to Barnesville, where they run a small retreat center.

AGNES L. TIERNEY (1868-1947) *[#77]* served on the board of the Friends Freedman's Association from 1909 until her death in 1947. Her chief concern was education and she frequently visited the Christiansburg Industrial Institute. "Her concern for her Negro friends was based on a deep religious conviction of racial equality which was like that of John Woolman, and, like him, led her to a friendly relationship that made no distinction of color and was so accepted." She had been a teacher and was a member of the Germantown Friends School board.

FREDERICK B. TOLLES (1915-1975) *[#206]* was a distinguished Quaker historian and scholar. He was director of the Friends Historical Library at Swarthmore College. His books included **Quakers and the Atlantic Culture** and **Meeting House and Counting House.** During World War II he was a C.O.

N. JEAN TOOMER (1894-1967) *[#64 and 164]*, being of mixed racial heritage, worked hard to promote the concept of "universal man" who was representative of all people. He published a novel, **Caine,** and was active with Friends in the 1940s, when he wrote for *Friends Intelligencer* and was a popular leader of the high school group at Friends General Conference.

MARGARET TORRIE *[#182]* with the help of her psychiatrist husband, **Alfred,** and others, founded CRUSE in 1958 to help widows and their families. Its work helped to change social attitudes towards widowhood in England and to break through the existing taboos on death.

FREDERICK J. TRITTON (1887-1968) *[#82]* was a British Friend active in the Spiritual Healing Fellowship. He wrote pamphlets and also articles for *The Friend* (London) in the 1950s, often about intercessory prayer.

CAROL REILLY URNER *[#123 and 279]* worked with her husband, Jack, in international aid and development projects in many countries, including the Philippines, Egypt, Bangladesh and Bhutan. Since Jack's death in an auto accident in South Africa in which she was seriously injured, she divides her time between Oregon and California and works on disarmament issues for the Women's International League for Peace & Freedom. She is a member of Sarasota (FL) Meeting.

JAMES G. VAIL (1886-1951) *[#216]* was a chemical engineer and a leading authority on soluble silicates in industry. A member of 3rd St. Meeting in Media (PA), he worked throughout his life on short-term assignments for the AFSC. From 1940-45 his title was foreign secretary and he travelled widely. He died in Delhi, India while serving as head of the Delhi International Friends Center.

JO VALLENTINE (1946---) *[#219]* is a member of the Australian Parliament. She refers to herself as an "eco-feminist."

ELIZABETH GRAY VINING (1902-1999) *[#90, 108 and 188]* was a librarian, a widow and the author of nine children's books when she was asked to serve as a tutor to the crown prince of Japan during the American occupation (1946-50). The book she wrote about that experience, **Windows for the Crown Prince,** was a best-seller. Friends also value her biography of Rufus Jones, her novel **The Virginia Exiles,** and her devotional anthologies.

ELIZABETH WATSON (1914---) *[#184]* had a call to preach early in childhood, but was told "girls don't do that." She studied theology and learned she was expected to become a director of religious education. Instead, she became a Quaker speaker, writer, retreat leader and wise woman. Her book **Wisdom's Dauqhters** imagines the stories of the women around Jesus. Anyone who has heard Elizabeth read these in her fine, deep voice will not forget the experience.

MIRIAM WERE *[#266]* grew up in a Quaker village in Kenya. For six years she represented the World Health Organization in Ethiopia. At the FWCC Triennial in 1992, she spoke like a prophet of old. She wondered why liberal Friends were not sure they were Christians when George Fox had said Christ had the keys to the kingdom. Then, breaking down in tears, she told her fellow Kenyans that none of their new yearly meetings were founded in love.

HENRY W. WILBUR (1850-1914) *[#200]* was general secretary of FGC when he died suddenly of a hemorrhage during their conference at Saratoga Springs (NY). He was also President of the National Federation of Religious Liberals. Living in Swarthmore (PA), he was allied with the Progressive Friends of Longwood Meeting (PA) and worked for improved race relations, Prohibition, Women's Suffrage, and peace.

JOHN WILBUR (1774-1856) *[#102]* was a Rhode Island farmer, land surveyor and Quaker minister. After the separations of 1827, Wilbur thought that New Englanders, reacting against the ideas of Elias Hicks, were leaning toward an overemphasis on outward forms and a weakening of the experience of the indwelling of the Holy Spirit. When Joseph John Gurney visited America in 1838, Wilbur tried to get him to recant and go home. Evangelicals in New England Yearly Meeting managed to have Wilbur disowned. Wilbur and 500 supporters then formed a competing yearly meeting. Wilbur's letters to George Crosfield in 1832 provided a summary of the quietist view.

DAN WILSON (1913---) *[#60]* and his wife, Rosalie, were in residence at Pendle Hill from 1950-1970. For fifteen of those years, he was the director. A graduate of Kansas Wesleyan University, he had previously spent 10 years with the AFSC. After leaving Pendle Hill, he was founding curator of the Mohonk Mountain House Museum, and a VISTA volunteer.

LLOYD LEE WILSON (1947---) *[#260]* is an acknowledged minister of the gospel in Virginia Beach Friends Meeting. He is a former clerk of North Carolina Yearly Meeting Conservative and a former general secretary of FGC. In 1992 he and a fellow Quaker formed Friendly Management Services to provide management and financial assistance to non-profit organizations.

ROGER WILSON (1906-1991) *[#199]* was in charge of British Friends' relief work in France and Germany after World War II as secretary of the Friends War Victims Relief Committee. He was later clerk of London Yearly Meeting and much respected both for his practical abilities and his speaking in meeting for worship.

JOHN WOOLMAN (1720-1772) *[#17, 72, 74, 97, 129, 142, 230, 235, 263, 265 and 276]* has been called "America's Quaker saint." This tailor from Mount Holly (NJ) fruitfully combined simplicity of life-style and transcendent spirituality in the service of strong social concerns -- particularly for the abolition of slavery.

JILLIAN WYCHEL and DAVID JAMES *[#256]* are clerks of Whanganui/Taranaki Monthly Meeting in Australia. They founded the Rowan Partnership, a freelance consulting business that works mainly with public bodies and voluntary organizations on team development, conflict resolution and social justice issues.

TAYEKO YAMANOUCHI *[#66]* was a member of Japan Yearly Meeting, having joined Friends in 1947 while she was in Shanghai, China. From 1971-76 she was associate secretary of the FWCC. She wrote **Ways of Worship** as background material for a study group at the 1979 Triennial.

ELIZABETH YATES (1905-2001) *[#174]* was an American Quaker author of historical novels, a biography of Prudence Crandall, and books of memoirs about her husband's blindness and their New Hampshire home. She was a member of Monadnock (NH) Monthly Meeting. Her **Book of Hours**, unlike the medieval ones, embraces the ordinary and finds it holy.

MILDRED BINNS YOUNG (1901-1995) *[#237 and 277]* grew up among Wilburite Friends in the mid-west. She spent some time at Westtown School, where her husband, Wilmer, was dean of boys. They then worked for AFSC in the South and for fifteen years they lived with sharecroppers and took up voluntary poverty in order to share the hardships of their lives. They were in residence at Pendle Hill from 1955-1961. Mildred said, "Poverty can be taken up. True simplicity comes by the grace of God."

JOHN YUNGBLUT (1913-1995) *[#115]* served twenty years in the Episcopal ministry before becoming a Quaker in 1960. He became director of Quaker House in Atlanta (GA), a faculty member at Pendle Hill and later headed two retreat centers. A life-long student of mysticism, he was inspired by Rufus Jones, Teilhard de Chardin and C.C. Jung. He did spiritual guidance and counseling and conducted seminars and retreats.

INDEX

Extract 23
on earthly possessions, 80
Orthodox Friends' emphasis on, 7
Journal keeping, *Extract 187*

Keith, George, 6–7

Leadings, 65–67, *Extracts 198, 207, 212–213*. *See also* Concerns
Letters
of intention of marriage, 52–53
of introduction, 56
of transfer, 39–40
Light Within, 16–17, *Extracts 6, 10, 13, 17, 24–26, 35*
Advices on, 82, 84
conscience distinguished from, 16
Hicksite Friends' emphasis on, 7–8
Listening, 18, *Extracts 67, 258*
Living wills, 58
Love, *Extracts 5, 30, 32, 38, 141, 165, 173, 192, 246, 251, 279, 290*

Marriage, 68–70
Advices on, 84
ceremonies not conforming to
civil law, 50
certificate. See Marriage certificate
clearness process, 47–50, 54
clerk's responsibilities, 53–54
conduct of wedding, 50–51
dissolution of, 69–70, 183
not under the care of the Meeting, 52
of non–members, 48, 52
overseers' responsibilities, 183
oversight committee, 50, 54–55
preparative meetings, 201
procedure for, 47–56
responsibilities of persons to be
married, 52–53
when two meetings are involved, 47–48, 52
wording of promises, 53, 54
Marriage certificate
during wedding, 51
oversight committee's responsibilities
for, 50, 55
preparation of, 50, 53
wording of, 54, 55–56
Marriage license
clearness committee's responsibility

for, 54
correct form for, 50, 53
oversight committee's responsibility
for, 50, 55
signing and return of, 51, 53, 55
Meeting for business, 177, *Extracts 126–130, 133–137*. *See also* Decision–making
Advices on, 83
clerk's role in, 24–25
conflict in, 27–28. *See also* Conflict
non–members' participation in, 24
participants' responsibilities for, 23–24
procedures for, 26–28
query on, 207
recording clerk's role in, 25–26
Meeting for Sufferings, 194–195
Meeting for worship, 18–21, *Extracts 45–69, 145–150*. *See also* Worship
Advices on, 83
query on, 206
worship and ministry committee's
responsibilities for, 180–181
Meetings. *See also* Monthly meetings
changes in formal relationships of, 200–203
Membership, 34–43
application for, 35–37, 184–185
associate, 38–39
dual, 41
in absentia, 37
in other organizations, 214
meaning of, 34
neglect of obligations of, 185
nominal, 43
of children, 37–39
preparative meetings, 201
records of, 43, 190
overseers' responsibilities
for, 185
recorder's responsibilities for, 40, 186–187
reporting statistics on, 176
sojourning, 40–41
termination of, 41–43
transfer of, 39–40, 184–185
yearly meeting structure, 175
Memorial meetings, 58, 59, 184
Military activity. *See* War
Ministers, recording of, 181–182
Ministry, *Extracts 68, 131*